FLY-TYING
METHODS

FLY-TYING METHODS

DARREL MARTIN

NICK LYONS BOOKS

Lyons & Burford, Publishers

Every book is a product of people and places. So it is with *Methods*. To my parents who gave me the western wilderness. To my wife, Sandra, who waited on lonely riverbanks. To my son, Michael, and another generation of tyers. To Ron Wilton, valued friend and keeper of the Itchen, who showed me the riparian world. To Alain Franck, who shared evening hatches and won the wine. To Dave Whitlock, forever the teacher of tyers. To John Merwin, my first reader and critic. To Taff Price, who, like another Welshman, can call the demons from the deep. To Philip Hager, who taught me the value of things small. To Nick Lyons, who writes like clear water over summer stones. To the late Cyril Bellman, who tolerated my patterns and my questions. To the late John French, who will forever fish at Highbridge. And finally, to the master of us all, *Salmo trutta*, whose shy shadow is the ring giver.

All drawings and photographs in this book are by the author.

Printed in the United States of America

10 9 8 7 6 5 4 3 2 1

Library of Congress Cataloging-in-Publication-Data

Martin, Darrel.
  Fly-tying methods.

  Bibliography: p.
  1. Fly tying.   I. Title.
SH451.M386   1987   688.7'912   87–2652
ISBN 0–941130–40–1

Note: Some portions of this book have previously appeared in various publications including: *Rod & Reel, Fly Fisherman, Fly Fishing the West, The Flyfisher, Flugfiske i Norden,* and *FliegenFischen.*

Contents

A NOTE ON LINE DRAWINGS

Line drawings generally present a clearer picture of the tying process than do photographs. However, it is important to understand the system behind these procedural drawings. The sequencing of materials indicates their position relative to the hook shank. Although it may appear that the materials are wrapped on together, because the thread passes over them at the same time, such may not be the case. The material that is wrapped on first is drawn closest to the hook shank. The tying thread is purposefully enlarged to show its placement. Not all thread wraps are indicated, nor do the drawings always depict the correct diameter or number of fibers. This is done to keep the drawings uncluttered and clear. Miscellaneous and obvious wraps have been omitted for procedural clarity—complete drawings would only obscure the tying process. The text should clarify all requirements of materials and methods.

It should be remembered that the thread, during tying, is kept ahead of (i.e., to the right of) the tying position in order to lap material ends. Some drawings may be enlarged for clarity. Other drawings, such as an off-wing, may be shown only in outline or omitted, while fuller detail may be reserved only for the final illustration. All illustrations demonstrate right-handed tying. A right-handed tyer mounts the hook in the vise so that the eye points to the right, and winds the thread **clockwise** when facing the eye. Left-handed tyers may find it helpful to study complicated drawings by reflecting them in a mirror.

Foreword

The almost ancient sport of fly fishing has experienced amazing growth in popularity throughout the world over the last half century. Mainly, this is because of its ability to diversify and encompass all areas of fresh and saltwater fishing. If a fish will strike and take a particular natural food, then that food can be imitated by a hand-tied fly and presented with fly tackle. Today, fly tying, one of the keys to this universal fascination with fly fishing, has taken great strides; the tools, the materials, the methods, and the designs are evolving dramatically, building and modifying the rich foundations of fly tying.

With so enormous an interest in fly tying today, only well-written and illustrated books can satisfy the serious fly tyer. Composing and illustrating a clear and broad-based book requires a lifetime of special skills, knowledge, and experiences. Such a task is seldom possible by just one person—unless that person is my friend Darrel Martin. I know of no one who understands and bridges so well the span between tying history and the present. Darrel is deeply committed to the entire spectrum of the history, the traditions, and the interaction of past and present—as well as the special problems of practical fly tying, to tie flies that will catch today's difficult trout. Darrel uses pen, pencil, brush, vise, and fly rod brilliantly. His new book *Fly-Tying Methods* is a rare masterpiece of fly-tying literature!

I've often wondered why Darrel could have such interest in me, a more or less crude, self-taught fly fisher who knows little of the history and traditions of fly tying and fly fishing. But after reading this work I know. His initial interest in me was as a researcher observing someone currently developing in the sport in much the same pattern as many of the first angling artists, tyers, and writers of centuries ago. His quest neither began nor ended with me. This book reflects similar interest in countless tyers and anglers through the written past and the active present. After reading this book, so many questions I have had about the uniqueness of Darrel and our friendship find clear answers. For years this relationship has worked beautifully for both of us.

This book is Darrel Martin at his best. His stature is established with *Methods*. He cherishes all that is tying and trout fishing. He constantly ties and ''fishes'' flies in his vise and in his mind. He sees each fraction of the total clearly and concisely, and he is able to share it because he is a fine artist, writer, teacher, historian, naturalist, conservationist, and explorer. He has produced a book for trout-fly tyers that beautifully answers the physical and mental needs of present and future fly tyers regardless of their skill or background.

This book reads clearly and precisely; it is as though Darrel were comparing each line from a selected staff of artists, writers, teachers, and historians. Whatever you or I are as fly tyers, we can relate to his work and see a true, more complex and complete picture of each subject covered than we realized possible. While it is true that each of the many fractions of tying is important, it is hard to communicate the parts to most people. The three-dimensional style of writing that Darrel uses in this book does just that. Examine his statements from any perspective and you will be amazed how complete they are.

The strongest appeal fly tying has is its visual attraction. The tools and materials that are used to sculpt, to wrap, and to weave flies have shapes, patterns, colors, and texture that fascinate us. Darrel has long appreciated this fact and has been a leader in promoting the art and illustration of fly tying through functional and realistic methods. He has done us all an enormous service.

Most of today's efforts to write and illustrate instructional books on fly tying are inadequate in combining clear and concise reflections on traditional and modern tying methods. To do so requires a most special talent and a dedication few of us possess. It requires a sacrifice of time and energy. But here is one man who has done just that.

Everyone who reads and studies this book will be fortunate and enriched by the devotion to tying and fly fishing of a special man named Darrel Martin. It is certainly the next best thing to spending time at his side as he ties and teaches his "fly tying methods."

DAVE WHITLOCK
February 1987

Introduction

I want to see and hear and understand. I want to feel that I know something of where the fish are and what they are doing and why. I want to be able to name the birds I see and take time out to watch them. I want to feel the river about me and fill my mind with the infinity of lights that breaks from its surface and its depth.
—RODERICK L. HAIG-BROWN

I always open the letters with foreign postmarks first. And one that came today told me of two elderly gentlemen in Italy who dress flies on bent needles, of flies that incorporate the silk from the gathered cocoons of certain moths indigenous to Northern Italy, of patterns that use dormouse tail hairs, and of others that use preen feathers. Enclosed in the letter was a neatly wrought Yugoslavian pattern winged with a feather glued to nylon backing. And in another letter there were some turkey beard fibers and a proclamation of their virtues as nymph legs. There can be no end to a book whose subject grows faster than its pages. There can be no end to a book when so many experimental tyers search for the perfect pattern.

Fly tying often includes the selection of methods and materials that best serve the pattern, as well as the ability to modify or create patterns that satisfy both tyer and trout. And a tyer can be as selective as a trout. Our successes are small, even to a size 24. But the quest for the perfect pattern, material, and method continues. It is a quest that may never be realized. Fly tying is our modest attempt to imitate the subtle and complex forces of nature, to share a world of animals, plants and water, to match the morning hatches. It is an excuse to be afield, an excuse to covet a glimpse of water, and an excuse to hear the "peent" of whispering night hawks. Fly tying has invited me into distant homes, made friends in an instant, and spoken all languages.

Fly tying converts the fragments of fur and feather into new shapes. Despite the comments to the contrary, tying is seldom restful—it is fraught with creative intensity. However, it does divert the mind to another world with other problems. Flies are pleasant to hold and trout are remarkably attractive. But we do not ultimately seek trout. We seek knowledge and experience. All our creations are imperfect and float upon mixed currents. And we become solemn when we encounter smooth water, drifting rings, and a well-wrought fly. Perhaps it allows the tyer to be a God in his own galaxy of gnats, to clamp a small world in the jaws of a vise. But my passion for tying is not unique; the patterns and methods in this book come from others who share this passion of tying and trouting.

As a tying teacher, I believe that the enjoyment of any subject is directly related to one's knowledge and skill. For this reason, this book roams through fields not usually traveled in a single tying text. It contains keystones for tying. It blends art and science into an eclectic approach for the inexperienced and experienced tyer alike. Here is a gathering of information on insects, plants, methods, and materials. It includes a generous glossary of angling terms and extensive photographs and drawings. It illustrates such subjects as hand tying and weaving. As an international approach, it includes European as well as American methods and materials. I want a single text that does more than just show a process; I want a text that works with theory and history, a text that offers tradition and innovation. I hope this book increases the reader's tying prowess. But I would like to think that it also serves the "complete angler"—the angler who finds pleasure in science and art, in history and theory.

These pages contain not only methods for doing, but also methods for understanding. Some chapters even glance into the graceful, sepia past. Like others, I enjoy that lost world of angling, a world where anglers in aquatints walk the river meadows, where swallows hawk and scythe the phantom hatches, where greenhearts muscle shadows that will never come to net. Some past patterns engage my spirit and my skill. When winter rain makes trout rings on the window, I search through the past and through my furs and feathers for a trout rise. Tying is a form of fishing; tying "traditionals" is fishing with friends. Traditional patterns allow the tyer to be part of the past. As Arthur Ransome once wrote, "Poor as it may be, it has its family prestige. Even if it catch no fish in summer it has caught plenty in winter, while it was still in the vise." I make no apology for the past.

Yet this is a modern book too, filled with new methods and new materials. The body of the book may be divided into chapters on equipment (tying tools and materials, the vise), chapters on methods (the patterns and problems), chapters on theory (the way of a fly, proportions, the hypothetical hook), chapters on reference (feathers and fluff, hairs and furs, the fly hook, the angler's lexicon), and chapters on natural history (the insect and the plant, the naturals). As the bibliography suggests, many works were freely drawn on as references and, whenever possible, credit has been granted throughout the text.

There is always some danger of construing any text to be a collection of methods and theories that, if precisely followed and applied, will result in perfect tying and trouting. There is always the temptation to copy rather than to create. It should be clear that these methods form no absolute system—they are variations of which only a few may be demonstrated in this or any other book. These methods, ranging from the simple to the complex, and from the past to the present, should be a beginning for original tying. As long as the stream of methods flow, the waters will be deep. They will have holding power. The tying methods presented in this book may be used in different and creative ways. It is important that a tyer collect methods just as he collects materials. Whether or not the tyer exactly follows the methods is not as important as the skill and knowledge gained by the process. My purpose in writing this book is to encourage critical and independent thinking. What Roderick Haig-Brown wrote of angling is also true of tying: "One of the charms of the sport is its infinite complexity. . . . The pattern of discovery may vary widely; that does not matter. The important thing is that the wood has depth and richness to reward a lifetime of quiet, perceptive searching."

Suggestions as to hooks and materials are only recommendations. Where there is significant reason for a particular method or material, it will be stated in the text. Otherwise, the tyer should match the hatch of his home waters. Insects will vary somewhat in color, size, and even habit due to temperatures, food, light, and the chemical character of the water. The proper study of tying is nature, and looking is learning. Creative tying is seldom prescriptive. So let this book draw together those elements of tying that have given me pleasure.

Consider what is done to dress a fly. The tyer comes to know the beauty and variety of fur, feather, and steel. He comes to know the traditions and theories of tying. He becomes a naturalist and a hunter. He is no mere observer of nature; he is neither photographer nor hiker. He is a link in the chain. With more imitative methods and materials, specialized hooks, improved rods, efficient lines, and greater knowledge of insects and trout, the modern tyer-angler is able to harvest trout with remarkable consistency. The element of chance exists, but no angler wants chance to be part of a trouting strategy. Therefore, he learns. He learns the materials, the methods, and the insects. And then he nets more than trout; he brings to net his time with nature. Perhaps that complete angler, Sir Izaak Walton, said it best so long ago: ". . . he that hopes to be a good Angler must not only bring an inquiring, searching, observing wit; but he must bring a large measure of hope and patience, and a love and propensity to the Art itself."

Many have told us that trout serve a greater role in nature than just to fill a creel. Truly, there is a fragile wilderness in the trout we hold for a moment. Tying makes us hunters again, but catching does not mean killing. Fly fishing may be done with little harm to nature. Yet, it is possible, at times, to trout so skillfully as to change the pattern of life in our lakes and streams. Therefore, let us fill our minds more than our creels. Let us pass to the future this literate and graceful field sport, angling with a fly.

What would the world be, once bereft
Of wet and of wildness? Let them be left,
Oh, let them be left, wildness and wet;
Long live the weeds and the wilderness yet.
—GERARD MANLEY HOPKINS

DARREL MARTIN
1986

ACKNOWLEDGMENTS

A sincere effort has been made to grant credit for original methods and concepts and to assure the accuracy of all statements made. However, with the legions of experimenting tyers, similar methods can evolve from different vises and credit errors can occur. Where a method or pattern has been attributed to several tyers and its origin is obscure, no credit has been ascribed.

The following companies have been most generous with their time and their products. I wish to thank Alan Bramley and the Partridge Hook Company; Scott Sanford and L. L. Bean; Henry Hoffman and Hoffman's Hackle Farm; Mustad of Norway; Metz Hackle Farms; Susan Stein and VMC; Tom Rosenbauer and Orvis; Deborah Burns and the D. H. Thompson Company; Ron Abby and Dyna-King; Laura A. Farley and the Danville Chenille Company; Piero Lumini, Riccardo Lumini, and Roberto Pragliola; Peter Mackenzie-Philps and Mackenzie-Philps Ltd.; Rafael De Madariaga and AFTEC; John Foust and Fishaus; Paul Burgess and Sue Burgess Ltd.; Pat Dunlap and Rogue River Anglers; Lee Wulff; Phillis McComber and the Normark Company; Zangs Corporation of South Carolina; Kathy Johnson and the F. A. Johnson Company; John Bork and River Systems; Randall Kauffman and Streamborn; A. Renzetti; Fred Matarelli; Roman Moser and Traun River Products; API Angling Products; Craig Mathews and Blue Ribbon Flies; McNeese's Fly Fishing Shop; Dennis Black and Umpqua Feather Merchants; Robert Borden; David M. McCann and Fly Rite; Len Codella and Thomas & Thomas; Richard Hays and Dan's Fly Tying Enterprises.

And I wish to thank those who gave their time and talents for the book: John Betts, Dave Biddison, Stewart Canham, Donald Downs, Larry Duckwall, Tim England, Graham Gaches, John Goddard, Hans P.C. deGroot, Dave Hughes, Dave Inks, Ingo Karwath, Harry Lemire, Wayne Luallen, Robert McHaffie, Donald Overfield, Neil Patterson, Garry Sandstrom, Colin Steele-Perkins, David Tait, and John Veniard.

Finally, a special thanks to Dr. Alfred M. Lucas for permission to print the feather coat of the white leghorn chicken, Lucas and Stettenheim, 1972; to Dr. Gordon Alcorn for his scientific clarity and suggestions; to Dave Ruetz, aquatic biologist, for his comments and corrections of the entomological data; and to Dr. J. Stewart Lowther and the University of Puget Sound for the microscopy.

PART ONE

TACKLE
and
TRIM

Tying Tackle and Trim

The range of tying tools and tying trim available is more comprehensive than essential. Tying does not require many tools. Some tools may even decrease the speed and quality of tying. Seldom will a tool compensate for poor methods and materials. Even so, tying tools are fascinating, and many tyers find pleasure in possessing and experimenting with various tying tackle. Tyers and shops constantly confront a changing market of tools, materials, and methods. The tying table changes rapidly as new tools and materials are introduced. Consequently, any list I could draw up would be immediately dated; however, the present renaissance in oddments makes this an interesting time for the tyer. Some of the tackle and trim discussed herein will endure, some will not. And a few items listed will be academic, due to cost or limited distribution. But high cost and limited distribution often encourage substitutions that, in turn, may produce new products and new demands. The American tyer now encounters the foreign market through publications, travel, and distributors. Companies, both foreign and domestic, produce quality products for tyers. Although this chapter precludes any extended assessment, I have included those tying tools and special items that I have found unique or useful. Furthermore, design features of the major tools are enumerated as a guide for cost and selection.

ALI IN QUILL

The *ali in quills*, introduced by Roberto Pragliola of Italy, are tapered transparent barbs, as long as 1½ inches, from the turkey wing. Piero Lumini's realistic *Imago di Plecottero* (adult stonefly) patterns wear ali in quill wings.

THREAD BOBBIN

A bobbin decreases thread waste and maintains constant wrapping tension. There are several excellent thread bobbins on the market. Made from chromed stainless steel and brass, the popular Matarelli bobbin is a standard of workmanship and beauty. The polished ends prevent thread fraying or cutting. A smooth thread tension is achieved by adjusting the flexure of the spool arms. The Matarelli Standard accepts a full spool, while the Midge

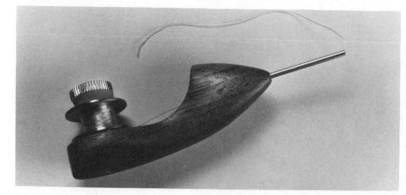

Moore-type bobbin made by Steve Jansen.

model takes the compact mini-bobbin. Care must be taken when adjusting tension to avoid springing the spool arms. J. Dorin's Dual Bobbin, with a removable midge extention tube inside the main tube, avoids the problem of threading by having the thread pass through a tip hole rather than through the complete length of the thread tube, as in a conventional bobbin. No special threader is required: threading is easily done by hand. Whitman-Wayne's Spring-Bob, which employs a similar tip nozzle, has a spring arm that yields during thread work. This increased "elasticity," a flex point just beneath the breaking point of a 6/0 Danville thread, discourages thread breàkage. The fingers may slide over the spool arms to increase tension when required. Handmade bobbins, such as those by Steve Jensen and the late Wayne Moore, have balance, weight, and delicate thread control crafted from attractive hardwoods.

The entry angle of the thread into the tube base is important. The thread angle may be so severe that the tube lip wipes the wax from the thread, thereby increasing wax accumulation at the base. An appropriate angle allows the thread straight entry into the tube base when the spool is half charged. This ensures that a near-empty or near-full spool avoids any acute thread angles. If the thread has a straight entry from a full spool, the near-empty spool thread angle will be too severe. Usually, this may be corrected by adjusting the spool arms. Carefully bend the spool arms, without placing pressure on the brazed joints, so that there is straight thread entry from a half-charged spool.

Bobbin Features:
1. Rigid spool arms to prevent twisting.
2. Adequate weight for thread pressure when "on the dangle."
3. Small-diameter thread tube for precise control, but not so small a diameter as to wipe the wax from the thread.
4. Adjustable spool tension and smooth thread flow. The angle should be such that the spool arms do not rub against the spool ends.
5. Polished tube lips and bore to preclude fraying or breaking of thread.
6. Close alignment of thread and tube to prevent acute thread bends and wax removal.
7. Comfortable balance and shape for the hand.
8. Minimum length for working beneath the vise head.
9. Appropriate spool size or spool range.

A bent Matarelli bobbin with straight thread entry into the tube.

Wing burners: Roberto Praglioli, Streamside Innovations, and Renzetti.

WING BURNERS

Wing burners offer several distinct advantages over cutters—a variety of wing shapes, realistic wing shapes, adequate sizes, no blades to dull, and speed. Due to the bend of the blade, wing cutters often place the widest part of the wing near the top, unlike many naturals. However, cutters are essential for folded synthetics; a burner would fuse the edges together.

Several quality burners are available. The stainless steel Streamlife Innovations burners, especially designed for the Iwamasa Duns, come in three sizes: 10 to 12, 14 to 16 and 18 to 20. Streamlife recommends that the feather sections be held "curve to curve" and that a drop of cyanoacrylate glue be added to the feather stems near the wing base. After about five seconds drying time, both feathers may be burned and mounted as a unit.

The brass Renzetti Wing Formers include mayfly, caddisfly and stonefly-nymph wings, four sizes for each insect: mayfly-stonefly nymph wings in 16 to 12, 12 to 10, 10 to 8, and 6 to 4; mayfly wings in 22 to 18, 18 to 14, 14 to 10, and 10 to 8; caddis wings in 20 to 18, 18 to 16, 16 to 14, and 14 to 10.

Available in three sizes, the stainless steel Roberto Pragliola Wing Burners, distributed in America by River Systems, are slightly offset to accommodate two small patches that grip the stem. For wing burning, I prefer a hen cape that has the barbs at right angles, or nearly right angles, to the shaft. If they are acutely angled, the barbs may be burned through at the base, resulting in angular edges.

The result of a wing with acutely angled barbs.

Wing Burner Features:
1. Appropriate wing sizes and shapes.
2. Well-matched template edges for clean wing shapes.
3. Correct metal thickness to prevent warp or fuzzed wing edges.
4. Adequate length for cool handling.
5. Adequate clamping of the feather.
6. Variable feather positions to accommodate dun, thoracic dun, and spinner wings. You should be able to angle the stem in various positions without burning it.

The result of a wing with right-angled barbs.

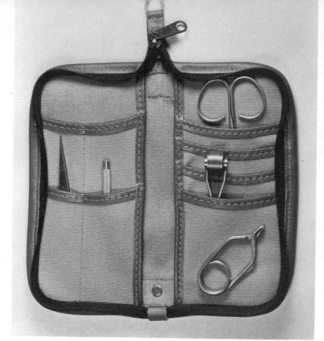

L. L. Bean tool wallet.

TOOL AND MATERIAL CASES

Tool and material cases gather those oddments often lost or misplaced. The popular River Systems Fur File consists of thirty-six transparent ziplock compartments sealed in stacks of six. A tyer merely flips through the "pages" to find the correct dubbing. With a Velcro fastener, the heavy pack-cloth Fur File folds down to a convenient $4\frac{1}{2} \times 10 \times 2$-inch wallet.

L. L. Bean has introduced two excellent tool cases. Made from durable, mildew-resistant Propex III cloth, the Leader and Tool Case is trimmed with full-grain leather, and the four slot and four compartment pockets open flat for easy access. The L. L. Bean Fly Tying Tool Case, made from Propex III and fabric trimmed, holds a complete muster of tools and yet folds into a 7×3-inch wallet that secures with a Velcro strap.

HEAD CEMENT

Head cement is used for more than heads—it molds spun bodies, shapes pheasant-tail legs, and glazes shellbacks. I made a casual comparison, in which a drop of cement was placed on porcelain and on whipped heads to determine drying time and penetration. The drop size, dependent upon the liquidity of the formula and the air temperature, has a profound effect on results. (Because many head cements contain hydrocarbons, ketones, esters, toluene, and xylol, adequate ventilation is required. Also, avoid open flames and skin contact.)

Price's Angler's Corner cement skinned over in about twenty minutes on porcelain and penetrated the wraps quickly. Pharmacist Formula, described as "semi-flexible," dried in about fifteen minutes. Dave's Fleximent dried in about ten minutes and penetrated rapidly. Because it is highly flexible when dry, it is recommended for spun bodies, Dahlberg Divers, terrestrials, and wing cases. River System Cement—with its intelligently designed dispenser cap and squat, no-spill bottle—skinned quickly and dried in about twelve minutes. Although it is not a head cement, mention should be made of Grumbacher's matte Tuffilm, a fast-drying acrylic art spray that prevents splitting and splaying of feather fibers.

CHENILLE

Tying chenilles from the Danville Chenille Company of New Hampshire are available in four sizes, from the small 0 to the large 3, and in a comprehensive variety of colors and combinations, including fluorescent, sparkle, variegated, and tinsel chenilles. Sparkle chenille has a strand of tinsel woven in. Variegated chenilles include multicolored combinations such as black-white and black-yellow. Tinsel chenille is pure spun-tinsel strands most commonly used for marabou muddler patterns. The fluffy and dense U. L. chenille from Traun River Products is perfect for large muddler heads.

HAIR COMPACTOR

A hair compactor packs spun deer-hair bodies. Ron Abby produces a static-free Delrin hair compactor in two sizes. Delrin, an acetal holopolymer with Teflon fibers developed for bearing applications, has a lubricity that makes it ideal for compactors and half-hitch tools. Its slickness prevents thread fray. The A-Y Deer Hair Packing Tool, available in three sizes (for anything from a 2/0 bass bug down to a 16 dry fly), has, unlike the traditional tube type, a slot channel for the head and shank. Landmark's compactor, made from impregnated agatewood, also has a hook groove so that compacting may be done over the heel or point of the hook.

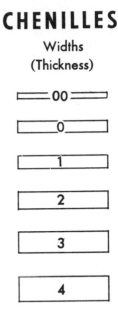

CHENILLES

Widths
(Thickness)

00

0

1

2

3

4

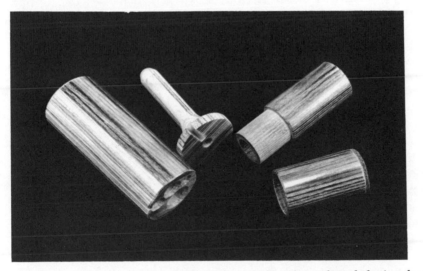

Hair patterns have expanded during the last decade and tool design has changed to meet the demands of the new methods. Shown are Landmark's hair compressor, compactor, and stacker, made from static proof, impregnated agatewood. The compactor has a hook grove so that compacting may be done over the heel of the hook. The mesquite agatewood compressor is a six-in-one tool with eccentric holes so that it will not roll off the table. The compressor allows uniform folding of bullet-heads for streamers, poppers, beetles, and hoppers.

HAIR COMPRESSOR

This tool compresses the folded deer "bullet heads" while the thread collar is wrapped. An attractive and traditional compressor, made from agatewood, comes from Landmark. The John Foust compressor has a short rubber tube that slips over the head. There are two advantages to an elastic tube: it fits a variety of head diameters and constantly compresses the fibers.

HAIR STACKER

A stacker aligns the natural hair tips for tying. It is indispensable for Humpy and bundled-hair patterns. Crinkled and soft-tipped fibers, such as calf tail, are usually finger-stacked. Such fibers cling to each other and their soft tips fold rather than align. However, a large-bore stacker, which does not bundle the fibers in the bore, can align about 80 percent of the fibers. Stacker design is actually rather complex. There are, generally, two different stacker types: open and closed. Although most stackers are made from aluminum, there are a few made from wood, especially rosewood, and plastics. One unusual stacker comes from John Foust of Fishaus Tackle, also the maker of a compact swing-away, extended-body tool. The Foust stacker, made from oak, brass, and Delrin, has a base that rotates away to expose the aligned tips. The hair enters one end and comes out the other.

Hair Stacker Features:
1. A small-bore hair chamber, from .250- to .437-inch diameter, to "bundle" the hairs. This is especially important when only a few hairs are stacked. A wide bore allows the hairs to cross rather than pile parallel. Large-bore stackers, like the Gausdal stacker, are excellent for mixing variously colored hairs for some of the Whitlock patterns.
2. A smooth, nonstatic hair chamber.
3. The male lip of the hair chamber should be thick enough, about .062-inch diameter or more, so that the fibers are not disturbed as the female section withdraws.
4. The "free-bore" space between the bottom of the stacker and the male lip should be close enough, from .375- to .187-inch diameter, to prevent the fibers from moving or falling during removal. In other words, the natural tips should be exposed enough for easy pick-up, yet not so much as to allow them to touch the female wall during withdrawal of the base.
5. The open-end stackers should have a tapered or flared lip for easy hair entry.
6. A wide, stable base cushioned for tamping.
7. A positive grip.

DUBBING

There are myriad combinations of natural and synthetic dubbings on the market. Fly-Rite is a fine denier dubbing in forty colors keyed to the hatches. Spectrum dubbing, a soft synthetic, appears in fifty colors, including the basic pattern shades of cahill, sulfur, gray fox, and caddis green. Nature-

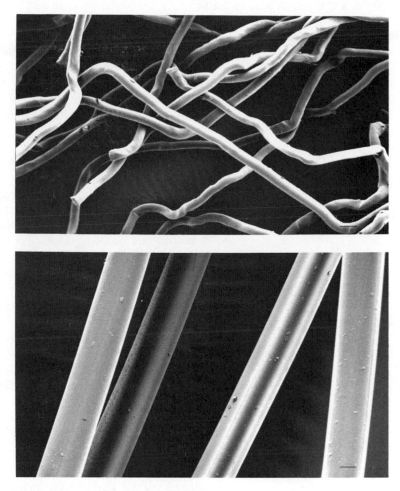

Polypropylene dubbing (54X): the fine diameter makes poly soft, while the irregular crinkle causes it to cord during dubbing. The smooth surface and uniform diameter are typical of synthetic fibers.

DuPont Antron fibers (53X): the smooth, faceted fibers of Antron reflect light. The material was popularized by Gary LaFontaine's *Challenge of the Trout* (1976). According to LaFontaine, Antron imitates the "dazzle sheath," or air cloak, worn by the emergent caddis and submerged female caddis. Antron has also been found effective for spinner and midge wings.

blend, developed by Jack Mickievic and Eric Leiser, consists of twelve natural fur blends for the major dun and spinner hatches of North America. Natureblend colors include pale watery dun, caenis, and light Hendrickson.

Robert Borden's Hare Line, which appeared in 1980, are long-cut fibers (about .75 inch), natural and dyed, blended in thirty-six "earthy" colors. Some colors, like black 22, are eighty percent guard hairs for tying the large bushy stoneflies. Black 7 is the underfur for smaller patterns. The sparkle and sheen of Antron blends, typified by Gary LaFontaine's translucent caddis pupa patterns, have increased in availability. Dupont's Antron has been described as trilobal, and also as rectangular, with four lateral channels. In any case, the popular Hare-Tron, another Borden product, blends rabbit fur with fifteen to twenty percent clear Antron. More than twenty percent clear Antron would weaken the color and decrease dubbing properties. Hare-Tron is an excellent compromise between the dubbing ease of natural fiber and the inherent luster of a synthetic.

FILO PLUME

Filo (or philo) plume, the aftershaft or secondary feather found at the base of a body feather, usually comes from the Chinese pheasant. Ted Niemeyer and, more recently, Gene Armstrong and Jack Gartside, have advocated its use for dubbing, the tails and gills of nymphs, and pupa patterns. Gartside's Pheasant Nymph has a filo-plume collar and his Philo Caddis Pupa has filo wings and thorax. The soft, diaphanous filo plumes imitate the pupa wings better than any rigid quill wings. If the filo is "hackle" wrapped, care must be taken with the tender filo stem—it will not tolerate a heavy hand. Filo's softness makes it remarkably easy to dub.

FLASHABOU

Flashabou, a flexible, metalized mylar that adds life and flash, is incorporated into wings for saltwater, bass, and streamer patterns. Larry Dahlberg, who first introduced it under the name of "metallic hair," used it as a tail on his burbling Dahlberg Diver. Other patterns quickly followed, including Whitlock's streamers and muddlers. The suppleness of the fine strands, which combine well with feather and fur, and the reflective flash have created a new generation of patterns. The popular Pearlescent tinsel, used for attractor and bait imitations, comes in a range of pastel shades. Dyed Pearlescent tinsels, called Fly Flash, have introduced touches of harder color, such as blue, yellow, red, and green, while still retaining the sparkle and spectrum of Pearlescent tinsel. Fly Flash is available in flexible strands for wings as well as tubes for bodies. Small baitfish patterns have increased for bass, trout, and salmon. The fine spooled strands have even been used for small midges and dries.

FLEXIBODY

Created by Hans P. C. de Groot of Holland in about 1977, Flexibody—colored plastic sheets .008 inch in thickness—is soft, elastic, and molds with pressure. A single strip, .25 inches wide and 5 inches long, stretches over 12 inches and recovers to under 6 inches. Because it stretches and avoids bulk, Flexibody is excellent for patterns down to a size 18. It may be cut into appropriate strips with a dual cutter, such as the Grifhold, number 161–B.

Flexibody comes in plastic sheets of approximately two inches by six inches, and may be cut to size on the cardboard backing. The elasticity, thinness, and color make excellent chironomid, larva, and nymph patterns. The transparent sheets allow the undercolors to show. Over twenty-one colors are available, including olive brown, amber, claret, clear, transparent black, light gray, and phosphorescent green.

Stripping Flexi-body with the adjustable Grifhold dualflex cutter (product number 161), Griffin Manufacturing Company.

FLOAT POD

Orvis has recently introduced the Emerger float pod, a minicylinder of balsa wood with a plastic stem for mounting. It is appropriate for light-hook emerging mayfly and *Chironomid* patterns.

FLOCK YARN

Nylon flock yarn comes under various names, including Ultra-chenille and Vernille. Unlike the typical double-threaded chenille, the fine fibers of nylon flock are projected, in an electrostatic field, onto an adhesive-coated carrier yarn. The flock particles, .5 to 1.5 millimeters long, are thus anchored by the adhesive at right angles to the nylon core. The yarn is remarkably soft, yet extremely strong, suitable for weaving and wrapping fly bodies. It is made by Kuhn, Vierhaus & Cie of West Germany in sixty-three colors, some of which are not available on the tying market. There is an excellent range of natural colors, especially the various shades of brown, green, and tan. KVC Nylon Flock Yarn was originally created for the automobile and upholstery trade where strength and durability are paramount.

Like chenille, the yarn should be mounted by the core threads. The best tools to strip the core with are your teeth as any sharp edge cuts the core thread. Flies with flock yarn absorb water well, thereby producing fast-sinking patterns, and the nature of the yarn creates volume without hardness. It is excellent for nymphs and larva patterns.

FOTO-FEATHERS

Due to the scarcity of oak turkey wings, River Systems developed, after first using a silk-screen process, a modified printing process that turns white turkey wings into mottled brown oak wings. Other print patterns have followed, including an olive-yellow-and-brown hopper wing, the tan-and-brown caddis wing, and the ebony-brown nymph wing.

FURRY FOAM

Furry Foam, two layers of poly foam bonded together and with nylon hairs electrostatically attached, was placed on the tying table by the Californian Darwin Atkin. The material, which rips easily and reacts to ketone-based cements, is usually stripped and wound on the shank like chenille. Frank Johnson, who developed the dying process and color range, first marketed the product under the present name. Various patterns, such as Johnson's damsel and Atkin's caddis, incorporate Furry Foam. Traun River Products offers Body-gills, a thin furry foam stripped and wrapped like chenille.

GALLOWS TOOL

Various methods may be used to wrap a parachute hackle: tying the hackle around a rigid wing base, tying the hackle around a vertical support such

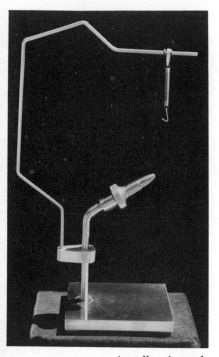

A gallow's tool.

as the hackle stalk, using fine wire, monofilament, or a hook extension. Most modern methods, such as Chauncy Lively's bunched-parachute spinner, which employs a 4X monofilament loop to form the wing division and thorax, are produced without gallows. However, the gallows tool maintains tension on the extension while the hackle is wrapped. Both the Veniard-Downs and Olsson methods are described in the text. In *Flytying Techniques* (1981), Jackie Wakeford describes the wire-loop method. After the body is completed, a wire loop is tied in and tightened by the gallows hook. The hackle, dull side down, spins around the loop base. After sufficient hackle turns, the hackle tip passes through the wire loop and the gallows hook is disengaged. Both ends of the wire loop are pulled taut to tie the parachute into a knot. It is also possible, especially for micropatterns, to loop the tying thread over the gallows hook and wrap the hackle around the loop base. Fine-tipped pliers pull the hackle tip through the loop. The thread dismounts the hook, tightens and then whip-finishes the fly. A drop of cement at the hackle hub secures the parachute.

Gallows Tool Features:
1. Vertical and horizontal adjustment of the hanging hook for correct placement.
2. A hanging hook with an open bend and soft spring for loop disengagement.
3. Adequate free space around the vise head for hand and material movement.
4. A vise clamp, with thumb or recessed hex screw, which accommodates a variety of vise-stem diameters and bends.
5. A hanging hook that slides to the vertical bar for mounting extended-body patterns.
6. A compact and portable unit.

HOCK

Hock hair, from either elk or deer, has increased in popularity. It is short, dense hair suitable for tails, wings, and bodies on small patterns such as the Humpy, Caddis, and Wulff. Because it lacks the buoyancy of body hair, hock-hair caddis float best in the smaller hook sizes. Most hock colors range in the ruddy tans and blacks. Hock works well wherever short, stiff wings and tails are required.

HOOKS

The tying demand for specialized hooks has brought to market Eagle Claw's "Stinger" hooks, designed in 1943 by Garvice Loucks of Tulsa, Oklahoma. These light-wire, wide-gap hooks have proven popular for bass flies. Tiemco has enlarged its range to include heavy-wire streamer and nymph hooks (TMC 300, TMC 5262, TMC 5263, TMC 3769, TMC 3761); a 1X fine, humped-shank hopper and terrestrial hook (TMC 2312, TMC 2302); a 2X short shrimp and pupa hook (TMC 2487); and light- and heavy-wire salmon-steelhead hooks (TMC 7989, TMC 7999). Kamatsu of Japan has recently introduced a range of chemically sharpened, high-carbon fly hooks. The Kamatsu "whisker" barb has a length about half that of a Mustad barb. Kamatsu also produces a fine-pointed, barbless fly hook.

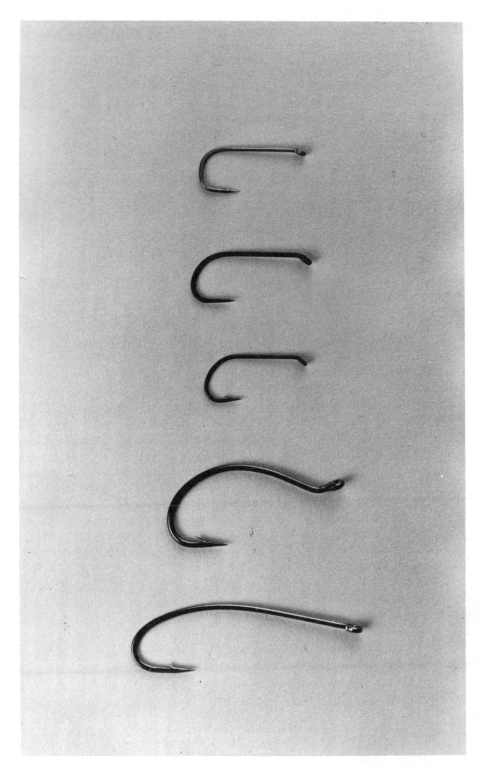

Innovations in hook design: Partridge Sneck Midge Hook, Roman Moser's Spearpoint Hook, Tiemco Dry Fly Hook (TMC 102Y), Mackenzie-Philps's Yorkshire Sedge Hook (Partridge), Tiemco's Nymph Hook (TMC 200).

MICRO FIBETTS

Micro Fibetts, popularized by John Betts, are tapered, conical filaments about .004 inch at the base and 2 inches long. These synthetic fibers, under Toray Industries' "White Sable" trademark, were originally produced for watercolor brushes. They are used for dun and spinner tails, nymph legs, and caddis antennae, and are now available in barred and solid colors. One tying concern is that the rigidity of Micro Fibetts may actually prevent the trout from taking the pattern. The problem does not appear in small patterns with a few tail fibers.

Other natural and synthetic brush fibers may be employed in tying. Red sable, actually the tail hair from the Asian weasel, and the expensive kolinsky sable, the tail hair from the male Siberian kolinsky or red Tartar marten, has excellent spring and resiliency for small dry-fly tails. The sable tail hair is thick in the belly and tapers at both ends. It is this shape that gives the watercolor brush its characteristic shape—the outward swell and sweep into a fine point. Because the base diameter of the natural sable is fine, it springs away during the take.

HACKLE PLIERS

Hackle pliers are simple and useful tools if designed correctly. Poor pliers can make tying a chore. The English-type pliers require care in design and construction. Often this is lacking. Sharp, ill-matched jaws slip or snip the hackle tip. The late Herb Howard made excellent English pliers; however, some modern imitations seldom match the materials and perfection of the past. Due to some poorly designed English-type pliers, the American tyer has embraced a new generation of pliers, especially the tear drop and J-jaw. J. Dorin's tear-drop hackle pliers are remarkably strong and excellent for fine and delicate hackles. Although they lack weight when "on the dangle," they hold well and the polished tips prevent hackle breakage. They open by pressing a jaw length beneath the pivot. Dorin also produces a looped-wire or J-jaw hackle pliers. These have large, circular jaw surfaces that hold well without breaking hackle tips. Most hackle pliers have the

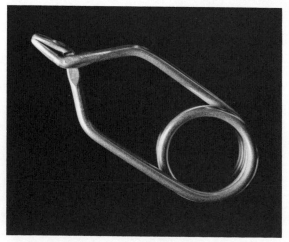

The traditional English hackle pliers with indexed jaws.

jaw axis at a right angle to the finger-hole axis. This encourages the hackle stem to twist during mounting. Roberto Pragliola of Italy produces pliers whose jaws rotate independently, thereby decreasing hackle-stem twist. Several hackle pliers have springs to cushion the heavy hand. It is best, perhaps, to learn the light touch.

Hackle Pliers Features:
1. Well-indexed jaws that hold well without cutting.
2. Adequate weight to maintain tension when "on the dangle."
3. Adequate point of grip. Many have a finger hole for hackle rotation.
4. Firm jaw tension with easy opening.
5. Large enough for comfort, yet compact for maneuvering.

SCISSORS

The ideal tying scissors should be short for manipulation, have finely tapered points for close cutting, and large finger loops for comfort. I prefer scissors about 4½ inches long, that place the pivot point just beyond the forefinger. Scissors blades touch at only two points—the pivot point and the cut point. The cut point, much like the center of a cross, moves along the edges of the shear bars as both blades wrap around each other while closing. Thus, a single cut or shear point passes down the blades when closing. The edge bevel is usually about thirty degrees with a variance determined by the material to be cut. Some of the finest scissors are stainless steel with a pivot screw that is locked yet adjustable. Several high-quality scissors have an insert edge of tungsten-carbide steel for superior cutting. Those with serrated edges are excellent for cutting such resistant materials as synthetics and deer hair. The serrations trap the fibers in the closing V so that the material is not pushed away.

No single pair of scissors can do all that is required in tying. Some tyers find that curved blades increase visibility and require less arm movement. Curved blades are also used for "carving" spun-hair patterns. Heavy materials such as moose mane, thick stems, heavy synthetics and tinsels require heavy shears for yeoman duty. This will prolong the life of the

Thompson Supreme Scissors showing the micro-serrations on the blade.

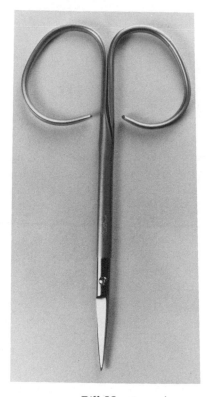

Bill Hunter scissors.

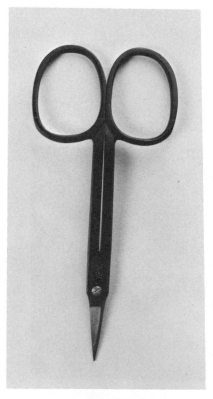

Orvis curved-handled scissors.

more delicate and expensive tying scissors. In the trade, scissors are usually not longer than six inches and the finger loops, correctly called rings, are equal in size. Shears, which have an oval loop for two or three fingers and a round loop for the thumb, are over six inches. Also, unlike scissors, shears have one sharply tapered and one semirounded point.

For a right-hander, the round ring section is the top blade, and the oval is the bottom blade. Right-handed scissors are identified so that if the scissors point north, the top blade ring is on the right.

There is a difference between right- and left-handed scissors. Right-handed scissors used in the right hand slightly orbit the top finger-loop to the left, thereby increasing the pressure at the shear point. Right-handed scissors used in the left hand orbit the top finger-loop to the right, thereby decreasing the pressure at the shear point. Scissors used in this manner may not cut well at the tips. Some tyers use the blade V to cut wire and metallic tinsel. Such use can spring the blades or cause the edges to catch or stutter as they close. Fine materials like hackle barbs and 6/0 thread require fine scissors; heavy or coarse materials require shears.

Some tyers, especially commercial tyers whose time is money, place the ring finger through the lower loop and allow the top loop to nestle in the palm. During tying, the scissors can be rotated beneath the wrist where the small finger controls them when not in use. If the index finger is used for the lower loop, then the forefinger is free for tying. When cutting, the scissors rotate into the hand and cradle in the natural fold formed by the thumb and forefinger. The thumb is then placed on, or in, the upper loop for cutting. After cutting, the scissors rotate again beneath the hand while tying continues. Some tyers cut away sections of the rings closest to the blades for greater comfort and finger space. Point tips may be matched by taping the rings where they touch, or by grinding.

Wearing scissors may seem awkward at first, but after time, they become extensions of the hand and their uses increase. A single blade can scalpel a thread closely and a fine point can rough thoracic dubbing. Safety glasses should be worn while using scissors.

Because of cost, the selection and care of scissors is important. "Serious" scissors have adjustable screw pivots, not rivets. A rivet cannot be adjusted easily when the blades become too tight or too loose. The finish should be smooth and free from casting pits. The blades should be sharpened at a uniform angle and depth down the blade. To snip a single barb, scissors must be pointed; no flat surface should appear when the tip is pointed directly at you. When worked, quality scissors have a solid swishing sound without stuttering. They have a comfortable sense of weight and balance. They should be kept clean and dry. A drop of light machine oil at the pivot will maintain their ease of operation, and a storage case will protect their edges from other tools in the tying kit. Scissors are the center of tying—never compromise on their quality.

There are many fine scissors on the tying market. Bill Hunter's light-weight stainless steel scissors from West Germany are four inches long with adjustable finger loops. Although too light for heavy cutting, the fine twelve-degree tips are excellent for detail work. Hunter also markets 4½-inch serrated-blade deer-hair scissors. These feature tungsten-carbide inserts and semicurved blades. Tungsten-carbide blades are remarkably sharp, but also remarkably brittle. They can be snapped. The Dorin Nippers are extremely light and compact, perfect for a streamside tying kit. They have an adjustable loop that fits the middle finger while the blades pass between the thumb and the index finger. The Nippers, which remain in the palm while tying, close by thumb action and spring open. The comfortable Normark FlyTyer Scissors, both straight and curved models, have a rivet and magnetic tips. The Kershaw Fly Tying Scissors have screw pivots, high-carbon blades, and wide contoured ABS finger loops. C. F. Orvis Tying Scissors feature a black oxide finish to reduce glare, large rectangular rings, fine points, and angled handles for easy pick-up. The comfortable handle curves for accurate cutting. The popular Thompson Supreme Scissors, 4½ inches long with a fifteen degree point, have coated handles, sharp Ice blades and limited-adjustable rings. One blade has fine serrations for hair work. The compact, 3.5-inch Thompson Midge scissors have Ice stainless steel blades, dipped handles, adjustable rings, and a serrated edge.

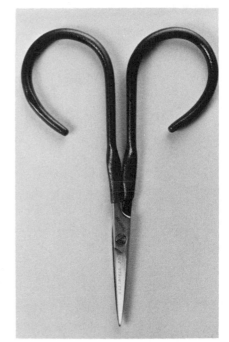

Thompson midge scissors.

Tying Scissors Features:
1. Finely tapered, sharp points. A fifteen-degree tapered point is best for fine work.
2. Large, comfortable rings.
3. Well-meshing blades with a smooth shear action.
4. Points register correctly when closed.
5. Surgical quality stainless steel.
6. Lightweight with a total length of four to five inches.
7. Serrated edge or edges for hair work.
8. Curved or straight blades.
9. Magnetic tips for selecting small hooks.
10. Uniform angle and width to the cutting bevel. The normal bevel angle is about twenty-five degrees, but scissors designed for special materials may be ground down as far as forty degrees.

SWANNUNDAZE AND V-RIB

Used either for ribbing or body, Swannundaze and V-Rib are semicircular vinyl strands. Swannundaze comes in twenty-three colors. Similar to Swannundaze, V-Rib is finer, softer, and more elastic. Under tension, V-Rib stretches to a finer diameter, making it suitable for smaller patterns.

SWISS STRAW

Dave Whitlock inaugurated Swiss straw for nymph backs and wings. This "onionskin" synthetic is 1.625 inches wide when unfolded, and comes in a variety of colors, including light olive, gold, cream, and copper.

From twelve o'clock: Vernille or Flock-Yarn, Micro-Fibetts, Swiss Straw, Chinese boar bristles, Swannundaze, and Sparkle Yarn. Thompson Monobond spools centered with Furry foam beneath.

SYNTHETIC QUILL

Synthetic Quill, marketed by Roberto Pragliola, is a fine plastic strip about one millimeter in width and five inches long. It comes in various contrasting colors, including green, brown, yellow, and red. Its width and weight make it appropriate for size 12 hooks and larger. Butt bulk is avoided by trimming the strip at a sharp angle and wrapping the angled tip in first.

TYING THREAD

Several new threads have appeared. One of the strongest threads available is the 3/0 flat Kevlar. It has become popular for spun-hair bodies, bass, salmon, and steelhead patterns. The colors include olive, brown, pale yellow, orange, red, and black. Thompson's 3/0 and 6/0 Monobond come in twelve colors including deer, burnt orange, nickel, and old gold. Their thread kit contains 900 yards of thread on twelve mini-spools. The 6/0 Danville prewaxed thread, also referred to as Herb Howard or Flymaster, has excellent strength for diameter and is available in a wide range of colors including fire orange, olive, tan, cream, beige, gray, pale yellow, and maroon. Dave Engerbretson's one-ply Ultra Midge, unfortunately limited to white, is rated between 15/0 and 20/0 for size 22 to 28 patterns. Danville's Spider Web, which is .003 inch, has only marginal bulk for extra turns.

Thread Features:
1. Strength.
2. Flat, multistrand, or single strand and twist.
3. Color range.
4. Spooled length and spool sizes.

Thompson multi-strand Monobond tying thread (161X): waxed Monobond has a uniform diameter and a slight twist. Twisted threads are generally stronger than straight threads.

Multi-strand, twisted Pearsal tying silk (160X): unlike a slick synthetic, the irregularities of natural silk fiber increase the cling. Even without wax, silk has a natural "adhesiveness" for tying.

WAX

Some tyers use supplemental wax. Most modern waxes are soft with adhesive resins. Hard waxes, through which the thread is pulled, are seldom used. Overton's Wonder Wax, which increases its tack with pressure, is very adhesive with a convenient twist-up container. Fly-Rite's Dilly Wax with low tack liquifies in the fingers for application. D. H. Thompson's high-tack dubbing wax, available in the popular twist-up container, always retains a degree of flexibility; it is particularly suitable for adhering stiff furs and synthetics to the thread.

DUBBING WHIRL

Several dubbing twisters are available. The Engerbretson Dubbing Twister has a single hook and finger loop. To use the Engerbretson Twister, hang the thread from the hook bend and apply a soft, sticky wax. Then, distribute the dubbing evenly on the thread. Place the hook of the Twister below the dubbed strand and, with the bobbin, fold the thread back to the hook bend, thereby making a loop. Only one strand will have dubbing. Make several wraps of thread to secure the loop to the hook shank and wrap the bobbin forward. Spin the Twister. When the dubbing is twisted tightly, place a finger in the loop and wrap the dubbed cord directly on the shank. The T-shaped Kaufmann Hair-Flair makes clipped-hair bass bodies, muddler heads, and spinner hairwings. Matarelli's Dubbing Loop Needle and D. H. Thompson's Dubbing Twister work similar to the Engerbretson Twister.

Dubbing Whirl Features:
1. Adequate weight and design for stable spinning.
2. Thread hooks that will not slip.
3. Thread hooks that close the spinning loop by a light pull.
4. An adequate extension for spinning.
5. Short length to pass under the vise head.
6. Finger loop or grip for wrapping bodies.

WINGS

Roman Moser's Traun River Wings, the most durable and realistic synthetic wings yet for mayfly, caddis, and stonefly patterns, are printed sheets, complete with venation. The tyer merely cuts the wing out, folds it, and ties it in. Stonefly wings are gray, brown, yellow, dun, or black, sized from 6 through 16. The caddis wings appear in black, various browns, grays, tan, and olive brown, and come in sizes 10 to 18. The dun wings cover a variety of dun shades to match sizes 10 through 18. Depending on the pattern, the wings are tied in either before or after the hackle. In America, John Betts has developed various tying techniques for synthetics, including Organza mayfly wings.

Other tying trim includes Zelon, heralded by John Betts, for sparkle-dun shucks, spinner wings, sparkle caddis sheaths, and deer-hair caddis underwings. Crystal hair adds "electricity" to Wooley Buggers, streamers, steelhead and salmon patterns. Polycelon, a closed-cell foam used for hopper bodies, is a surrogate for the polypropylene wing pads of floating nymphs. The fine and dubbable camel hair is available in a variety of colors, including natural. Some old patterns have been revisited with new materials, such as the Blue Ribbon Woolhead Sculpin that incorporates a spun wool head for improved casting and sinking. The marriage between synthetic and natural fibers continues. The marketplace will always offer hundreds of new materials waiting for methods and tyers.

The Vise

Part of the pleasure of tying comes from the beauty, form, and function of tools. Many tyers collect tools as they collect methods and materials— and the vise is at the center of tying. Vise selection is important. Not only must a vise hold thousands of hooks well, but it may also be required to perform special operations in tying. A vise should accommodate the various attachments and methods with fast, positive action. The jaws should be tempered correctly and be adjustable for the full range of common hooks. All adjustments should be simple and secure. Most important, the hook should not move during the tying process. A vise should grant long and faithful service. Some tyers prefer a vise that has interchangeable jaws for different size hooks; this allows the added advantage of replacing a jaw immediately if one becomes sprung or chipped. A variety of materials— including aluminum, steel, Delrin, brass, and nylon—may be found on the modern vise. Price range is wide, ranging from the less expensive synthetic castings to the precision-milled stainless steels. Price may or may not be a factor in the quality and function of a vise. The quality of a vise is determined, in part, by materials, manufacturing process, and design. Certain materials and manufacturing processes will necessitate a higher cost. In any case, when selecting a vise, the following features should be considered:

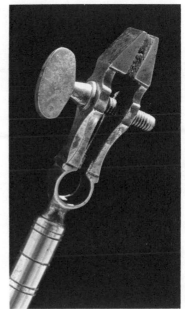

An antique vise.

1. Any knurling should be clean and precise.
2. The threads should be fine, adequately deep, and acutely angled to prevent backoff of adjustments. Lock rings may be added to snug adjustment rings.
3. The finish should be durable and pleasant. Some tyers find that a no-glare matte finish prevents eye strain.
4. The vise should have an adequate mounting system. C-clamps should accommodate most tables. The quality vises usually have a pedestal base as well as a C-clamp system.
5. The vise should accept supplementary tools, such as gallows, material clips, lamp mounts, and others. A standard diameter standrod, usually ⅜ inch, should accept future products, even those designed by manufacturers for different vises.
6. The jaw should firmly hold the standard range of hooks with minimal adjustments for maximum hold. This is the primary purpose of a vise.

In some vises, hook placement is paramount for maximum hold.

7. The vise should be esthetically pleasing. A finely tapered jaw, a lustrous brass base, and the touch of fine workmanship can turn a vise into a work of art.

8. There should be an adequate jaw opening. Vises with interchangeable jaws may accommodate different hook diameters, such as 6/0 to 32, by jaw change. Few single-jawed vises can adapt from midge to salt-water patterns. Fixed-jaw vises may have a limited hook range.

9. The jaw shape should allow adequate hook access while tying.

10. All special functions, such as jaw rotation, jaw angle adjustment, and gallows attachment should be simple and convenient to perform. All adjustments should be smooth over their entire operating range.

11. Jaws should be tempered for strength yet soft enough to hold well.

12. There should be readily available replacement parts.

13. There should be an adequate guarantee of parts and workmanship.

14. The axial rotation of the jaw should be without roughness or wobble.

15. Metal parts should resist rust and chromed parts should resist peeling. Chromed jaws, which are usually not recommended, reflect light and flake at the edge when under pressure.

16. Jaws with grooves, serrations, or pins for holding and positioning hooks should accommodate an adequate hook range.

Although most vises have the traditional draw-cam system, recent decades have seen some innovative designs and complex features. There are four fundamental vice systems based upon the manner in which the jaws close.

1. *Draw-Cam Lever*, where the rotating lever, an increasing-radius cam or "wiper cam," draws the tapered rear of the jaw bolt into a collet or sleeve, thereby closing the jaws. A typical example is the Thompson A.

2. *Push-Cam Lever*, where the cam lever pushes the jaw bolt through the sleeve collet, thereby compressing and closing the jaws. The jaw that must exit a collet is usually smaller in diameter than the typical draw-cam jaw. Dyna-King by Abby is an example of this "reverse system."

3. *Spring Lever*, in which there is continuous pressure on the jaws exerted by a powerful wedging or spring action. The jaws require no adjustments other than opening to accept the hook. A typical example of this unique system is the Regal vise.

4. *Screw Knob*, in which the rotation of a screw handle draws the jaw bolt against a collet, thereby closing the jaws. This is a variant of the draw system. An example of this system is the Sequoia 2000 and the Thompson B. Although generally slower than a lever system, it is one of the simplest and most reliable closure systems.

Most vises adjust the jaw setting (the distance between the jaw faces) by a threaded sleeve to accommodate various hook diameters. The push-cam system usually has the adjustment sleeve immediately behind the jaws; the draw-cam system, immediately in front of the cam lever.

Generally speaking, a tying vise should require little upkeep. A periodic wiping with a silicone cloth, some light oil on working threads, and a lubricant on any bearing surfaces should suffice. A vise should be constructed of rust-resistant metals; if it is not, then a light polish should restore any part to perfection. Care should be taken not to drop a vise. Usually, depending upon the operating system, a vise should not be left with pressure on the jaws. On vises with interchangeable jaws, make certain that the appropriate jaw is used for the particular hook. Do not spring the jaws to accept larger hooks than possible. Do not over-tighten a vise. It should hold securely with minimal pressure. The better vises usually come with a lifetime guarantee that will repair or replace any defective parts as long as there is no evidence of misuse or abuse. Travel vises take the journey best in a soft case, but care must be taken so that parts do not collide.

The following vises are typical of the price range and features of the modern vise. All of these vises, listed alphabetically, may be considered representative of the various systems.

DYNA-KING FLY VISE

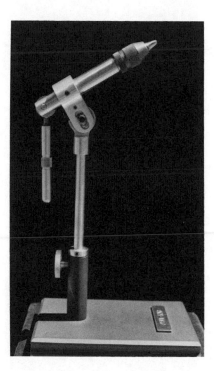

The Dyna-King vise by Abby Precision Manufacturing Company has no casting, and all workings have polished tolerances and operating surfaces. Care of design and construction is evident. A smooth cam motion closes the blunt bullet jaws that have a small radius. The vise head has full axial rotation, and may be tilted on the horizontal axis to 0, 30, 60, and 90 degrees, the useful angles. The vise may be converted for the left-handed tyer. A lock ring on the stem adjusts for permanent height on the pedestal or C-clamp base. A unique characteristic of this vise is the two different sized "nests" or grooves in the jaws. The straight nests accommodate large hooks easily. Some special hook designs, such as the Limerick and arched caddis bends, may require the available, smooth jaw. The straight vertical nests work very well if the hook heel fits them. Some hooks that match the nest may fit low in the jaws in order to clear the barb and point. Jaw change may be required to expose enough of the hook heel for tying some patterns. A very fine, serrated tip holds small hooks well. The jaws are adjusted easily and fast, next to the hook. The smooth mechanics and appearance of this vise mark it as one of America's finest.

Features
1. Base or C-clamp
2. Adjustable head angle
3. Axial rotation of the jaws
4. Fine polished finish
5. Adjustable height on standrod
6. Infinitely adjustable jaw angle that can accept salmon doubles.

HMH STANDARD PEDESTAL VISE

Bill Hunter, of New Boston, New Hampshire, set out in 1975 to perfect the tying vise. Created with the help of a corps of tyers who submitted commentary, the HMH vise was marketed in 1977. The different vise parts were manufactured by various subcontractors while Hunter performed the finishing process and fitting. In 1981 HMH vise production was purchased by Angling Products, Incorporated, which had supplied parts for the orig-

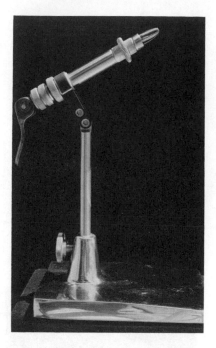

inal vise. It is cam-operated and draw-collet, the traditional system, with interchangeable chrome-moly jaws. The vise comes with two jaws: a serrated Magnum jaw for hook sizes 6/0 through 16, and a Midge jaw for hook sizes 12 through 32. Two other jaws are available—the Trout Jaw for hook sizes 2 through 22, and the Restricted Jaw for hook sizes 18 through 32. The C-clamp model comes with a 9-inch standrod. The pedestal-base model comes with a brass base that weights slightly more than 4½ pounds. The polished brass base is remarkably attractive and stable.

It is a simple matter to change HMH jaws. The cam pressure is released and the adjusting knob is screwed forward. The jaw may then be unscrewed from the collet sleeve. A new jar is inserted and screwed home until it stops. It is then backed off and positioned for tying. Changing and adjusting a jaw takes less than half a minute. The jaw may be rotated by loosening a locking ring; the head then rotates against Delrin washers. There are three grooves for positioning a stainless steel spring material clip at the forward end of the collet sleeve. The angle of the head is adjusted with a hex wrench.

The jaws may be rotated for hackling, dubbing, lacquering, or examining by adjusting a brass lockout ring against a Delrin spacer. As with most cam-lever vises, the flip lever that tightens the jaws should be parallel with the standrod when correctly adjusted. For nearly a decade the HMH vise has set a milling standard for all vises.

Features:

1. Machined construction and polished parts
2. Interchangeable jaws
3. Solid-brass base or cast-aluminum C-clamp with a 2½-inch gap
4. Head-angle adjustment by hex key
5. Full axial rotation of the jaw

ORVIS FLY TYING VISE

The Orvis vise, which accepts hook sizes 2 through 28, has full-jaw rotation, and the angle may be adjusted anywhere from zero to twenty-five degrees above the horizon. The jaws are locked in the normal or inverted positions with a sliding detent bolt. Furthermore, with the rotary locking screw, the jaws may be locked in any position throughout its axial rotation, so that special hooks, such as salmon doubles, may be tied. The C-clamp adjusts from 1¼ to ¼ inch, and the vise height is adjustable up to 8 inches above the table. The Delrin head as well as the collet and jaws is black to reduce glare. The Orvis vise operates by a draw cam with the jaw-width adjustment immediately in front of the cam lever. It is a simple and functional design.

Features:

1. Full jaw rotation
2. C-clamp mount
3. Black finish
4. Limited but adjustable jaw angle
5. Standrod height adjustment
6. Suitable for right or left-handed tyers
7. Accepts salmon doubles

REGAL PEDESTAL VISE

The colletless Regal vise is unusual in its operating system. The jaws are always under tension. Mounting and dismounting a hook is accomplished by squeezing a lever that opens the jaws. The system is extremely fast and no jaw adjustment is required. One jaw half has a circular nest with a Delrin pin stop at the rear. When the jaw lever is slowly released, the hook nestles correctly in the pocket. It has what might be called a self-adjusting jaw that will accommodate hook sizes 6/0 to 32. Because the jaw is an integral part of the head, it is not interchangeable. Care, therefore, must be exercised in mounting the hook correctly. A hook should never be placed close to the jaw edge on this or any vise. The hook may work loose, snap out, and cause damage to the jaw edge. The base is bronze, and the lever handle, brass. The vise, complete with table base, weighs 5½ pounds for solid stability. Small hooks are held by the tip and not nestled. It comes with a removable stainless steel material spring. The anodized head cants left and right for fly examination. It has a 5½ inch standbar. The C-clamp model, which opens to 2⅛ inches, has a long, 10-inch standbar. There is a hex-tool storage hole in the base. The forty-five-degree jaw point ends in a small radius tip for fine hooks. The Regal is fast and unique.

Features:
1. Fast hook mount and exit with self-adjusting jaws
2. C-clamp or heavy pedestal mounts
3. Jaw cants left or right
4. Accepts wide range of hooks
5. Wide jawed C-clamp and long standbar

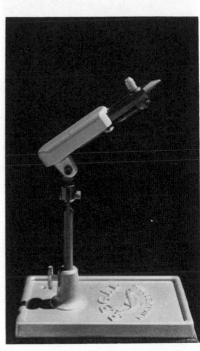

SEQUOIA 2000

The Italian Sequoia 2000 vise by Roberto Pragliola is a well-designed tool. It adapts to a C-clamp (1¾ inch clamp spread), or to a unique table base with two vise settings, one vertical and one approximately forty-five degrees. The table base can house three tools for convenient access. The head rotates on its own axis by means of a spinning extension, and the jaws may be fully rotated on its axial plane. The head has, in fact, infinite adjustments. Two thumb screws on the far side set the head angle and release the jaws for spinning. With the center screw, the jaws may be locked at any point of full rotation. The vise comes with a gallows attachment that screws into the head assembly and locks with a set screw. The hanging gallows hook is fully adjustable along the gallows bar. This is an appropriate vise for extended-body and spinning methods. Three interchangeable jaws include a fine midge taper, a standard taper, and a wide streamer jaw. The standrod is 8¼ inches long. The standard jaw has a 30-degree taper and, like all the jaws, is made from soft steel to hold firmly. This import is engineered for various tying methods.

Features:
1. Spinning jaw system
3. Three mounting systems (a C-clamp and a two-position pedestal)
4. Long adjustable standbar
5. Three interchangeable jaws
6. Detachable and adjustable gallows system

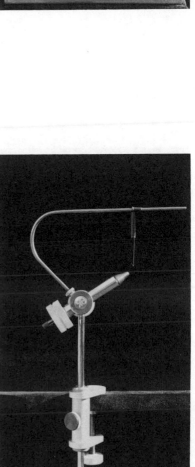

THOMPSON THREE-SIXTY

There have been more flies tied on Thompson vises than on any other vise available. The model A, much like that vintage Ford, has stood the test of time and taste. D. H. Thompson is credited with the invention of the "collet" type vise where a single cam lever closes or opens the jaws. The standard model A has been clamped to tying tables for over sixty years. Thompson makes several variations on the model A. There is the no-glare, black matte finish on the Pro-Vise, which accepts all Thompson collet jaws and a C-clamp, or the black-matte finished Pro II, which has a weighted base. To accommodate intricate body tying and special hook bends, the Ultra Vise has an adjustable head angle from the horizontal to the vertical. In addition to the standard Thompson jaw, there are special-purpose jaws—the Midge Jaw for hook sizes 18 to 32, and for the saltwater fly tyer, the Super Jaw for 4/0 to 6/0 hooks. There is also a conversion base, which changes the C-clamp vise into a pedestal model. This weighted base will accept many other manufacturers' vises. Pro-Vise, with a no-glare, black-matte finish, is available with either a C-clamp or pedestal. The Three-Sixty vise is a rotating Pro II vise. The collet rotates against Delrin wafers, and the jaw is positioned by a brass screw ring. The standrod is tightened to the base by a heavy screw sleeve. In all, the cost and quality still makes the Thompson an attractive standard.

Features:
1. C-clamp or pedestal base
2. Complete axial rotation of the jaw
3. Accepts specialized, interchangeable jaws
4. No-glare finish

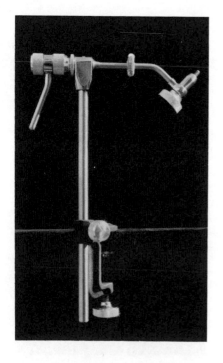

THE RENZETTI PRESENTATION VISE

The Renzetti Presentation Vise, available with either a C-clamp or base mount, is unique in design and function. This attractive vise, made from stainless steel, tool steel, brass, and aluminum, employs the "reverse" jaw system of the push-cam. The C-clamp opens to over four centimeters and has a finely textured matte finish. Other parts are polished, and the milling and knurling are precise. Three interchangeable jaws, each no longer than three centimeters, are furnished: the RVJ–1 jaw (for hook sizes 18 to 28); the RVJ–2 (for hook sizes 2 to 16); and the RVJ–3 (for hook sizes 1 to 5/0). The jaw is quickly changed by unscrewing the jaw actuator knob, dropping the jaw out, and inserting the desired one. The angled jaw head offers excellent tying clearance around the hook. This vise comes complete with a material spring and a bobbin cradle. The bobbin cradle, with an O-ring embedded in the slip clamp to maintain adjustment, supports the thread or bobbin when using the unique rotary system. A jam-ring adjusts the rotary tension or locks the system. Most rotary vises rotate on the jaw axis; however, because of the offset jaw, the Renzetti rotary system is different. When a hook is mounted, its shank is in direct line with the rotary shaft, allowing the shank to rotate on its own axis. Consequently, the thread, hackle, or dubbing may be applied, not by orbiting the hand around the hook shank in the conventional manner, but by turning the shank itself with the rotating arm. In a manner of speaking, the material is not so much wound on the hook shank as the hook shank is wound on the material. Some tyers have found these two features—tying space around the jaw and axial shank rotation—creative additions to an attractive tying tool.

Features:
1. Base and C-clamp
2. Axial hook shank rotation
3. Fine finish and milling
4. 8¼-inch standrod shaft
5. Three interchangeable jaw heads
6. Excellent tying clearance around the tying space
7. Adjustable material clip and bobbin cradle

The Fly Hook

The hook has been aptly described by Richard W. Talleur, in his thoughtful *Mastering the Art of Fly-tying*, as "the canvas" on which the fly dresser composes his "masterpieces." Yet even a naked hook can be an *objet d'art*. Without the fur and feather, a hook may possess that attractive accelerated sweep, that tapered swirl of eye, that sharp and delicate spear that marks it a masterpiece.

Like many tyers, I react to hook styles. I prefer some merely because I tie on them, and I tie on them merely because I prefer them. Some are old friends. They have a familiar grace and I know what to expect from them in terms of space and shape. I find history in the sneck and salmon music in the Limerick. But the hook is more than emotion; it is said that the history of man may be seen in the history of the hook. If so, then the history of man is complex and growing ever specialized.

The general process of hook making is simple, yet complex. It is done by touch and by theory. First, the wires are honed sharp, then barbed and bent. In bending, the barb connects with a "template," and the wire is bent around to fashion the particular bend. Traditional bends—such as Limerick, perfect, sneck, and Sproat—are often modified for modern taste. For example, Partridge's Redditch bend is a modified perfect bend to maintain an adequate gap essential for hooking. Many modern bends are variations, often variations and combinations of the perfect and sproat. Some hooks are then cold-slammed, the so-called "forged" hooks, on the heel. The bowing or eyeing must be as round as possible, tightly closed, and centered on the shank. The inside diameter of the eye is usually the diameter of the particular hook wire used. The eye is set at thirty-five degrees, either up or down. The hooks are hardened and tempered. This gives the correct spring and strength. The balance between hardness and softness is delicate. If a hook is too brittle, it will snap; if it is too soft, it may open. In either case, the hook has failed. Finally, each hook is inspected and packaged.

The Partridge Hook Company cuts the high-carbon steel wire to length.

To avoid over-heating, three grinding passes form the cone point. In most cases the wire is pointed at both ends.

Antique hook from *The Book of St. Albans*, 1496.

To produce the tapered eye, the center of the wire is pennelled or tapered. The wire may now be cut to produce two hooks.

The wire is then barbed or "bearded" by automation or by hand. Partridge cuts about 20% into the wire at the base of the point and lifts the barb to align with the point.

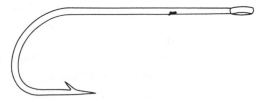

If required, the hook heel is forged flat for extra strength.

The hook wire then wraps around a template to form the bend.

The eye is formed in the bowing process around a small pin, usually the same diameter as the hook wire.

The eye is normally set up or down about 30°.

CHARACTERISTICS OF THE FLY HOOK

THE SIZE

Hook selection is shrouded in mystery and tradition. Usually a hook is selected, not by the gap size, but by the shank length for the particular pattern or insect. Understanding basic terminology allows the tyer to select the corresponding shape and size for the natural. Hooks numbered 2 through 28 grow smaller as the numbers become larger. Usually only even-numbered hooks are manufactured, although it may be possible to find the elderly odd-numbered hook on occasion. Sizes 1 through 30/0 grow larger as the number becomes larger.

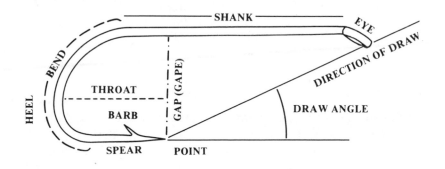

Modified hook lengths, either shorter or longer than the "standard," are indicated by an "X" rating. Each X notation means the standard-length shank has been lengthened without a gap change to the shank size of a standard hook one size larger. For example, a number 12 1X would have a size 12 gap, but would have a shank length of a size 10 hook. Conversely, a number 12 1X short hook would have a gap equal to a standard size 12 hook and a shank length equal to a standard size 14 hook.

The wire-weight system is similar. A 1X heavy wire is equal to the wire-weight used in a hook one size larger; a 1X light wire, equal to the wire-weight used in a hook one size smaller. Light wire forms dry-fly hooks, and heavy wire makes wet and nymph hooks.

There is no universal or absolute measurement for hook sizing. If the hook is of the same type, such as a dry-fly hook, then the size designation is usually enough. However, the scale does differ among manufacturers and, sometimes, among countries. Therefore, it is always best to speak of the manufacturer and hook style as well—that is, a Partridge Code A, size 14, or a Mustad 94842, size 12. This avoids confusion. Various hook makers base the size scale on different parts of the hook. Mustad, for example, primarily bases the hook size on the gap width, the distance from point to shank. Other firms, such as Partridge, have based the scale on the shank length. Descriptions such as 2XL, meaning that the shank length is equal to the shank length of a regular hook two sizes larger, are seldom accurate because of different bends, mensurations, and manufacturers. When hook variations—bends (perfect, Sproat, Limerick, sneck, or Wilson); shank length (regular or extra long or extra short); shank formations (straight, curved, angled, or "broken"); eye angles (up, down, or ringed); eye formations (looped, ball, tapered, or flat); wire diameters (regular, extra heavy, or extra light); gap width; spear length or throat; barbed or barbless; point formations (hollow, superior, or Dublin); offsets (kirbed or reversed); shank sections (regular or forged); and shank tapers (regular or low-water)—are considered, it is no wonder that hooks appear in thousands of shapes and sizes.

APPROXIMATE STANDARD HOOK LENGTHS

5/0	2"	4	$^{15}/_{16}$"	18	$^4/_{16}$"
4/0	1$^7/_8$"	6	$^{13}/_{16}$"	20	$^7/_{32}$"
3/0	1$^3/_4$"	8	$^{11}/_{16}$"	22	$^6/_{32}$"
2/0	1$^5/_8$"	10	$^9/_{16}$"	24	$^{11}/_{64}$"
1/0	1$^1/_2$"	12	$^7/_{16}$"	26	$^{10}/_{64}$"
1	1$^1/_4$"	14	$^6/_{16}$"	28	$^9/_{64}$"
2	1$^1/_8$"	16	$^5/_{16}$"		

THE OFFSET

The advantage of an offset point (kirbed or reversed) is moot. Flies are usually tied on straight-shanked hooks, i.e, shanks that align with the spear. However, some tyers consider the offset point an asset for the smaller size hooks, especially for hooks smaller than size 18. A kirbed spear points to the left if the hook is held with the bend up and the point facing

GAP/LENGTH COMBINATIONS FOR A TYPICAL NO. 8 HOOK

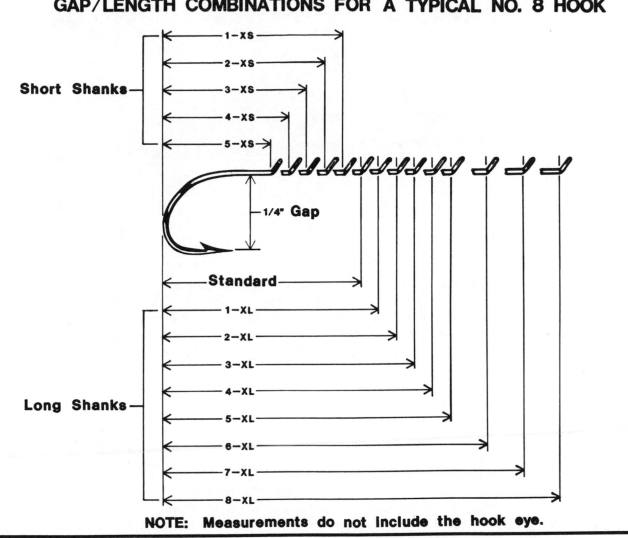

NOTE: Measurements do not include the hook eye.

you. A reverse spear, when held in the same manner, points to the right. A straight shank is one that aligns the spear with the shank. A kirbed point is perhaps better for right-handed tying because it offers the shank to the tyer. Some hooks, such as the older Bartleet salmon irons, are also distinguished by point lift, where the point rises toward and then parallels the shank. The wide gap on the salmon iron compensates for any "ricocheting" of the rounded "brow."

One way of increasing the gap and creating a "searching point" is to offset the spear. Although Datus Proper doubts the effectiveness of a kirbed or reversed point, it is one way of increasing the gap on a small hook. However, the increase is not as significant as might be expected. If the

Reversed

Kirbed

Straight

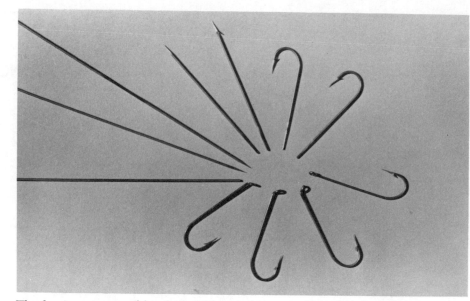

The basic process of hook-making, starting at nine o'clock and proceeding clockwise.

offset is one-half the gap distance (a hypothetical exaggeration), then the gap increase is only about twelve percent. This is not a significant gap increase when considering the distorted hook shape. Nevertheless, the offset spear does increase hooking potential. The spear spirals in for a greater hold. A spear bent away from the shank axis will also create a searching point and increase the hold.

THE FORGE

The cold-slammed, flat-forged bend thickens the metal on the axis in which the greatest stress may arise. Tradition claims that forged hooks are fished dry and unforged hooks are fished wet. There may be more important factors, such as wire weight, that determine whether a hook is fished wet or dry. Traditional forging has dubious value. The increased metal on the vertical axis is at the expense of the metal on the horizontal axis, metal which would have to be bent against in the first place. If forging is done to a significant extent, then some strength may be gained on a single axis. But what is gained on one axis is lost on the other axis. The Partridge company has forged some hooks on the inside curve only, thereby preserving a strong vertical and horizontal axis.

THE EYE

There are three methods in forming and positioning hook eyes. They may be tapered, ball, looped, and up, down, or ringed, and even combinations of these, such as a tapered up-eye. A tapered eye has the eye-wire tapered before the eye is formed. This produces a delicate, light eye. If the wire is not tapered before forming, a ball eye results. Looped-eye hooks, where the eye-wire doubles back and extends a short distance along the shank, adds weight and prevents leader wear by eliminating the critical and abrasive wire end at the head. Up-eyes are usually used for salmon, steelhead, and dries, down-eyes for streamers and wets. The ringed or straight eyes are often used for saltwater, bass, and midge patterns where effective hooking is paramount. To a limited degree, the down-eye hook makes the draw angle more acute and, consequently, more effective. In the smaller sizes, the up-eye grants a wider gap, but on some patterns the body diameter of the pattern may extend as far as or farther than the eye does from the shank. A mild down-eye is usually preferred on all hooks for this reason.

THE BARB

A wide or long barb may actually impede penetration. The increased surface of a large barb, sometimes described as the "resistant wedge," requires greater penetrative force. The entry furrow caused by a large barb may actually allow the spear to escape. The primary penetration resistance occurs on the top of the spear where the barb is located. This, of course, allows the barb to hold under pressure; however, this resistance may also preclude deep entry by a large barb. When in doubt, cut the barb out. A sharp point and a flattened barb may actually increase retention because the spear sinks deeper into trout tissue. If a barb is present, it should be small and far enough from the hook heel to allow deep penetration. The only advantage of a small, delicate barb may be for airborne trout on slack line.

H. G. McClelland's *How to Tie Flies* (1939) discusses the Hardy "harpoon" hook, which had the barbs cut into the near and far sides of the point. Roman Moser's recent "spear point," produced by Partridge, is similar. The spear point has a lateral flange on each side of the point. This is an excellent idea in that it increases the horizontal width, thereby decreasing tissue tear. It is for this reason that I sharpen hooks on a horizontal plane

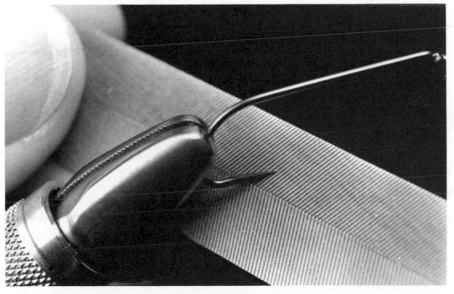

Rather than folding the barb down, hook-debarbing is best done by filing the barb off, leaving a flat surface on the point. The flat top prevents the point from ripping or cutting the holding tissue. The silicone-treated Luhr-Jensen four-inch hook file cleanly wipes the barb off all but the smallest hooks.

across the top of the point. However, a cutting edge should be avoided on the sides of the point. McClelland believed that "while all cutting edges aid penetration immensely, those at the side might start a tear in the flesh, and aid the hook's pulling out."

Partridge of Redditch believes that the optimum barb depth should be twenty percent of the wire diameter, and certainly never more than twenty-five percent. Less than twenty percent is acceptable for trout hooks. Note that the barb is cut from the full diameter of the hook wire (where the point begins) and angled from twenty-five to thirty degrees. The Partridge

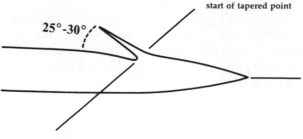

barb is delicate and severs minimal wire. The points will vary in shape and length. Time and trial will determine the value of "chemical sharpening," an acid-erosion process. Usually a short, steep point with the entry point on the lower edge of the wire is desirable. The lower point will cause the point to seek tissue rather than merely slip or skip.

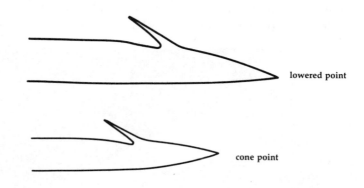

THE GAP

A wide gap may have as much effect, perhaps even more, as a barb does in holding trout. A wide gap allows the hook to secure enough tissue so that it will not pull free. A "narrow" hook that captures only a morsel will invariably pull free during the struggle. A gap must be great enough to secure a hold, but not so great as to diminish the draw angle. Many small hooks have a narrow gap unsuitable for the selective, muscular trout that require small patterns. For hooks smaller than a size 18, the ratio between the effective shank length and the gap may be in favor of the gap to increase the holding power. Perhaps tyers should speak in terms of the "effective gap," the distance between the down eye and the point.

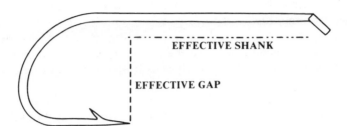

EFFECTIVE SHANK

EFFECTIVE GAP

The effective gap is the vertical distance between the down eye and the hook point. The effective gap, perhaps, should be the actual distance between the body of the dressed pattern and the hook point. It is surprising how often this distance is critically diminished by body mass, especially on such patterns as shrimp and Irresistibles. In the standard size 12 (Mustad 94840), the eye droop occupies one-third of the distance from shank to point. A two-thirds effective gap must be a consideration when tying and trouting. It becomes even more critical with smaller hooks—so critical, in fact, that the effective gap of hooks in the 20 range may have a fifty percent or less effective gap. An up-eyed hook, obviously, has an effective gap equal to the true gap. But what is gained in effective gap is often lost in effective penetration.

THE TEMPER AND HARDNESS

In terms of hook strength, the modern tippet can actually surpass the breaking strength of some small hooks. Metal technology is virtually the same as it has been in the last several decades, but research in polymers has produced a tippet stronger than some hooks on which it is tied. Much depends on the hook shape, the wire diameter, the degree of forging, and the hardening and tempering process. Under controlled conditions the hooks are hardened and then tempered for the correct strength and spring. A hook should yield to a certain point and then break, rather than straighten out. In other words, a hook should bend before it breaks and then break before it bends farther. Many anglers prefer a hard temper with limited spring. One test method used by Partridge is to place the point into the end of a wooden dowel and pull until the hook opens or bends. Experienced feel determines whether more or less "cooking" is required.

THE MECHANICS OF STRESS

In his perceptive *What the Trout Said*, Datus Proper establishes the failure angle of a hook. In his testing, sample hooks are weighted along the pull line until they break, or open to forty-five degrees, whichever comes first. Certainly, a hook that opens to forty-five degrees is an unreliable fishholder. It should be noted that Proper's stress analysis is, as he admits, a "worse-case scenario," based on the hook before penetration. He indicates that hook failure usually comes before the point penetrates past the barb. Certainly the initial entry angle, which is what he stresses, is important in terms of ease of entry. But the stress instantly shifts, however, into new geometry as soon as the point has penetrated. His reasoning is solid, but

I do believe that significant trout loss can occur even after the point has sunk home. For me, *that* is the worse-case scenario. If, due to a narrow gap, the hook has not gathered enough holding tissue, then it may pull out. If the design mechanics stress the hook, then it may either yield or break. For this reason, my bend analysis is based upon complete penetration.

The "effective shank length," a creative phrase from Datus Proper, is that portion of the shank "in front of the point of the hook." Proper concludes that the minimum leverage for adequate hooking power is about 1½ to 1. That is, the effective shank length should be about half again greater than the gap. The resulting angle, from point line to line of pull, is thirty-five percent. This experiential figure is adequate for most fishing. But as the point penetrates, the angle becomes more acute and, consequently, more effective. Therefore, it may be possible to have a 1¼ to 1 ratio, which some small hooks have, without significant trout loss, especially if the spear is offset. The Orvis Supreme Dry Fly Hook (size 22, regular shank) has a gap ratio less than 1¼ to 1. Mustad's 94842 (size 20) has a gap ratio approximately 1½ to 1. Partridge's Code B Wide Gape (slight reverse), which I have used on spring creeks and chalk streams for years, has an Effective Shank Length actually shorter than the gap itself. Once the penetration is complete, the "Final Direction of Draw" (A–C) exerts maximum stress. The more acute the angle E is, the more efficient is the penetration, and the less effective is the hold, which gathers less tissue. From this arises the fundamental paradox of hook design: the wider the gap, the more effective the hold, and the less efficient the hooking leverage.

The following hooks illustrate three distinct "geometries" of stress. The line A–C is the final direction of draw. Angle E is the penetration angle; the more acute this angle, the more efficient the spear entry. The holding force is dependent upon the resistance of tissue, the area and flatness of the spear top, and the depth of penetration. A hook with "quick penetration"—i.e., a short spear—has less holding force than a longer spear. Line D, always the longest right angle line to line A–C, is the stress line. The longer A–C is, the greater the force passed to the wire at B. The more angular the bend at B, the more this force is concentrated. The tendency of a hook to break at the upper bend is dependent upon the distance between the upper bend and the final draw line.

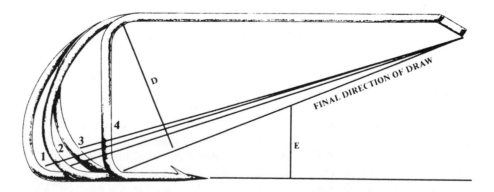

Comparison of hook bends with a given gap and shank length. As the "Final Direction of Draw" lines vary in length and angle according to the particular bends—(1) Limerick, (2) Sproat, (3) Perfect, and (4) Sneck—so does the D, the stress line, and E, the penetration angle.

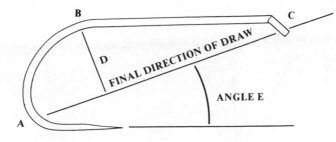

The sproat has a moderate length of line D and a mild curve at B, making it a relatively strong hook design.

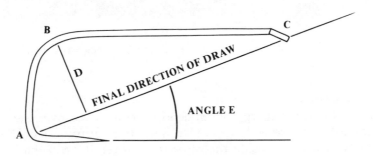

The sneck has a longish D and an angular B, which gathers the stress, making it a relatively weak design. However, heavy wire and a milder heel-shank bend can improve the sneck.

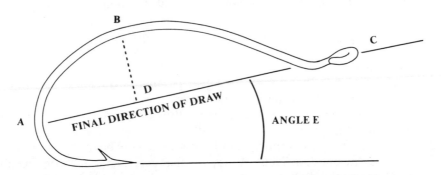

By way of contrast, the Partridge Yorkshire Caddis hook has a short D line, a shallow B bend, and heavy wire that make it a remarkably strong and efficient hook.

THE HOOK BENDS:
THE ADVANTAGES AND DISADVANTAGES

THE LIMERICK

Advantages
1. The attractive "rakish" lines
2. The hook "trails" well in heavy water
3. The set-back point produces a superior penetration angle

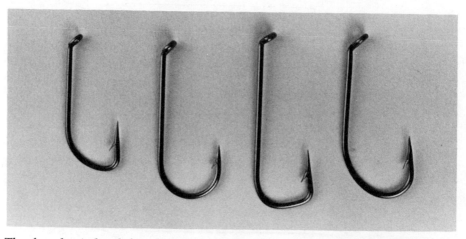

The four basic hook bends: Limerick, Perfect, Sneck, and Sproat.

Disadvantages

1. Limericks with a sharp bottom bend are considered by some to be less strong than those with a rounded heel. The abruptness of the bottom bend varies from manufacturer to manufacturer. It is true that an angular bend gathers more mechanical stress; however, the heavy wire used for salmon and streamer hooks produces a strong bend.
2. There is a significant extension of steel beyond the body of the fly, which may be a key to selective rejection. However, the trailing feathers and fibers of wets and streamers may cloak the bend.

THE PERFECT

Advantages

1. This semicircular bend with the spear parallel to the shank distributes the stress throughout most of the curve.
2. The perfect opens the distance between the point and the shank, thereby increasing the gap.
3. The perfect has a medium bite and a moderate heel beyond the fly body.
4. Ernest Schwiebert, in *Trout*, comments that perfect bends "offer optimal strength in the light-wire hooks designed for high-floating performance."
5. Because of the wide gap, the perfect bend is appropriate for patterns that bulk the shank, such as the Humpy or Irresistible.
6. The perfect bend is esthetically pleasing to many tyers.
7. The rear shank bend is less angular than the sneck.

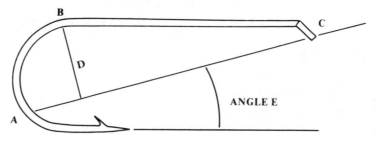

Disadvantages

1. Compared to the sneck, there is a significant extension of steel beyond the fly body.
2. The spear of the perfect is curved, perhaps allowing the trout to twist or turn upon it, and the spear length may be significantly short, thereby restricting the depth of penetration.
3. The weak point, at the rear shank bend, is more angular than a sproat.

THE SNECK

Advantages

1. The fundamental advantage of the sneck bend is that the heel and spear hide directly beneath the fly body. Perhaps the effectiveness of a caddis pattern is due to the overwing and body tending to conceal the heel and spear, making them less visible to selective trout.
2. Unlike the Perfect and Sproat, the increase in gap does not increase the steel beyond the fly body. Any shank length may have any gap width.

Disadvantages

1. The sharp angle, where the bend meets the shank, gathers the mechanical stress to a single point.
2. The sneck bend usually requires heavy wire, which violates the lightness requirement on medium and large dry-fly hooks, to compensate for the angular bends.

THE SPROAT

Advantages

1. The gradual curve at the weak point, where the shank meets the bend, makes the sproat a relatively strong design. The Sproat is actually a modified-perfect bend, with the upper bend, where the major stress would occur, more gradual, and the bottom bend, where minor stress would occur, more abrupt. It preserves some advantages of both bends—the gentle upper curve of the perfect and the wide gap of the sneck. As a "compromise" bend, the Sproat moves the spear to the rear for adequate length and superior hooking leverage.
2. The Sproat has more bite than a perfect bend.
3. The Sproat has no abrupt bend, such as does a Limerick or sneck, which might magnify the mechanical stress.
4. A wide variety of sizes and weights are available for fly tying.

Disadvantages

1. The Sproat exposes a significant amount of heel beyond the fly body. When used for wet flies, bucktails, and streamers, the extension may be insignificant.
2. The Sproat usually does not have the gap or the throat of a perfect bend.

MEDITATIONS ON A MIDGE HOOK

To demonstrate the logic essential for good hook design, let us, for a moment, construct a hypothetical hook. Not all tyers will agree to the arguments and compromises set forth, but all will understand the rationale behind them. A design should be based on the implied purpose of the hook—in this case, a size 20 midge hook, designed for slow clear waters and selective trout. Once the purpose is established, then three principles of hook design come under consideration: 1) for every design gain there is a corresponding loss; 2) compromise must be made between two opposite and equal merits that best accommodate the design; and 3) compromise must be made between two opposite and equal weaknesses that appear. Our hypothetical hook is "ideal" only for the purpose and the compromises that we accept. It might be added that these "meditations" form the rationale behind the Partridge Sneck Midge CS21.

THE HYPOTHETICAL MIDGE HOOK

The Eye: A fifteen-degree down-eye would maintain an adequate gap and an acute draw angle. Most body diameters would extend no farther from the shank than the eye; therefore, this slight down-eye would not decrease the gap.

The Bend: Because of the selectivity of midging trout, the hook heel should hide beneath the body. The weakness of the traditional Sneck design is the abrupt angle between the bend and shank. To minimize the "weak angularity," the upper bend would be slightly rounded to distribute the stress. The bend would leave the shank with a mild curve, immediately seek a straight heel line, and abruptly bend into the spear. The angular bottom bend may be tolerated because most of the stress would be on a vertical axis against the heel, rather than on a horizontal axis against the spear.

The Offset: The spear would be slightly kirbed; that is, the spear points to the left when the bend is up and the hook eye points to you. As a right-handed angler who fishes upstream, I want the spear pointing directly downstream into the trout's mouth. Furthermore, such a bend makes it appropriate for tying because the shank is offered to the tyer while the spear points away. However, the direction of offset, kirbed or reverse, is perhaps not as important as that fact that it *is* offset. And, unlike the extended heel, the offset spear hides beneath the wings and body.

Highly selective trout may have a significant period of "mouth-time," the lapse interval between the envelopment of the fly and the actual entrapment of the fly by the mouth. Only when a shy trout is fairly certain of the fly's authenticity by taste or texture will it exert mouth pressure. Mouth-time, of course, is a survival mechanism. During ascent, the mouth may be open and any tippet tightening may only pull the pattern through trout lips. As previously indicated, the offset is one method of increasing the gap and creating a "searching" point. The searching point will have a tendency to bury into tissue rather than, like a "flat" hook, to slip between trout lips. A soft-tipped rod, an elastic shock-cord tippet, and an offset hook usually increase spring creek success.

The Gap: In small hook sizes, the gap is seldom adequate. The standard size 20 (Mustad 94842 up-eyed dry-fly hook) has an approximate gap of a scant two millimeters. The "effective shank length" is often equal to or smaller than the gap. The effective shank length of our hypothetical midge hook might be about 1¼ the gap. I would accept anything up to about 1⅓ the gap. This would encourage effective hooking and adequate hold. An excessively wide gap would only make the draw angle less acute and less effective. Minute patterns, such as the dry midge, would match the short shank.

The Spear: The ideal hook would be barbless, with a searching point on the lower edge. It is easy, especially in the small hook sizes, to fracture the hook by bending the barb down. And such small sizes normally do not accommodate files well. Quality waters advocate quality angling. A barbless hook penetrates quicker, sinks deeper, and holds better with less tissue damage than most barbed hooks. The spear length should be about three-fourths the gap width. It should be long enough to hold well, yet short enough for effective hooking leverage.

The Wire: The hook wire should be slightly heavy to accommodate large trout on small patterns; therefore, in a size 20, the wire diameter should be a least .015 inch. The angular sneck bends also demand slightly heavier wire. Mustad's 94842 in size 20 is .013 inch, and VMC's 9288 in size 20 is .012 inch. On a size 20, the heavier wire will float as well as a standard wire hook. American tyers often reject effective small patterns because of ineffective small hooks.

The Temper and Hardening: As indicated earlier, a hook should bend before it breaks and break before it opens. The hypothetical midge hook should have slightly more hardness than springiness. Large trout on a small hook demand controlled spring, so that the maximum hook strength is exerted (unto the breaking point) before it opens.

A hypothetical midge hook.

THE CHARACTERISTICS OF THE GOOD HOOK

Although an effective hook is a compromise and balance of opposites, the following list includes many of the desirable manufacturing and design features:

1. An adequate strength for design and wire weight. Datus Proper estimates a 3-pound-test for a size 14 as adequate.
2. A searching point, that is, a point that seeks entry.
3. A design that accommodates the fly pattern.
4. An adequate gap spaced appropriately for that particular hook.
5. The minimal weight with maximum strength.
6. A neat, centered, and tightly formed eye.
7. A minimal spring.

8. A short and sharp point.
9. An adequate spear length.
10. If barbed, a small, delicate barb that severs twenty-five percent or less of the wire diameter.
11. A fine finish.
12. A penetrating point on the lower edge of the spear.

THE FLY HOOKS

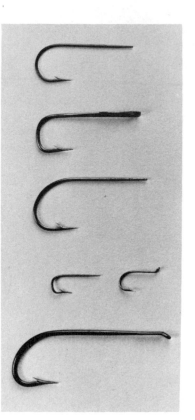

Within the last few decades the hook has become increasingly specialized. There are, of course, wet and dry hooks. But now we have shrimp, pupa, midge, dun, upside down, emerger, swimming nymph, floating nymph, flat-bodied nymph, caddis, keel, stinger, and others of their ilk. The trinity of Mustad, Partridge, and VMC (Viellard, Migeon et Cie) bless the marketplace with a remarkable variety of hook sizes and shapes. Wright & McGill, under the Eagle Claw label, produces some fly hooks, including several dry and streamer styles. And more hooks wait to be canonized by tyers. All companies continue research and development and will continue to introduce manufacturing improvements and new styles that the marketplace sanctions. Tyers should constantly experiment with hook manufacturers and designs just as they do with materials and methods. This will encourage and support creative hook making.

HISTORIC BENDS
Fine wire, Round Blue, size 6 (1935)
Spring Loop Hook, size 6 (1936)
Straight shank, Forged Bend, size 3 (1937)
Sneck Hand Bend, size 14 (1933)   Helical Trout, size 0 (1936)
Partridge Salmon, size 2 (*c.* 1935)

MUSTAD OF NORWAY

According to Hans Jorgen Hurum's *A History of the Fish Hook* (1977), the water wheels of the Huns River spun O. Mustad & Son's first hook machine, designed by Mathias Topp, in November of 1877. Gifted metal workers, creative machine designers, English hook-making skills, quality hooks, aggressive international marketing, and secrecy made Mustad. Perhaps more patterns appear on a Mustad than on any other hook. Mustad's dry fly hooks include the 3913, 94833, 94836, 94837, 94840, 94842, and the barbless 94845. Mustad's 94840 is claimed as the most common fly hook in the world. The wet-fly and small nymph hooks are 3906, 3908, 7948, 9671, and 9672. The large nymph and streamer hooks include the 3665, 9575, 38941, 79580, and 94720. Special patterns, such as a plump Humpy, may be tied on the 94838. The extra-long shank 3906B creates nymphs, and the 2X long 9671 makes medium nymphs. Larger nymphs and Woolly Worms often use the 3X long 9672. Muddler minnows are wrapped on a

38941 or the 4X long 79580. The 9575 is one-half inch longer than a regular shank and is used for large streamer patterns. The Viking bend is a perfect or round bend. The most common point shapes are hollow and superior. The outer edge of the hollow point is straight, while the line curves between the point and the innermost part of the barb. The superior point is opposite with the outer edge curved and the inner edge, between the point and barb, straight. The widely distributed Mustad hooks include a full range for the fly tyer.

STANDARD MUSTAD FLY HOOKS

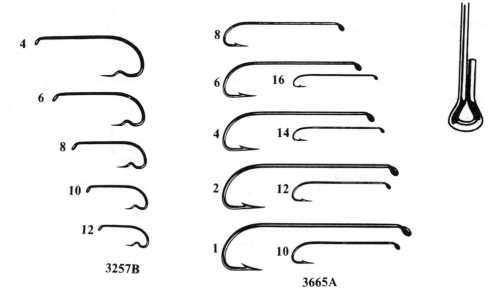

3257B

3665A

3257B	Barbless, superior point, turned-down tapered eye, bronzed, extra-fine wire, kink instead of barb, sizes 8–16
3665A	Limerick, hollow point, turned-down tapered eye, bronzed, one-half inch longer than regular, sizes 2–14
3906B	Sproat, hollow point, turned-down tapered eye, bronzed, extra-long shank, wet-fly and nymph hook, sizes 4–18
3913B	Special Sproat, hollow point, slightly reversed, turned-up tapered eye, bronzed, wide gap, European distribution

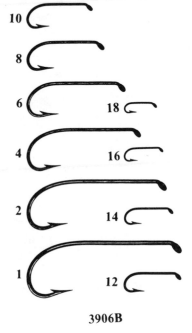

3906B

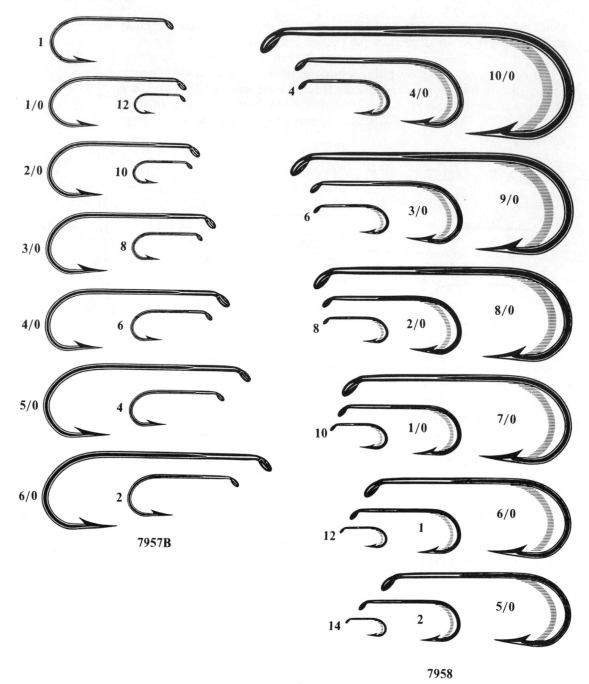

7957B

7958

7957B   Hollow point Viking, forged, straight, turned-down tapered
         eye, bronzed, long shank, sizes 2–18

7957BX   Hollow point Viking, forged, straight, turned-down tapered
         eye, long shank, extra-strong wire, sizes 2–8

7958   Hollow point Viking, forged, reversed, turned-down tapered
         eye, bronzed, sizes 2/0 and 6–20

9523 Hollow point Viking, 5X extra-short shank, turned-up eye, extra-fine wire, spider hook, sizes 8–16

9671 Hollow point Viking, forged, straight, turned-down tapered eye, bronzed, 2X extra-long shank, sizes 2–18

9672 Hollow point Viking, forged, straight, turned-down tapered eye, bronzed, 3X extra-long shank, sizes 2–18

9674 Hollow point Viking, forged, straight, ringed eye, bronzed, 4X extra-long shank, sizes 1–14

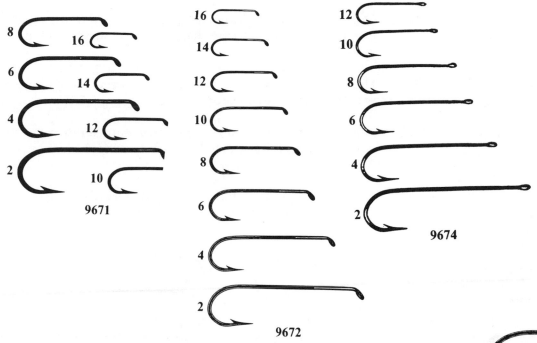

36620 Limerick, one-half inch longer than standard, ringed eye, Thunder Creek hook, sizes 4–10

36890 Turned-up, looped-oval eye, Limerick bend, Dublin point, forged, black, for Atlantic salmon and steelhead flies, sizes 1–12

33960 Sproat, turned-down ball eye, 4X extra-long, streamer and nymph hook, sizes 2–12

37160 Hollow point, wide gap, slightly reversed, upturned ball eye, bronzed, sizes 7/0 and 2–20

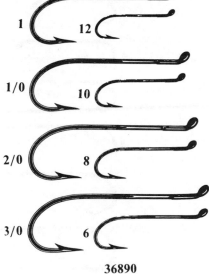

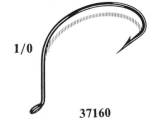

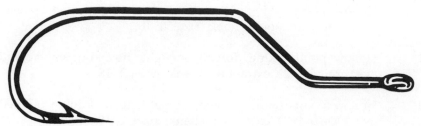

38972

37187	Hollow point, open bend, straight, ringed and bronzed, the "stinger," sizes 1/0, 2, 6 and 10
79580	Hollow point Viking, forged, straight, turned-down tapered eye, bronzed, 4X extra-long shank, streamer and nymph hook, sizes 2–16
79791	Hollow point Viking, forged, reversed, turned-down tapered eye, bronzed, 5X extra-short shank, extra-fine wire, sizes 2–16
79792	Hollow point Viking, forged, reversed, turned-down tapered eye, gold plated, 5X extra-short shank, extra-fine wire, sizes 2–18
94720	Hollow point Viking, forged, straight, turned-down tapered eye, bronzed, 8X extra-long shank, sizes 2–8

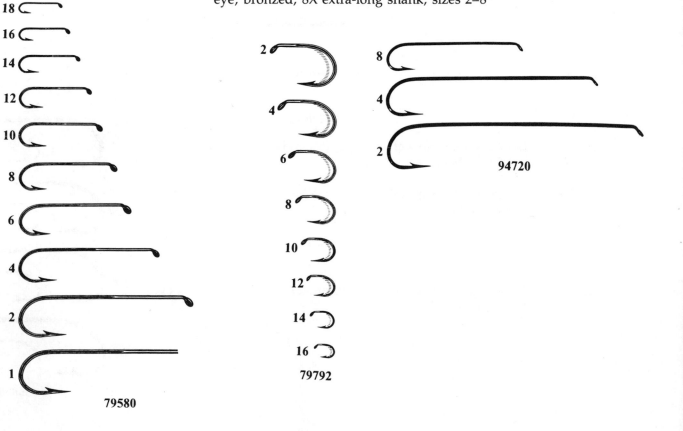

94831   Hollow point Viking, forged, straight, turned-down tapered eye, bronzed, 2X extra-fine wire, 2X extra-long shank, sizes 4–16

94833   Hollow point Viking, forged, straight, turned-down tapered eye, bronzed, 3X extra-fine wire, sizes 2–20

94836   Hollow point Viking, forged, straight, turned-down tapered eye, bronzed, short-shank, extra-fine wire, sizes 10–20

94838   Hollow point Viking, forged, straight, turned-down tapered eye, bronzed, extra-fine wire, sizes 10–20

94842   Hollow point Viking, forged, straight, turned-up and tapered eye, bronzed, extra-fine wire, sizes 6–28

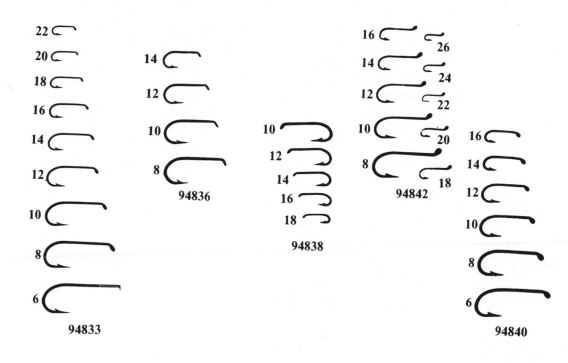

94845   Hollow point Viking, forged, straight, turned-down tapered eye, bronzed, fine wire, barbless, sizes 8–20

94840   Hollow-point Viking, model Perfect bend, extra-fine wire, forged, straight, bronzed, turned-down tapered eye, claimed to be the most popular fly hook in America, sizes 8–28

94859   Hollow point Viking, forged, straight, ringed eye, bronzed, extra-fine wire, midge, sizes 20–28

94863   Hollow point Viking, forged, straight, bronzed, barbless, extra-fine wire, turned-down looped eye, sizes 6–16

PARTRIDGE OF REDDITCH

Partridge of Redditch is perhaps the most creative company producing modern hooks. It had been in hook making for well over one hundred years when the firm was sold to Pickering and Bramley in 1970. It now has a product range of about four hundred different hook models. Despite the small company size and reliance on individual handwork, they produce a remarkable range of unique fly hooks, and have led the way in inventive design, introducing up to twenty new hook styles each year. Redditch, one hundred years ago, was a major hook-making center that included firms like Allcock, Bartleet, Hewitt, Millward, and Sealey. The "Redditch bend" used by Partridge on most of their trout hooks is based on the old Allcock "model perfect" and the revived Captain Hamilton bend. Both roundish bends produce a good gap and allow the hook to pivot, easily precluding "the possibility of tearing out during the struggle." Partridge fly hooks are made from high-carbon, Sheffield steel wire covered with a rust preventative for the course of production. It is this coating that gives the hooks a lustrous bronze color. The characteristics of a Partridge hook are the fine point, the delicate barb, the neat eye, and the strength. Partridge's "Connoisseur Series" includes their finely wrought specialty hooks.

Partridge hooks cover a wide range. The Draper Flat-Bodied Nymph hook, developed by Keith Draper of New Zealand in 1977, incorporates a wide gap, short point and barb, as well as a looped shank bronzed at the bend. The Captain Hamilton hooks, both in dry and wet weights, feature the perfect bend, large gap, short point, and delicate barb. The Yorkshire Caddis hook, which was developed by Peter Mackenzie-Philps, is considered by some tyers to be the finest sloped-shank hook on the market. The Yorkshire Caddis hook is, by no means, solely for larval and pupa patterns. It is a superb hook for shrimp, stonefly, and dragonfly patterns. It is a curved-shank hook in bronze, sizes 16 to 8. Perhaps some larger sizes would be advantageous for our stonefly and dragonfly patterns. The hook point is not in line with the eye. And with a wider-than-standard gap, the "open gap" design makes a superior hooker. It is available in a medium-weight wire, called "2X fine" by Partridge, except for size 8, which is a standard, heavyweight wire. The Yorkshire is flat-forged with a slightly turned-up eye.

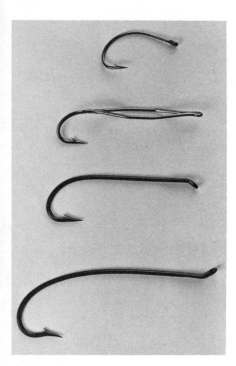

Innovation in hook design: Partridge Grumb-Shrimp Hook, Partridge Draper Flat-bodied Nymph Hook, Partridge SEB Steelhead and Salmon Hook, Partridge Bartleet Salmon Hook.

Standard Partridge Fly Hooks

For comparison, the following table describes the Partridge trout and single salmon hook range with designations, uses, and specifications (body length, gap, wire diameter, and hook weight) for a size 12 (with exception of the size 24 K1A midge).

CODE	LENGTH MM	GAP MM	DIAMETER MM	WEIGHT MG
A	8	4.5	.56	36

Albert Partridge, widegape, down-eye hook, offset bend, short point, wet fly, short nymph and medium-weight dry fly, developed about 1930

B	8	4.5	.56	36

Albert Partridge, medium-weight, up-eye dry fly

D3ST	12	5.5	.61	64

Partridge straight-eye streamer hook, streamer, still-water nymphs, muddler minnow, 4X long, developed 1978

D4A	14	5.5	.61	68

Partridge bucktail/streamer hook, streamer, still-water nymphs, muddler minnow, patterns with bucktail wings, 4X long, flat-forged Redditch bend, down-eye, developed in 1980

D5B	11	5.3	.56	44

Partridge mayfly hook, offset bend, up- or down-eye, 1980 modification of an older pattern

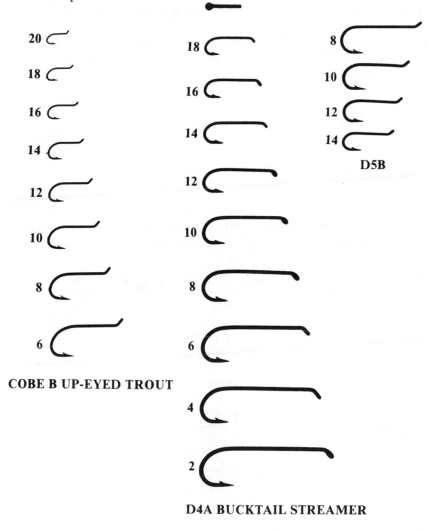

COBE B UP-EYED TROUT

D5B

D4A BUCKTAIL STREAMER

| D74 | 14 | 5.3 | .56 | 54 |

Captain Hamilton streamer hook, still-water nymph, wet fly, medium-weight wire, 2X fine, 2½X long, flat-forged, down-eye, same as the Partridge nymph hook H1A

| E1A | 10 | 4.8 | .51 | 36 |

Hooper L/S 4X fine, dry fly, down-eye, ½X long, flat-forged, Redditch bend. Ken Hooper, who worked with Partridge during the last six years of his fifty years in Redditch hook making, was involved in the original design of this range for Sealey. The specifications are almost identical to the "Premium" hook that Sealey made for Orvis.

| E3AY | 10 | 4.8 | .51 | 36 |

Except that these hooks are barbless, they are identical in every way with the Code E1A range. These "needle point" hooks have no hump or barb substitute.

| E4A | 9 | 4.8 | .51 | 32 |

Andre Ragot, dry-fly hook, made for the French firm Mouches Ragot, 4X fine, about ½X short, forged, offset, down-eye, Redditch bend

| E6A | 9 | 4.8 | .51 | 32 |

Hooper 1X short, 4X fine, dry fly, down-eye, evolved from the E1A about 1960, for high-riding patterns, about ½X short, Redditch bend

| E6B | 9 | 4.8 | .51 | 32 |

Hooper 1X short, 4X fine, dry fly, up-eye version of E6A

| E6AY | 9 | 4.8 | .51 | 32 |

Barbless version of E6A

| G3A | 8 | 4.8 | .61 | 48 |

Sproat, forged, wet fly, nymph, down-eye, standard wire and length. In about 1880, Mr. Sproat of Ambleside approached Hutchinsons of Kendal with the Sproat bend, which has since become popular.

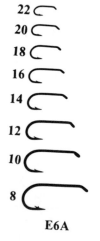

E3AY

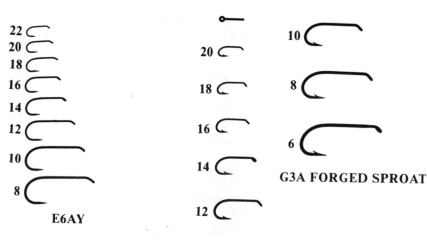

E6A

E6AY

G3A FORGED SPROAT

H1A   14   5.3   .56   54
Captain Hamilton, nymph hook, wet fly and nymph, light streamers, 2X
fine, 2½X long, flat-forged, Captain Hamilton bend, wide gap, down-eye,
developed in 1980

H3ST   15   5.5   .61   116
Draper flat-bodied nymph hook, 6X long, flat-forged, low-water salmon
bend, wide gap, straight double-type eye, special shape, developed by
Keith Draper of New Zealand

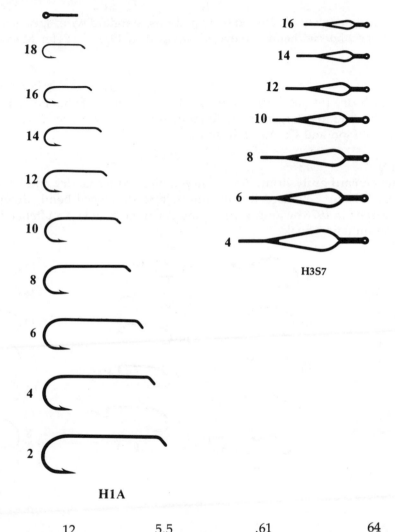

H1A

H3S7

H4ST   12   5.5   .61   64
Partridge straight eye L/S nymph hook, streamers, nymphs, and muddler
minnows, 4X long, flat-forged, wide gap, straight ball eye, same as Partridge D3ST

H5A   14   5.5   .61   68
Partridge long-shank nymph hook, nymph, streamer, and muddler minnow hook, 4X long, flat-forged, Redditch bend, wide gap, down-eye, same
as D4A

J1A 8 4.8 .61 48
Partridge Limerick, wet-fly hook, standard weight and length, flat-forged,
down-eye, popular in New Zealand and Australia

K1A 3.5 2 .31 5
SIZE 24
Vince Marinaro, midge hook, small dry-fly and nymph hook, 4X fine,
standard length, offset, forged, Captain Hamilton bend, wide gap, down-
eye, developed in 1978

K2B 14 5.8 .61 44
Yorkshire sedge hook, curved body patterns, standard wire, special length,
flat-forged special bend, up-eye, developed in 1979 by Peter Mackenzie-
Philps

K3A 14 5 .51 52
Swedish dry-fly hook, upside-down dry-fly hook, LaFontaine caddis, 4X
fine, 2X long, flat-forged, modified Sproat bend, down-eye, developed by
Nils Eriksson and Gunnar Johnson in 1979

K4A 13 5.5 .56 40
John Veniard grub/shrimp hook, curved body patterns, dry and larva patterns, 2X fine, standard length, offset, forged, special bend, down-eye,
developed in 1976 by John Veniard and Partridge based on an Italian blood-
worm-imitation hook

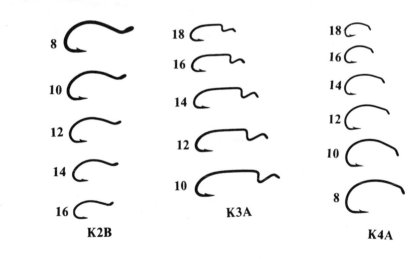

K5ST 10 5.3 .51 44
J. G. upside-down hook, for USD patterns developed by John Goddard
and Brian Clark, also nymph and wet-fly hook, 2X fine, standard length,
forged, offset, Captain Hamilton bend, wide gap, straight-eye

K6ST 12 5.3 .56 48
Taff Price swimming-nymph hook, medium-length nymphs, 2X fine, about
4X long, Sproat bend, straight-eye

K9A   14   5.5   .61   68

Trevor Housby, dog knobbler L/S hook, dog knobbler patterns, 4X long, flat-forged Redditch bend, wide gap, down-eye, dog knobbler patterns were originally tied on American-type jig hooks

L1A   9   5.3   .61   48

Captain Hamilton standard H/W wet-fly hook, standard wet patterns, flat-forged, wide gap, down-eye, Captain Hamilton near-round bend. Captain Hamilton, a Scot living in New Zealand at the turn of the century, asked Hardy for a range of hooks to match the heavy New Zealand trout. Albert Partridge made them for Hardy.

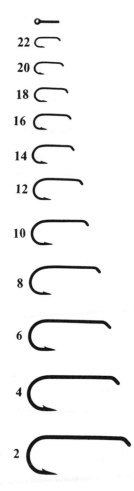

CODE L CAPTAIN HAMILTON

L2A   9   5.3   .56   40

Captain Hamilton standard M/H wet fly hook, medium-weight wet- or dry-fly hook developed in 1978, 2X fine, flat-forged, wide gap, down-eye

L3A   9   5.3   .51   32

Captain Hamilton standard dry fly, down-eye hook, 4X fine, standard length, flat-forged, Captain Hamilton bend, wide gap

L3B	9	5.3	.51	32

Captain Hamilton standard dry fly, up-eye version of L3A

L4A	9	5.3	.46	28

Captain Hamilton featherweight dry fly, down-eye hook, for lightly hackled or no-hackle dry flies, 6X fine, flat-forged, wide gap, Captain Hamilton bend

L4B	9	5.3	.46	28

Captain Hamilton featherweight dry fly, up-eye version of L4A

M	9	5	.69	60

Partridge single salmon hook, heavyweight, fast-sinking flies in fast water, black finish, 2X heavy, flat-forged salmon bend, loop up-eye. Note that the Partridge salmon hook codes are M (single salmon, heavyweight, standard length); N (single, low-water, heavyweight, 2X long); and 01 (single Wilson, medium-weight, about 6X long).

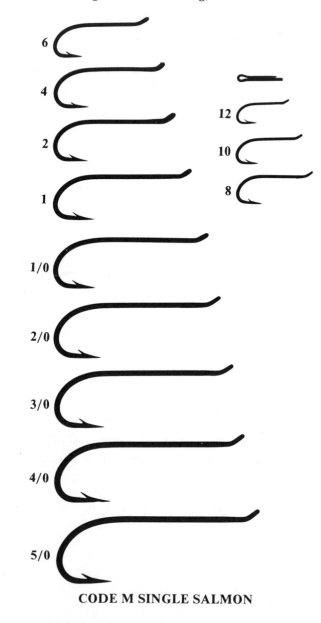

CODE M SINGLE SALMON

N   11   5   .64   60

Partridge single low-water hook, medium-weight, dressed lightly and short for salmon and sea trout, black finish, 1X heavy, 2X long on salmon scale, flat-forged, low-water bend, looped up-eye, developed about 1920 for low-water conditions.

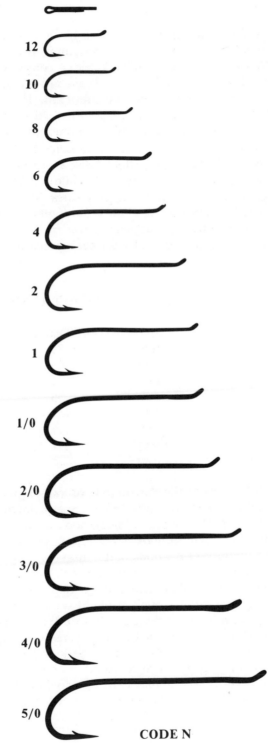

12

10

8

6

4

2

1

1/0

2/0

3/0

4/0

5/0

CODE N

16

14

12

10

8

6

4

2

CODE 01 SINGLE WILSON

| 01 | 14.5 | 6.8 | .64 | 85 |

Partridge single Wilson hook, lightweight salmon and sea trout in low-water conditions, black finish, medium-weight wire, about 6X long on salmon scale, flat-forged, sweeping Wilson bend, wide gap, looped up-eye, developed about 1930. Minto Wilson believed that he would catch more salmon with a fine-wire salmon fly hook that stayed near the surface, almost a dry fly.

The Partridge Grub-Shrimp hook (code K4A) is another sloped-shank hook that is suitable for all small, curved imitations. It is 2X fine, medium-weight, slightly offset, and unforged. Partridge continues to market the Marinaro Midge hooks in size 24 to 28. These are 4X fine (lightweight), wide gap, turned-down eye, offset, and unforged. They are appropriate for micro-dries as well as minute nymph patterns. Also, the less expensive Sealey brand hooks are now made and distributed by Partridge.

The Partridge up-eyed, wide-gap trout hook (code B) is considered by some tyers to be the finest small-pattern hook available. The 2X fine wire (medium-weight) lends superior strength, while the 1X short shank and 1X wide gap grants improved hooking properties. The code A is a down-eyed version of code B; both are medium-weight, offset, dry-fly hooks with an "improved" or modified sproat bend. Occasionally, code B is available down to size 20. This range of hooks has been produced by Partridge for almost fifty years.

CODE A, ALBERT PARTRIDGE WIDEGAPE DIMENSIONS

Size	Body Length	Gap	Wire Diameter	Weight (mg)
6	14 mm	7.5 mm	.74	100
8	12 mm	6.5 mm	.66	74
10	10 mm	5.5 mm	.61	52
12	8 mm	4.5 mm	.56	36
14	6.5 mm	4.0 mm	.51	24
16	5.5 mm	3.5 mm	.46	18
18	4.5 mm	3.0 mm	.41	14
20	3.5 mm	2.5 mm	.38	12

More recent additions to the Partridge hook catalog include the Andre Ragot dry-fly hook (sizes 8 to 22); the Skues Sneck down-eye hook (sizes 12, 13, 14, 15, 16, and 17); the Sneck Midge hook (code CS21, sizes 18 and 20); the T. S. Floating Nymph hook (sizes 12, 14, 16, and 17); the S. E. B. Steelhead and Salmon Wet Fly hook, a down-eye in black or silver finish, (sizes 2 to 8); the Keith Fulsher Thunder Creek hook (sizes 4 to 8); the Adlington & Hutchinson Blind Eye Salmon hook (sizes 7/0 to 2/0); the Captain Hamilton International hook, super heavyweight and heavyweight (sizes 10 to 14), and middleweight (sizes 10 to 18); the Bartleet Salmon Fly hook (sizes 3/0 to 1/0 and 1 to 6); the Carrie Stevens 10X Long, Heavyweight Streamer (sizes 2/0, 2, and 4). The Skues sneck and the Bartleet salmon bends, rather historic styles, have returned to the congregation. Due to the demand for larger curved hooks, Partridge now produces a long-shank sedge-caddis hook (Code K12ST) in sizes 8, 10, 12, and 14. These 3X long slope-shanked hooks have a black finish, forged bend, and a straight, ball eye. While providing a backbone for caddis imitations, they lend themselves to a variety of nymphal, emerger, and larval patterns, including woven dragonfly nymphs and soft-hackle wets. Another Partridge addition is the Alec Jackson Spey Fly Hook (CS22) available in four sizes (1½, 3, 5 and 7) and five finishes (black, blue, bronze, nickel, and gold). This spey salmon and steelhead series, especially appropriate for presentational tying, features a tapered and looped up-eye, a graceful sweep, a short point, and a sliver barb. Hook design is always continuous, even ancestral and anachronistic, but never complete.

VMC OF FRANCE

From my early tying days, I recall the small boxes of French hooks. Since 1796, the family firm of Viellard, Migeon et Cie, located in the Alsace Province of France, has manufactured steel products and, since 1910, "family made" fish hooks. VMC's National Round bend, evident in 9280, 9281, and 9282, is a modified perfect bend with a touch of Sproat. Three features that attract tyers are their short points, wide gaps, and flat forging. The 9280 (sizes 6–20) is a forged, bronzed, down-eyed, extra-fine-wire dry-fly hook. The 9281 (sizes 8–20) is an up-eyed 9280. The 9282 (sizes 8–18) is a forged, reversed, down-eyed, extra-short shank and extra-light-wire dry-fly hook. The 9288 (sizes 6–20) is a forged, straight, down-eyed, extra-fine-wire, short shank and short-point dry-fly hook. The 9289 is the up-eyed version of the 9288. In the appropriate sizes, the 9288 and 9289 are excellent basic dry-fly and midge hooks. The 9283 (sizes 2–18) is a forged, straight, down-eyed, extra-long-shank streamer hook. Other fly hooks include the Aberdeen and O'Shaughnessy range. New designs, for wet and nymph patterns, include the 8526 and the 8527 Sproat fly hooks. The 8527 is 1X long and both have appropriate-weight wires. VMC's English Wide Gaps, 9800 and 9801, have been used successfully for Alaskan steelhead and salmon patterns.

The short spear, flat forging, ball eye, and hard temper characterize the VMC hook. The "PP" designation, as in 9255PP and 9256PP, means "Perma Plate." VMC claims that Perma Plate proves more corrosion-resistant than unplated stainless steel and is less point dulling than electroplating. VMC's hard temper prevents breakage during quick and heavy commercial tying. Improved distribution has increased the popularity of the VMC hook. The VMC range interchanges with Mustad in the following table:

VMC	MUSTAD
8526	3906
8527	3906B
9255PS	3407, 34007
9279	9671
9280	94840
9281	94842
9288	94838
9800	37140, 37141
9800N	37140, 37141
9801	37161, 37162
9801N	37161, 37162

REDDITCH HOOK BENDER

Even during the second half of the nineteenth century, when mechanical hook making flourished, considerable handwork was required in making hooks. Redditch hook benders, small tools with a pin and template, shaped the soft, pointed, barbed hook wires into a standard bend. Women and children, working at home, did piecework for such companies as Sealey, Allcock, and Partridge. Even today, Partridge of England may still do some handwork on certain hook types to maintain their high standards.

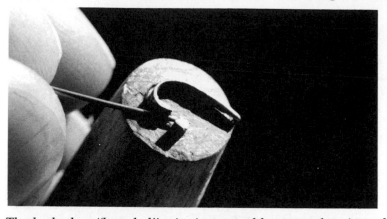

The barbed or "bearded" wire is trapped between the pin and template.

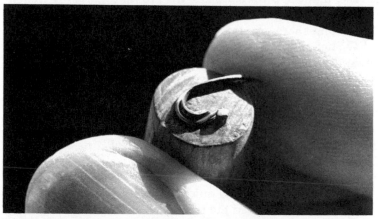

The tool is rotated counterclockwise, pressing the soft wire over the template to form the hook bend.

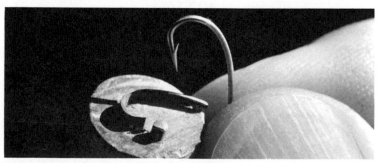

The shaped hook is then lifted out of the template for forging, bowing (forming the eye), hardening, tempering, and bronzing by the company.

CHAPTER 2

Feathers and Fluff

The birth of a fly begins with a feather. The tyer will require time and experience to know the various feather types, their numerous names, and their craft possibilities. The fly at the end of your tippet should be the result of all your knowledge and skill; it is the touchstone that drifts over the mystery of water and trout. After all, a fly is more feather than steel. It is the different feathers and the different methods that make a different fly.

In any overview of feathers, the tyer should recognize the complex, branching structure of the feather. Feathers demonstrate a remarkable variety of shapes, structures, and sizes. Variety of size, for example, is clearly evident in that a rooster's tail feather may be one thousand times longer than its eyelid feather. And, according to Jaap and Turner, quoted in *Avian Anatomy* (1972), a single barred Plymouth Rock may have a total plumage count of 8,377 feathers. The fly-tying possibilities of feather variety has yet to be reached. A single bird bears the five main structural feather types, which include:

1. *The large, stiff feathers.* These feathers form the airfoil—the flight feathers (the remiges), and the large tail feathers (the rectrices). The barbs, usually stiff and tapered, make ''quill'' wings, body and tail strips.

2. *The moderate-sized body or contour feathers.* The contour feather, the most commonly used feather in tying, furnishes hackles, kidney feathers, breast feathers, and flank feathers. It varies greatly in size and shape. The rachis, or central shaft, is four-sided, somewhat rectangular, slightly wider than thick, and the underside has a ventral groove. The proximal barbs, those at the bottom of the vane, are soft and downy, suitable for dubbing. The contour feather has both the downy, plume texture, as well as the firm, tightly knit pennaceous texture. The contour feather serves for tail fibers, wings, hackles, and body strips for fly patterns.

3. *The small, fluffy, down feathers.* The silky fibers of the down feather, unlike the more rigid contour feather, grow out of a common center. The down feather has no rachis. The soft strands make excellent dubbing material.

4. *The fine, hairlike filoplumes.* These feathers are employed in a very limited way in fly tying.

5. *The minute face bristles.* These are seldom, if ever, used in tying.

Close examination of a bird will reveal various types of feathers of different

Auricular tract feathers (ear feathers)

Dorsal cervical tract feathers (hackle)

Upper median tail coverts
(tail-coverts)

Interscapular tract feathers
(cape)

Dorsopelvic tract feathers:
(saddle)
(back plumage)

Ventral cervical tract
feathers (front of
neck plumage)

Humeral tract feathers:
(wing front)
(shoulder plumage)

Upper marginal coverts of
prepatagium (wing-bow)

Pectoral tract feathers
(breast plumage)

Alular remiges

Upper median secondary coverts
Upper major secondary coverts } (wing-coverts
or wing-bar)

Secondary remiges (secondaries or wing-bay)

Primary remiges
(primaries or flight feathers)

Abdominal tract feathers (fluff)

Femoral tract feathers (rear body feathers)

Femoral tract feathers (lower thigh plumage)

Crural tract feathers (hock plumage)

C Jamroz

Rectrix 1 (greater sickle)
Rectrices 2 - 8 (main tail feathers)
Upper major tail coverts 1' - 6' (lesser sickles)

Feather coat associated with individual feather tracts of the Single Comb
White Leghorn Chicken. (Courtesy of Dr. Alfred M. Lucas, Lucas and
Stettenheim, 1972. Illustration by C. Jamroz.)

grades. The fly tyer should be familiar with the fundamental feather types, their structures, and tying properties.

The flat part of the feather, usually called the vane, is supported by the rachis. The rachis is that section of the shaft that bears the barbs. Unlike the calamus, or quill, the rachis is essentially solid instead of tubular. The vane is held together by parts called barb, barbule, and hooklet. Barbs branch out from the rachis in a single plane. The barbs are the common fiber strips of the feather. The barbules, several hundred on each barb, interlock with nearby hooklets to hold the vane together. The vane acts as a natural "zipper," holding the parts together. When preening, a bird "zips" the barbs together with its beak to reform the feather. What the tyer calls "webbing" is nothing other than a mat of dense barbules. These dense barbules trap moisture and increase the weight of the fly. Obviously, this characteristic is not preferred in a dry fly—and it is the dry fly that forms the basis for quality.

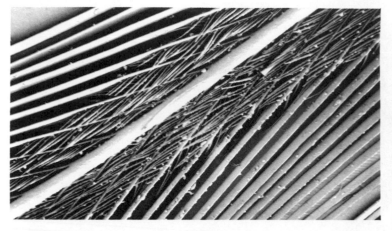

Hackle section showing barbs and webbing (30X): the matted webbing, the dense barbules, contrasts with the slender barbs. Where webbing appears, the barb base is softer and more absorbant.

Hackle section showing webbing (201X): the flanged barbules trap water and encourage sinking.

Hackle section showing webbing and oblong cross section of the rachis (30X): a stem wraps against the narrow side of the oblong cross-section. Sometimes tough care must be taken to keep the hackle stem from twisting or rolling on the broad side.

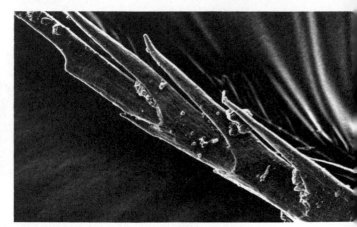

Grizzly feather barb (1000X): the barb extentions, the spines, aid floatation by increasing the surface area that supports the dry pattern. Cutting a dry hackle decreases the surface area and creates artificial "barbs" that penetrate the meniscus and absorb water.

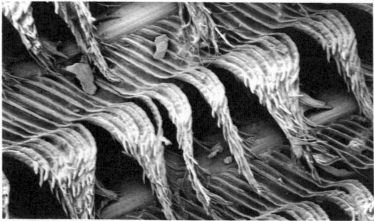

Duck quill section showing overlapping barbs (150X): the barbules, several hundred on each barb, interlock with nearby hooklets to hold the vane together. This interlock allows various feather srips to be married or zipped together.

Peacock herl cross-section (70X): the cross section of the peacock herl is asymmetrical. Make certain when wrapping that the fuller flue is exposed.

Cape selection is one of the most significant aspects of feather knowledge. Usually a numeric or alphabetic rating, with 1 or A as the superior cape, is employed for classification. In selecting a neck or cape, the tyer is confronted with a myriad of neck grades, numerous neck colors (including all the values and hues of natural and dyed capes), and several neck characteristics (such as listing, flecking, and taper). As yet, there is no universal grading system, nor may one be possible. Grading capes is a relative art —a neck is not only graded according to its own merits but also in relation to the properties of similar necks available. Selecting a fine feather is like selecting a vintage wine: there is a season and a time. Like a fine wine, there are "tastes" in color and qualities. A feather is selected by a balance of properties and personal taste. Also like a fine wine, a classic cape is enhanced through correct care and storage.

The following is a fundamental list of "tasting" characteristics often used in cape selection:

1. The cape should come from a mature bird, killed in prime condition. For domestic birds the best time usually is middle to late winter. There should be full winter plumage and few, if any, pinfeathers (the short, immature feathers about to emerge). There was a time when most tying necks were imported; however, the finest capes, the genetic capes produced for the tying trade, are now native. And, through proper care and storage, a year-long supply is available. A feather is a protein that can easily rot without correct care. The supplier should make certain that the neck is clean and free from broken or twisted feathers.

2. The outer surface of the feather, the convex side away from the bird body, should have a gloss or sheen but be without brittleness. The concave underside of the feather should be close in color to the outer surface. However, the underside will always have a dull, dunlike appearance and never match perfectly.

3. A superior dry-fly neck will have resilient barbs and a slender, pliant stem. Fan the barbs to determine how quickly they return to position. But remember to bend the hackle forward away from the cape rather than bend the cape away from the feather. This will prevent breaking the cape. Heavy webbing slows resiliency and produces a soft hackle useful primarily for nymphs and wet flies.

4. Traditionally, webbing has been the prime consideration for dry-fly quality. Normally, as long as the webbing does not enter the tip one-third of the hackle, the hackle may serve for a dry fly. Keep in mind that a size 16 hook requires only one centimeter (about 6/16 of an inch) of hackle for five full wraps. And five full wraps, three behind the wings and two in front, produce a fully hackled fly. The standard Palmer hackling will require, on a size 6, 4X long hook, five centimeters (about two inches) for the four traveling wraps. If the hackle tip is tied in first, then very little, if any, of the webbing will be used. If the hackle is tied in butt first, then often the superior hackle tip is cut off. Even when wrapping in the Palmer hackle, many tyers tie in the hackle tip section at the hook bend first; this produces an unencumbered hook gap and a full thoracic wrapping.

5. Feather taper is a much more significant element than is generally considered. A fast taper makes an inferior hackle because the barb length will vary too rapidly for symmetrical hackling. A hackle may be quite deceptive—it may appear small and narrow, but the barbs, which can lie

parallel to the shaft, or rachis, may be quite long. Always notice the hackle taper and barb length; they can work independently of each other to produce a superior or inferior hackle. It is of value to note that the spacing of barbs varies among feathers and also varies along the rachis of a single feather. In the hackle, a typical contour feather, the spacing increases with the next higher barb. The barbs near the feather tip are farther apart than those at the feather base. The midway barbs may have the same spacing as the tip barbs, but usually the spacing is one-half of the tip spacing. *Avian Anatomy* calculates the average distance between barbs at three vane locations on a Mallard interscapular feather. The result is 119 microns at the base, 333 microns at the middle, and 625 microns at the tip. Consequently, hackles may vary in the number of barbs they carry and the appropriate spacing of them for tying. The length of the barbs increases for the first one-fourth or one-third of the feather. It remains consistent for a short distance until it decreases near the tip. The barb angle, which is greatest at the base, becomes more acute near the tip. Thus, generally speaking, as the barbs become farther apart, they become more acute to the rachis.

6. Hackle range within a size and throughout the various sizes is a consideration for a perfect neck. Whether you want a neck for a size 18 or 14 fly makes little difference: both may be high quality necks. But, in any case, there should be enough of an appropriate single size for your particular tying needs. Check the feather density by lifting the hackles. Some necks have more hackles than others, but also some necks are thicker or more dense than others. If you are in doubt, compare the density of several necks until you have an idea of what a fully dense neck is. The larger feathers on a neck may serve for tail fibers, streamer feathers, and other tying needs. Even in the finer grades of dry-fly necks, there are usually enough wet-grade feathers for many flies. There should be little waste, if any, in a good neck.

7. The neck should have consistent coloration and any contrasting marks, those marks that are sharply defined, ought to appear even in the smaller hackles. However, this may not be possible in some cape colors. Often a superior badger neck will not have the distinct black center in the smaller hackles. Also, coloration may be related to webbing. The black center of the badger is black webbing; therefore, it would be a contradiction to have a web-free badger. And even in dyed necks, coloration should be consistent. Dyed necks can be determined by noting whether the rachis or stem is also dyed.

8. By nature, some necks are high quality while others are low. Some white necks have a tendency to be soft, while a grizzly neck normally has excellent barb resiliency. Therefore, a good white neck might secure a better grade than will a grizzly of the same quality. And the light ginger, while often high in quality, is somewhat rare; even an otherwise mediocre natural ginger may receive a high grade. Odd necks can be excellent buys at times. And if you choose quality before colors, some excellent necks may be had. Several other aspects of necks may influence the grading. A flecked neck is any neck with dotting or flecking that is in contrast to the basic color of the neck. A variant is any neck with more than one color. This term should not be confused with a variant fly, which is a fly with exaggerated proportions. And a listed neck is any neck, regardless of color, except black, which has feathers edged in black.

9. A feather is a protein that will rot easily without correct care and storage. The supplier should have made certain that the cape is clean and free from broken or twisted feathers. Steaming the cape will normally straighten and "dress" the feathers. Heavy zip-lock plastic bags or airtight plastic containers make excellent storage containers for capes.

There is an expression in wine tasting that a fine wine must "blossom in the mouth and spread out its peacock tail." The metaphor that connects feather with wine is not all hyperbole. The finest feather is the rich, full-bodied, and mature feather. The feather connoisseur recognizes the sweet, rich mahogany of coachman brown and the cool, dry flavor of a light cahill. A warm and subtle bouquet of light explodes as it passes through a fine hackle. After all, the birth of a fly begins with a delicious hackle.

The plumage color and contrast will vary according to the age of the bird and season in which it was killed. Fly tyers place artificial limits on colors. Each individual color is usually a color range within a particular color. A grizzly, for example, is not merely a barred black-and-white feather. The black may range into gray and the white may enter cream. The barring may be straight across the feathers or V-shaped, and the colors may have high contrast or blend into each other.

Quality synthetic hackle, with the correct stiffness, taper, and length is, I have been assured, possible to produce. The real question is whether or not it is necessary or desirable to create the synthetic fly. Perhaps synthetic hackle—sold by the linear foot—will grace some future Cream Cahill. Certainly, attractive and effective synthetic patterns have been created by John Betts. And creative tying may be nothing more than using common materials with unusual methods. Yet, part of the pleasure, I believe, is in knowing the wildlife byproducts that constitute the beauty of tying.

Although the following list includes some unusual feathers and fluff, all are commercially distributed or may be derived from huntable populations:

BLUE GROUSE (*Dendragapus obscurus*). The dorsal plumage is black and grayish tan with fine black tip markings. The wing cover feathers may have a touch of white at the center edges, while the breast feathers may be slate gray with a white center or tip. The male generally has a dusty gray or bluish gray body with mottled wings. The light gray terminal tail band may be missing in the northern Rocky Mountain birds. The wing cover feathers may have tan or brown marks. The breast feathers have a general appearance of blue-gray, mottled or vermiculated with cream, tan, and black. This coniferous-forest grouse is often confused with the smaller spruce grouse where the ranges overlap in the Pacific Northwest. The fine markings make this plumage appropriate for soft-hackle, wet, and nymph patterns. The habitat of the blue grouse extends from the Alaskan and western Canadian coastal forests to San Francisco Bay and into the Sierra Nevadas and Rocky Mountains.

BOBWHITE (*Colinus virginianus*). The tawny plumage of the bobwhite is a rich splash of browns, creams, and blacks. The small hackle feathers are dusty brown with black speckled edges. The rump feathers are mottled gray-browns with black centers. The flank feathers have brown centers marked off with black strips and a cream edge. These are especially useful for small soft-hackled and wet-fly patterns. The cream-and-black-banded breast feathers make excellent wing pads for small nymphs, and they have been used for dry caddisfly wings. The bobwhite is a wide ranging bird inhabiting all of Mexico and eastern America. There are hunted populations through much of its range including the Snake and Columbia river basins of Washington, Oregon, and Idaho. Over twenty subspecies are listed in Paul A. Johnsgard's *Grouse and Quail of North America* (1973). The males of most subspecies have a white eye stripe or "mask" extending to the base of the neck. The northern American males usually have black-and-white irregular barring on the breast and abdomen; the southern Mexico males have dark unbarred abdomens. It may be of value to note that in Europe the term quail refers to several kinds of game birds related to the pheasant family; in America, the term quail refers to birds of the grouse family. But there may always be regional differences. The bobwhite is called a quail in northern and eastern America; in the American South, it is called a partridge.

CALIFORNIA QUAIL (*Lophortyx californicus*). The plumage has a variety of patterns and color. The dorsal contour feathers are slate gray, some with a slight olive tinge. The brown dun flank feathers have a distinct cream center that appears as a narrow "eye" near the tip, and ventral feathers are cream with black bars and cream with black and brown marks. Some breast feathers are cream near the tips with a black list. The feathers are small but varied—from the brown dorsal feathers to the brown-scaled cream ventral feathers. They produce some unusual midge and caddis larvae patterns. The black-plumed California quail claims territory from British Columbia to Baja, California.

CHINESE PHEASANT RUMP. The Gothic-window feathers of the cock, with the barred arches, are often used for nymphal wing cases or single-piece nymph legs.

CHINESE PHEASANT TAIL. The barbs from the cock Chinese pheasant tail are used for nymph tails and bodies as well as dry bodies. These strong barbs—strong enough for wing pads and shellbacks—are usually dyed in a variety of colors.

CHUKAR (*Alectoris chukar*). The chukar partridge, with its dun brown back and bold chestnut-and-black flank stripping, has a white throat framed by a broad black band. The feathers, usually of regional interest and limited distribution, have been used primarily for wet flies, including some estuary and saltwater patterns. Body feathers range from a pale dun through pale ginger to reddish brown dun. These are some of the finest dun creams and browns of any bird. The distinctive flank feathers have a gray base edged by a fine black line followed by a broad band of cream, then a bold black band with a rich chestnut-tip band. The bird's tan flanks are conspicuously marked with vertical black bars and bands that extend from the top of the beak backward through the eyes and down the sides of the neck to join on the upper breast. Other colors include a rusty brown tail, reddish beak, and brown ear tufts. The color and markings of both sexes are similar, but the puffy head and broad leg spurs distinguish the male. The chukar was first introduced in 1935 in Nevada with the first hunting season there in 1947. Washington state declared its first season in 1949, eighteen years after introduction, with the largest harvest of any state through 1967. Huntable populations were planted in eastern Oregon in 1951. The talus slopes and rock canyons of the Columbia basin proved superb habitat for this Eurasian transplant. It now occupies the Great Basin from British Columbia to Baja, California, and as far east as Colorado.

COQ DE LEON FEATHERS. There are no finer imitations, natural or synthetic, for tails, legs, and wings than the feathers of the Spanish coq de Leon. The coq de Leon flock was originally bred in a monastery in about 1620. The long barbs are stiff, glassy, and some are finely flecked. Two or three fibers make excellent mayfly tails. A small bundle creates a spinner's glassy wings, and a larger bundle imitates the mottled ambers and grays of a caddis wing. The coq de Leon feathers may be divided into two groups: the browns (*pardos*), and the grays (*indios*). Each group may then be subdivided into five browns (corzuno, sarrioso, langareto, aconchado, flor de escoba), and five grays (negrisco, acerado, plateado, rubion, palometa). The other coq de Leon feathers may be considered variations on these ten types. All of these feathers and various pattern types are described in *El Manuscrito de Astorga* (1624) by Juan de Bergara. The text has been translated into English by Claude Belloir and printed privately (1984) in Denmark by Preben Torp Jacobsen. The text includes a facsimile of the Old Spanish document, and modern translations in Spanish, French, and English. Jesus Pariente Diez's *La Pesca de la Trucha en los rios de Leon* (1984) describes the patterns from the Astorga manuscript, as well as patterns from another manuscript, by Luis Pena of Leon, dated 1825. The traditional Leon patterns, with or without tails, have thread ribbing, silk bodies, and hackles tied in a variety of color combinations. Some of the Astorga patterns, tied with wrapped hackles (turns of hackle), were used with a dapping rod: "This month [March] provides great sport for rod fishing because it is springtime and the zephyr and [the] 'favonio' [a pleasant breeze] blow and the waters become warmer." The rod, much like the modern Spanish "tralla" or whip cracker, was used like a blowline or dapping rod.

The translucency of the coq de Leon barbs is especially evident by rotating the feather in sunlight. The barbs appear to reflect all the gathered light until they burst into a particular subtle and rich color. The glossy translucency and rigidity of the barbs make them excellent for patterns that require extremely fine barbs, approximately .002 of an inch, under 15 millimeters long. Consequently, they make excellent tails for the dun and spinner of micro-mayflies such as the *Baetis*, the *Tricorythodes*, and the *Caenis*.

The pardos come from the Leon area and the indios from the extended highlands. For the modern tyer, the hackle fibers may be used as hackle barbs, tied according to the traditional Spanish patterns, or as tail fibers or spinner wings. There are various names for these Spanish feathers; however, most coq de Leon feathers may be classified according to five color categories within the gray or brown designation. Usually, and as previously noted, other coq de Leon feathers are variations of these ten color combinations. It should be noted that these feathers are "spade" feathers and not the dorsal cervical hackle feather.

The term *pardo* is the name of a Spanish cock and means "reddish brown." The *Diccionario de la Real Academia*, quoted by Claude Belloir, defines the color as "the tint of earth or that of the fur of the common brown bear, intermediate between white and black, tinged with cinnamon, and darker than grey." Surely, this is where color surpasses description.

Pardo Corzuno: The term comes from the Corzo, or European roebuck (*Capreolus capreolus*). The feather has very fine mottled marks of pale russet brown flecking against a dark background. The feather markings are, in fact, darker than the roebuck's coat. Sometimes this feather is also described in terms of the coloration of the fallow deer.

Pardo Sarrioso: The term comes from *sarrio*, a Spanish variety of the European wild goat or chamois (*Rupicapra rupicapra*). This feather is similar to a finely mottled corzuno, but with a light brown background.

Pardo Langareto: The original name was *longareto* from the Old Spanish *longo*, meaning long, with probable reference to a natural fly or to the rather large feather markings. On this feather, the markings are aligned or joined to form a pale, almost a pale Naples yellow strip, which appears as an inverted V.

Pardo Aconchado: This feather gets its name from the conch shell. The large markings on a light brown background are not aligned. In the commentary of the Astorga manuscript, *conchado* is defined as a "cock whose overall shade is speckled with another tint."

Pardo Flor de Escoba: The term comes from the coloration of the Spanish broom bush, genus *Genista*. The term *escoba* means broom. The dark background is nearly covered with reddish brown or pale burnt umber spots or strips.

The coq de Leon indios feathers, a gray feather ranging from chalk white to a glossy black, are indio negrisco (gray back to black), indio acerado (steel gray or ash gray), indio plateado (silver gray or pearl gray), indio rubion (blond gray), indio palometa, from *paloma*, meaning pigeon (gray-white to dusty white). The most interesting indios are the negrisco, the acerado, the avellanado, the perla, and the rubion.

Indio Negrisco: The indio negrisco is a gray black to a deep lustrous black. The webbing has a blue-green sheen similar to a peacock herl. Microscopic barbules form the webbing. The stem is a lustrous black.

Indio Acerado: The indio acerado is a silver steel gray. The webbing is pale gray. The term *ascerado* means steel and is also described as a silver ash gray.

Indio Avellanado: The indio avellanado is best described as a hazel nut color. It is a remarkable subtle blend of gray and brown that is apparent only in reflected light. The webbing is a light gray to a near white. The stem is usually gray.

Indio Perla: The indio perla is, as the name suggests, a pearl color. It is similar to the avellanado, but slightly stronger in the metallic pearl sheen of the barbs.

Indio Rubion: The barbs of the indio rubion are a bright ginger or a ruddy golden yellow. The webbing of this indio has, like the indio negrisco, the blue-green sheen of a peacock herl. *Rubion* is an Old Spanish term for red.

CUL DE CANARD. These feathers, from the "duck's derriere," are the oil gland feathers. When preening, the duck anoints the bill by stroking the oil gland, located on the dorsal surface of the tail. These feather tufts, the circlet of the uropygium, aid in transferring oil to the bill by capillary action. Although they appear as down feathers, even when dry the oil feathers are not as fluffy as other down or plumulaceous feathers. These feathers are plumulaceous, but are shorter and simpler than the down feather. The barbules lack the distinctive feathers of typical plumulaceous barbules, some being reduced to the stylet type. There are commonly eight to thirty feathers per bird, arranged in a circlet or oval around the oil duct orifice. The feather, when stuck together with oil, forms a paint brush tip or "wick." These feathers, when tied on a fly, are remarkably water repellent (hydrofuge) and buoyant. No silicone is required to float a fly tied with

The long, webby schlappen and three cul de canard "wick" feathers.

these feathers—they have naturally embedded oils. Because few are found on a single duck, the cost is high and distribution limited. This item was made commercially popular by Roberto Pragliola, the Italian firm that markets two natural colors, white and havana tan. The cul de canard feathers are especially effective for spinners and floating midges. They may be "soft-hackle" wrapped for mayfly emergers, tied as the overwing of small caddis or bundled and figure-eighted and cut to length for spinners. Such patterns, which float in the surface film, prove effective on challenging waters.

ENGLISH PARTRIDGE. (*Perdix perdix*). The speckled brown contour feathers are common for nymph legs, soft-hackled patterns, and wet-fly hackles. The American tyer often uses the more broadly marked grouse feather in place of the partridge.

GAMBEL'S QUAIL (*Lophortyx gambelii*). The Gambel's quail has the general appearance of blue dun with cream and reddish-brown ventral feathers and black mottled underparts. It is a buff white with unscaled belly feathers and with a chestnut brown crown and flanks. The feathers have an excellent range of blue and brown duns. However, the typical barb length, averaging about 12 millimeters, is appropriate only for small patterns. The narrow tail feathers are the same blue dun of the dorsal. The barbs may be used for small dries and soft-hackled patterns. This desert quail ranges through southwestern America and northwestern Mexico.

GOLDEN PHEASANT TIPPETS. The golden orange barbs with black bars are usually used for fancy fly tails. This "collar" feather barb is called for in a variety of traditional patterns, such as the Peter Ross, Fanwing Royal Coachman, and some fully dressed salmon patterns.

GOOSE BIOTS. These are the stiff, abruptly tapered barbs from the leading edge of a goose primary feather. They are used for nymph tails, legs, wing cases, and hatching-pupa wing pads.

GUINEA HEN. The natural contour feathers are black with bold white spots. The mottled contours are often used for wet and salmon patterns.

HEN PATCHES. These round, speckled saddle feathers, somewhat similar to brown partridge feathers, are economical and ideal for burnt wings, soft-hackles, nymph legs, and caddis wings. The hen patch has a wide range of colors and markings including speckled and barred patterns.

JUNGLE COCK FEATHERS. These eyed feathers, traditionally used for salmon and streamer flies as well as jassid wings, have a natural "lacquered" spot. Importation to America is prohibited, but some breeder-grown hackles have been available. There are photographic and painted imitations. Guinea fowl, starling breast, and the golden plover wing-coverlet feathers have been used in place of the eyed jungle cock. Many tyers, however, prefer to omit the feather rather than use any "unnatural" imitation.

MALLARD FLANK FEATHERS. Unlike the brown mallard bronze feathers and the small curved breast feather, the mallard flank feather has dark gray speckling over a pale gray vane. It is neither as delicate nor as "crisp" as the wood duck flank feather.

MANDARIN DUCK. The mandarin duck, distributed through China, Japan, and Korea, has a falling crest and uniform plumage. Feathers are scarce because the mandarin seldom hatches its eggs in captivity. The valuable flank feathers are a rich chestnut brown with delicate lines somewhat similar to the wood duck.

MARABOU. Marabou, originally the soft wing coverts and tail of the African marabou stork, is now the underdeveloped feather of the turkey. The soft, filamentous strands respond to current and fly movement. The feathers are taken from the legs and some immature contour feathers of the turkey.

MONTEZUMA QUAIL (*Cyrtonyx montezumae*). Also known as the Harlequin or Mearns, the Montezuma quail wears a distinctive and attractive coat of many colors. The dorsal contour feather has a white or cream center tapering to the tip with black bars or spots over brown and gray vane panels. The breast and ventral feathers are black with large, white spots or bars. The rare and lovely plumage, usually with high contrast, produces excellent feathers for nymph cases and soft-hackle wets. The paler breast and flank feathers have center marks and narrow, delicate bars. The flank feathers have the cream center, somewhat wide, with barbs banded in black on a brown wash. The male has distinctive black-and-white face marks and a bluish-black flank with heavy white spots. The female is a rich mottled brown. The Montezuma is the smallest quail and the only one without a crest. There are limited, but huntable, popultions in its range from southern Arizona to western Texas and as far south as Oaxaca, Mexico.

OAK TURKEY WING. This is a large fawn-and-brown-speckled feather. The secondary wing feather from a peacock is a darker substitute for the rare oak turkey wing. This feather creates the wings for the traditional Muddler Minnow and the "grouse-wing" caddis.

OSTRICH. The ostrich sports a long, soft, plumaceous herl used for salmon patterns, and nymphal and larval gill plates. It is also used as a substitute for marabou wings.

PEACOCK HERL. The popular peacock herl is a metallic green-bronze herl used for salmon butts, larva heads, dry-fly bodies, and wings. The short barbules are denser on one side than on the other. Wrap in so that the denser side is outside. Two or three strands are often twisted together or wrapped on the tying thread to produce a strong, plump underbody.

PEACOCK EYED TAIL. Used mainly for stripped "quill" bodies, the herls are selected from directly beneath the "eye" area. Various traditional methods are used to strip the flue from the herl—rubber on glass, liquid bleach, or a wax bath.

PEACOCK SWORD. The curved, bright green herls used for wings on the Alexandra and tail of the Spruce Fly.

GOLDEN PLOVER (*Pluvialis dominica*). A top wing feather, like the starling breast feather, is sometimes a substitute for jungle cock eyes when the tips are varnished with a white spot. The wing cover feathers are a deep gray with edge spots of yellowish ginger. In spring the mantle is dotted with gold flecks. The golden plover, along with the black-bellied plover, was greatly overgunned at the turn of the century.

RUFFED GROUSE (*Bonasa umbellus*). The ruffed grouse has attractive plumage of black, cream, tan, gray, and brown. The distinctive fan-shaped tail has contrasting cross barring of seven to nine alternating bands of black, brown, and buff on a gray or reddish brown base, and a broad subterminal black band with a light margin. The cover feathers for the wing may have cream centers near the tip. The tail feathers are barred with a wide black band near the tip. The tail tip ends in gray, peppered with black. The larger flank feathers may show the wide bands of cream, black, and dusty yellow. The breast feathers have a yellowish tinge with dark markings. There is a wide range of muted colors on the bird that makes it appropriate for soft-hackled and wet patterns. It also makes excellent nymph legs and caddis wings. The range of the ruffed grouse includes Alaska, Canada, and south through the coniferous forests into northern California, the Great Lakes, and the Appalachian range.

SAGE GROUSE (*Centrocercus urophasianus*). The general plumage appears in both sexes as a variegated black and gray. The wing-cover feather may have a cream or white center with erratic V barring of cream on a black field, while the edges may be speckled or striped tan. The female's barred breast feathers produce excellent soft-hackles, wet-fly hackles, and nymph legs. Some feathers may be more black-and-white while others are more black-and-tan. Tail fibers are black with tan markings and are most suitable for nymph bodies and some small dry bodies. The sage grouse inhabits the prairie lands from Alberta and Saskatchewan south to Utah, Nevada, and California.

SCALED QUAIL (*Callipepla squamata*). The plumage is similar to the Gambel's quail; however, the breast and mantle feathers are tipped in black and fan shaped, creating a scaled effect. The belly has brown "scales" on slate or blue dun plumage. The breast feathers are light gray and cream with a distinct black edge, hence the "scaled" quail. The flank feathers are blue dun with a distinct cream eye near the tip. While the population centers on the Chihuahua Desert of Mexico, it extends into Arizona, New Mexico, Utah, Colorado, and Texas.

SHARP-TAILED GROUSE (*Pedioecetes phasianellus*). The dorsal contour feathers are bold black splashes, and tan with black stipples. The wing coverlets have a distinct white patch. Some of the white breast feathers may sport the "gothic arch" markings. The ventral feathers are more distinctly whitish with black markings. The saddle contours are marked close to the edges, produce excellent soft-hackle or nymph legs. The sharp-tailed grouse ranges from the interior of Alaska to Hudson Bay, south to Utah, and as far east as Lake Huron.

STARLING (*Sturnus vulgaris*). The ubiquitous starling is an iridescent purple-green in the spring and wears pale speckles on a dull coat in winter. Fledged juveniles are grayish brown on top with a pale belly. Wing feathers have produced the standard dry-fly wings for decades. For small patterns they are still superior to duck wings. Contour feathers are used for soft-hackle and wet-fly patterns.

TEAL. The teal's flank and breast feathers are barred on a sandy white background. These feathers have done yeoman duty for soft-hackled patterns and dry-fly wings, and they are common feathers for wet-fly wings. This single feather has spawned a whole range of soft-hackled patterns.

WOODCOCK. The wing has a rich reddish brown plumage barred with black and cream. The wing underfeathers are used for nymph and wet-fly hackles. The reddish brown European woodcock (*Scolopax rusticola*) is larger than the American woodcock or "timber-doodle." The American woodcock (*Philohela minor*), with its plumage to match the soft rusty browns and grays of the dead leaves of the forest floor, inhabits the woods of eastern North America. Because of the woodcock's game-bird status, the plumage is locally available. The traditional Greenwell's Glory and Halford's Welshman's Button have English woodcock feather sections for wings.

Hairs and Furs

In the beginning, the unknown author of the *The Treatise of Fishing with an Angle* wrote of "donne," "blacke," "yelow," and "grene wull lappyd abowte wyth the herle of the pecoks tayle." The pattern comments, put to text by Wynkyn de Worde in 1496, began the formal history of fly-tying materials. And some natural materials, such as dyed wools, have a distinguished history. Certain coveted "body blends" and "fur formulas" have been family secrets. In addition, hairs and furs, coming as they do from attractive animals, have a charm and quality that may never be matched by synthetics. Natural fibers have characteristics that have traditionally filled the tying cabinet—they are long, short, soft, stiff, translucent, opaque, tapered, straight, crinkled, and colored. They are "complete" materials, making tails, bodies, wings, and even hackles. To a significant extent, knowing the hairs and furs is knowing the tying traditions.

The diameters and dimensions of natural fibers, as well as color and some other characteristics, may vary according to the maturity of the animal, the body location of the fiber, the individual animal, and the season in which it was taken. The hair diameters are measured at the widest section of the fiber. Because the natural materials will vary, especially in diameter and length, the value of the following table lies in its *comparisons* of hairs and furs. Among other things, the diameter and length will determine, to a significant extent, whether or not a particular hair is stiff enough and long enough to be used as a dry-fly tail. One must remember that a description, such as pale dun, may not mean the same thing to all tyers. Colors come in an infinite array, and language is all but inadequate in describing them. Therefore, intelligent and critical observation is essential.

There exists a multitude of available hairs and furs. Some materials are common, some are regionally available, and some are rare. A few unusual fibers have been included in my listing, such as yak hair, reindeer hair, and musk-ox underfur. They are worth finding and worth using. Intelligent substitution may be appropriate, if not necessary, at times. Experiment with the different natural materials to learn their properties and possibilities.

Most animals have a double-hair coat that consists of long coarse overhairs or guard hairs, and short fine underhairs. The guard hairs grow in primary follicles and underfur grows in secondary follicles. The ratio between the guard hairs and underfur is important in determining the dubbing characteristics. The hairy hill sheep has about three follicles of fine fibers for every one primary follicle of coarse hairs. The softer merino sheep has twenty follicles of fine fibers for every one primary follicle. Consequently, merino dubbing adheres well to the tying thread. The ratio between hair types determines to a large extent the tying uses of the hair. The classification of these two hair types is further expanded into subdivisions:

Guard Hairs:
1. Spines: the large, defensive hairs, such as quills.
2. Bristles: the stiff, protective outer hairs, such as manes.
3. Awns: the normal coarse guard hairs, often with a swelled and flattened tip and a fine base.

Under Hairs:
1. Vellus: the short, fine, "down" hair.
2. Fur: the thick, fine, and short hair.
3. Wool: the long, soft, and usually curly or crinkly hairs.

Typical guard hair shape (an awn): note the enlarged "shield" area.

Typical guard hairs, such as those found on rabbits, hares, and rodents, flatten toward the tip into a shieldlike section that projects beyond the underfur. Muskrat guard hairs are angular in cross section and the coarsest guard hairs may be oval with a frayed tip. Guard hairs vary. Three different guard hair types are recognized in rats and mice: the round monotrichs, the flat awns, and the short, fine auchenes. The "shield" section of otter hair may extend over half the total length. The guard hairs of the beaver and the otter are wavy, similar to crinkled wool. Pig bristle is stiff and is often triangular in section. The goat's double coat has overhairs that are much longer than those of deer and wild sheep. The coat of the angora goat, called mohair, is long and lustrous. The underhair of the cashmere goat is a very fine underwool. Sea otters and seals lack erector muscles, which allows the flattened guard hairs to overlap, an adaptation to prevent water from entering the insulating underfur. The crimped underfur probably traps air that increases buoyancy and insulation. The deer coat is comparable to the wild sheep coat with the exception that the overhairs are coarser.

The scale pattern, and sometimes the root structure, of the guard hair usually identifies the animal. Any hair with spiny scales that protrude from the hair shaft, such as seal and mink fur, makes excellent dubbing. The scales interlock during the dubbing process. This increases the twisting or "cording" effect in dubbing. Rabbit underfur has a flattened cross section and ribbonlike appearance. Although the scales are negligible, the fine, soft ribbon fibers bind together during dubbing. Though the scales determine the characteristics of dubbing only, it may be of some interest to note that whitetail and mule deer hairs have curved scales similar to fish. Caribou hair has hexagonal scales, and antelope scales are diamonds arranged in a diagonal row. The variety of hairs and their characteristics can be a complete study in itself.

ANTELOPE

Diameter: .012
Length: Four centimeters
Color: Range of pale creams to light brown
Characteristics: Guard hairs to six centimeters; dense dun underfur; coarse, but soft fibers compress and flare readily; the hair tips are often broken or shagged; sun bleaching can severely fade the natural colors
Uses: Caddis wings, Humpy bodies, general spinning, and hair-bug tying

BADGER

Diameter: .003 to .004, guard hairs and underfur approximately .0005
Length: two- to eight-centimeter guard hairs
Color: High-contrast colors ranging from the base of cream, tan, and black to a white tip
Characteristics: A strong hair with a slight curl on the longer hairs; underfur is firm and translucent and may have a mild crimp
Uses: Dry-fly wings, tailings and overwings for salmon patterns and streamers

BEAVER

Diameter: Guard hair .002 (base) and .005 (swelled tip)
Length: Five and a half centimeters (guard hair) and two and a half centimeters (underfur)
Color: Light to dark gray underfur with blue-gray back; the guard hairs have amber or cream tips
Characteristics: Like otter fur, beaver is water resistant; stiff, swelled, and flattened guard hairs; usually available in natural and dyed colors; beaver is easily dubbed if few guard hairs are present
Uses: Dry-fly and nymph dubbing

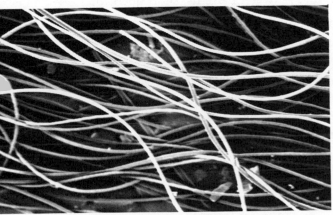

Beaver dubbing (102X): the fine diameter makes beaver soft and easily dubbed.

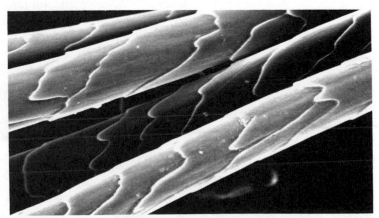

Beaver dubbing (2000X): under greater magnification, the clinging scales are evident. This characteristic enhances the fiber's ability to cling together and adhere to the thread.

BLACK BEAR

Diameter:	.003 guard hair and fine, .0005 underfur
Length:	Ten- to sixteen-centimeter overhair with four- to five-centimeter underfur; hair length varies according to the body location
Color:	Usually brown, brownish black, or black overhair with brownish black underfur; black bear hair has a wide color range including brown
Characteristics:	A slick, stiff, and reflective hair; often only regionally available; underfur is coarse with an errant, loose crinkle
Uses:	Winging material for wets and streamers

BLACK-TAILED DEER

Diameter:	.006
Length:	Five centimeters
Color:	Light gray stem with black bands on either side of amber tip
Characteristics:	Fine tips and dun underfur; standard tying material; wide color range on different body parts
Uses:	Speckled tips produce mottled caddis wings; a strong hair for Humpy patterns; for general spinning and hair-bug tying

BUCKTAIL (WHITE-TAILED DEER)

Diameter:	.005 to .018 base
Length:	To fourteen centimeters
Color:	Ventral white and dorsal cream-and-brown, may vary from gray-brown to dark brown; the hair has either a white or gray base with a dark band followed by an extended cream section ending in a black tip
Characteristics:	A long hair with a relatively soft base
Uses:	Wings for streamer and saltwater patterns; short fibers for caddis overwings and Wulff tails

Cross-section of whitetail deer body hair (75X): whitetail body hair has a fish-scaled surface and vacuous chambers.

CALF BODY

Diameter: Varies from approximately .0005 to .001
Length: Length varies according to body position, approximately two to three centimeters
Color: The natural colors are white, black, and brown; the most popular color is natural white
Characteristics: Calf body is a fine hair with minor curve; firm thread pressure must be used to position this slick and stiff hair
Uses: An excellent substitute for calf-tail wings and tails; this fine, relatively straight body hair is used for tails and wings of Wulff patterns and overwings of small streamers

CALF TAIL

Diameter: .002 to .003
Length: Three to five centimeters
Color: Natural white, brown, tan and black, and dyed; the common white tail often has a patch of brown or black at the base
Characteristics: Widely available; the hair length varies significantly; because of the soft tipped fibers, calf tail must be finger stacked; the straight, but tightly crinkled fibers near the tail base are preferred for tails and wings; the long hairs at the tail tip are curved and spiraled, unsuitable for most tying
Uses: Tail and wing material for the popular Wulff patterns; winging material for all hairwing patterns; an appropriate substitute for bucktail, especially on small patterns

CARIBOU

Diameter: .005
Length: Four centimeters
Color: Light gray stem with pale cream or tan tip
Characteristics: Silky soft fibers preferred by many for spinning; easily compressed and flared; fine texture and diameter; the soft fibers may be cut with fine single-strand tying threads
Uses: Particularly useful for small patterns that require spinning, such as Irresistibles, grasshoppers, and muddlers

Caribou body hair (200X): this chambered body hair compresses for dense spinning.

CHINESE BOAR

Diameter: .003 to .007 (varying diameters)
Length: Six to seven centimeters
Color: Mixed colors include black, brown, amber, yellow, and tan
Characteristics: Strong, stiff, translucent fibers often with split ends; one of the few natural fibers that may be soaked and knotted without breaking; the Chinese boar bristle, from the spinal section of the Chunking wild boar, has a natural curve and frayed tip; the frayed tip is called the "flag"
Uses: Tails, antennae, and legs on nymphs; "quill" body material

ELK

Diameter: .012
Length: Five to seven centimeters
Color: Range of natural browns mixed with cream tans; some hair tips may be black; stem colors usually either gray or light cream; medium dun underfur
Characteristics: Coarser and stronger than deer
Uses: Wings and tails for no-hackle patterns; caddis overwing; dubbable underfur

HARE'S MASK (EUROPEAN)

Diameter: .0015 (guard hairs)
Length: Nine millimeters (guard hairs at ear base), eight milimeters (underfur at ear base), twenty-four millimeters (cheek underfur), three centimeters (cheek guard hairs)
Color: Mixed colors including black, brown, tan, pale yellow, and gray, with the latter dominating; ear base may be peppered with black and cream; cheeks may be a rich tan, pale cream, or white; the patch from the nose to the ears is usually dark
Characteristics: Combination of soft and stiff hair fibers; dubbing for full, fuzzy, and spiked bodies; moderately translucent hairs; the English hare is approximately the size of our western jack rabbit
Uses: Common dubbing for the Gold Ribbed Hare's Ear Nymph; dubbing for medium to large shaggy nymphs and some dry patterns

European hare body fur (100X): hare body fur has a variety of diameters including broad guard hairs. A fur fiber cross-section is flattened and may have a ribbonlike appearance. It "felts" readily and, with the guard hairs removed, dubs easily.

Moose

Diameter: .010 (body) .012 (mane)
Length: Five centimeters (body), ten centimeters (mane)
Color: Wide color range, from black and brown to light tan and creamy white, colors often mixed; the moose mane has black underfur
Characteristics: Does not compress or spin well; moose mane is often a blackish brown with some tan and white hairs; moose body and mane hairs are extremely strong with a slick surface; depending upon body location, fibers will vary in length; hair fibers may be stacked for alignment
Uses: Moose mane may be used for ribbing and dry fly "quill" bodies; moose body fiber tips make strong tails for dry-fly patterns

Musk-ox Underfur

Diameter: .0005 and smaller
Length: Twelve centimeters
Color: Dark blue dun to pale dun
Characteristics: Extremely soft, tightly crinkled fiber called qiviut; high cost and limited availability; sometimes available in craft and weaving stores; perhaps the easiest natural dubbing material available
Uses: Dubbing material, especially useful for dry micro-patterns

Muskox underfur (75X): the superior dubbing characteristics of muskox underfur are the long length, the extremely fine diameter, and the irregular surface.

Muskrat

Diameter: .002 guard hair
Length: Three-and-a-half-centimeter guard hair and two-and-a-half-centimeter underfur
Color: Range of light cream, dark blue-gray, and dark browns; underfur is dun gray with cahill-colored (a tan cream) tips
Characteristics: Common material; fine dubbing; stiff guard hairs with sheen
Uses: Usually for nymphs and some dry patterns; muskrat guard hairs make excellent mayfly tails

OPOSSUM (AMERICAN)

Diameter: .003 guard hair
Length: Six-centimeter guard hair and three-centimeter underfur; opossum may have long guard hairs
Color: Rough, grayish white fur with good luster
Characteristics: Limited availability
Uses: Often limited use unless dyed; nymph and dry-fly dubbing

OPOSSUM (AUSTRALIAN)

Diameter: .002 guard-hair base to .003 swelled-tip section
Length: Six-centimeter guard hair and three-centimeter underfur
Color: Natural rust, browns, and grays, with cream and tan underfur; gray underfur; lustrous hair with the general appearance of cream over gray brown; guard-hair base is a blackish brown with a pale cream or dusty white swelled section and a black tip; some fur samples may be considerably lighter in color, tending toward white or cream; Eric Leiser, in *Fly-Tying Materials* (1973), describes the Australian opossum as "Medium gray fur over most of the animal, but a yellowish cream underside. . . ."
Characteristics: Versatile and easily dubbed; dubbing substitute for basic furs; excellent for larger nymphs, such as stonefly patterns; pale creams serve as a substitute for Light Cahill dubbing
Uses: A standard nymph dubbing

OTTER

Diameter: .003 guard hair, fine underfur of .0005
Length: Two-centimeter guard hair and one-centimeter underfur
Color: General appearance is dark brown; guard hairs have cream tips above a dark band; the lower guard hair stem is usually light brown to dusty white
Characteristics: A dense, well oiled, slick fur with stiff, prominent guard hairs and dense, fine underfur that is excellent dubbing; otter usually has a dusty white base that blends into a dark brown tip; the flattened section of the guard hair extends to over half the length of the hair, making the guard hairs difficult to dub; the hair stem may have as many as five different "petal" scale patterns; the underfur, like the beaver's underfur, is wavy and, as with crimped wool fibers, takes dye asymmetrically
Uses: A standard nymph and wet-fly dubbing

PECCARY (JAVELINA)

Diameter: Average hair diameter, approximately .025
Length: Varies according to location, average length approximately thirteen centimeters
Color: Peccary hairs are black, actually a deep brown-black, with approximately three narrow cream white bars; the hairs are usually black tipped; the white-lipped peccary, found in central Mexico to Paraguay, is larger and darker than

the collared peccary; the collared peccary, or javelina, has a coarse grizzled blackish gray coat with a gray collar; the collared peccary body bristles are available for tying

Characteristics: Not as commonly used as in the past; limited distribution; the stiff bristle hair grows in small, tight, separate clusters, usually four or six hairs to a clump with no underfur; like typical bristles, the hairs often have flags, the broken or split ends; the skin is recognized because the hair roots leave an evenly distributed three-holed pattern in the skin

Uses: Extended-body mayfly patterns, stonefly tails, and "quill" bodies

Polar Bear

Diameter: Approximately .003 to .005 body hair, .003 and finer underfur

Length: Varies, with the average approximately twenty-four centimeters with five to six centimeter underfur

Color: Usually a creamy white to natural white overhairs, often with a minor wave or swirl and white, crinkled underfur

Characteristics: Translucent, strong, stiff overhairs; rare and expensive, restricted and diminished availability

Uses: Traditionally used for hairwings on salmon, steelhead, and streamer patterns

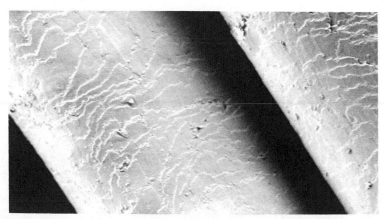

Polar bear hair (49X): the relatively smooth and glassy polar bear body hair.

Rabbit

Diameter: Guard hairs (shield area) .002, underfur .0005

Length: Varies significantly depending upon the maturity and breed, average approximately thirty-five millimeters

Color: Wide range of natural colors, especially black, brown, gray, and white; available in comprehensive range of dyed and blended colors

Characteristics: Most common and least expensive natural dubbing available in the widest color range; the soft, short fiber facilitates dubbing and spinning; the dense underfur and stiff guard hair may be combined for dubbing, or mixed with Antron

Uses: Dubbing material for all nymphs, wets, dries, streamers, and salmon patterns

REINDEER

Diameter:	A delicately tapered hair with a base approximately .008, and a very fine underfur approximately .0005
Length:	Body hair about forty millimeters with overhairs eighty millimeters or longer
Color:	The color varies from tan to a mouse dun coat with pale dun base and underfur
Characteristics:	A remarkably fine, soft, compressible, and slightly crinkled hair; limited availability; it is finer and softer than caribou body hair
Uses:	The finest spinning hair available, especially appropriate for small, spun-body patterns such as the Irresistible; this fragile body hair is not recommended for the folded Humpy body

SEAL

Diameter:	.002 guard hair and .001 underfur or less
Length:	Three-and-one-quarter-centimeter guard hair and approximately two-centimeter underfur
Color:	Various shades of cream and brown
Characteristics:	A stiff, spiky, and translucent guard hair; fine underfur with a distinct crinkle; seal fur may resist dubbing, especially with short, spiky guard hairs on a single thread, a well-waxed thread or dubbing loop may be required; the soft and creamy underfur from young seals is easily dubbed; the Greenland seal fur produces coarse dubbing; seal fur is remarkably translucent when properly dubbed; like the fur of most aquatic mammals, the fibers do not lose their luster in water; seal fur is in restricted and limited supply
Uses:	Traditional body material for all dubbing applications, especially for saltwater and salmon-fly patterns

Seal dubbing (102X): diameters vary for the soft and stiff fibers that make seal fur relatively difficult to dub. Some fibers have spiny scales that increase cling.

SHEEP WOOL

Diameter:	Diameters vary from .0660 to .0500
Length:	Varies considerably with the breed, "combing" wools are over five centimeters long and "clothing" wools are less than three centimeters long

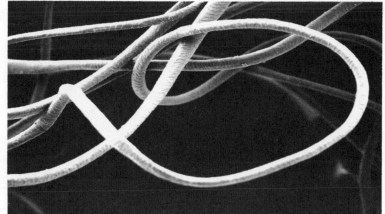

Sheep wool (105X): the soft, fine, and crinkled fibers make wool easily dubbed.

Color:	Natural colors of black and white with comprehensive range of dyed colors
Characteristics:	Sheep breeds are classified as fine wool, long wool, coarse wool and the like; consequently, the dubbing characteristics will vary; wool fibers have a microcrimp and are covered with irregular, pointed scales, unattached for almost two-thirds their length; these scales make the fibers cling together during the dubbing process; a protective film called yok, an oily mixture of lanolin (wool wax) and suint (dried perspiration), covers the raw wool; the elasticity of the fiber (it can stretch up to thirty percent of original dry length) facilitates dubbing; this elasticity keeps the hairs apart, thereby creating maximum air space for insulation; wool keratin is able to absorb up to thirty-five percent of its weight in water vapor before it begins to feel wet—actually, these properties of air space and water absorption make wool excellent for both dry and wet fly patterns; John Veniard, in *Fly Dressing Materials* (1977), lists the disadvantages of wool as bulkiness and the tendency to change color when wet; wild sheep have bristly overhairs known as ''kemps,'' as well as the typical soft underwool—kemps are the brittle white fibers often found in Harris tweeds
Uses:	The fine dubbing and yarn strands are used for various wet and dry bodies

SQUIRREL BODY (RED FOX AND GRAY)

Diameter:	.002 guard hairs
Length:	Two-centimeter guard hairs, one-centimeter underfur
Color:	Red-fox-squirrel guard hair has black-and-cream or reddish cream bands tipped with black; the belly fur is a fiery ginger or a reddish cream and may be sparse; the underfur is gray tipped in cream; the gray squirrel yields a pepper gray dubbing
Characteristics:	Belly hair is translucent and sparse
Uses:	Squirrel body hair creates shaggy nymphs and, with the underfur extracted, the guard hairs make excellent wings or tails for wet and dry patterns

Squirrel Tail (red fox and gray)

Diameter:	.003
Length:	Varies according to position, two and a half centimeters at base, six centimeters at ⅔ position, and as long as eight and a half centimeters at tail tip
Color:	Red-fox-squirrel tail hairs have black-and-ginger bars with a ginger or light red tip; the dorsal side has more black markings; gray squirrel hair has a tan, black, or brown base followed by a distinct black band and a white tip; the gray squirrel hair has a general badger appearance
Characteristics:	The long, strong hairs are fine for their length; hairs at the tip or near the tip may have a pronounced spiral; red fox squirrel tails and gray squirrel tails are common tying materials
Uses:	The hair length makes them appropriate for streamer and hairwinged patterns, especially tube flies; blue-gray underfur is easily dubbed; base hairs make hairwinged dry-fly wings

White-tailed Deer

Diameter:	.010
Length:	Six centimeters
Color:	Light gray stem with black bars on both sides of cream tip
Characteristics:	Wide color range, although often paler than blacktail standard, durable body hair with a minor crinkle and dun underfur
Uses:	Spinning, hair-bug bodies, and strand overbodies

Woodchuck

Diameter:	.003 base, .005 swelled tip guard hair
Length:	Four-centimeter guard hair and two-centimeter underfur
Color:	The general appearance is white or cream flecking on a black and ginger background; the guard hair has a pale cream tip, and the underfur has a black base beneath a ginger or cream tip
Characteristics:	The body fur of the woodchuck may have high-contrast markings; some samples may be more uniform in color due to sun conditions
Uses:	Woodchuck guard hairs make tails and wings for dries, while the body fur produces coarse dubbing

Yak

Diameter:	.003
Length:	Twelve to sixteen centimeters
Color:	Available in a variety of dyed colors
Characteristics:	A fine, long translucent fiber; a substitute for polar bear body hair; limited distribution
Uses:	Streamer, steelhead, and salmon-fly wings

An early Catskill pattern, tied by Theodore
Gordon, 1908–09.

A classic salmon fly

A wet fly tied by Charles F. Orvis

SOME MODERN PATTERNS

A Red Quill—originated by Art Flick, tied by Lawrence Duckwall

A Funneldun, originated and tied by Neil Patterson

An Emerging Caddis, tied by Darrel Martin

Three Woven-Bodied Nymphs—originated and tied by George Grant

Woven-Bodied Dragonfly Nymph, tied by Darrel Martin

A Whitlock Muddler—originated and tied by Dave Whitlock

COQ DE LEON FEATHERS

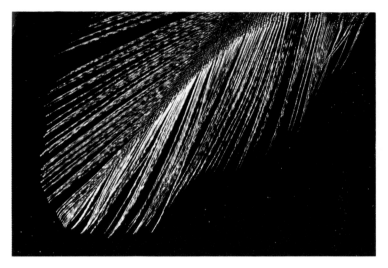

Pardo Corzuno

Pardo Sarriosa

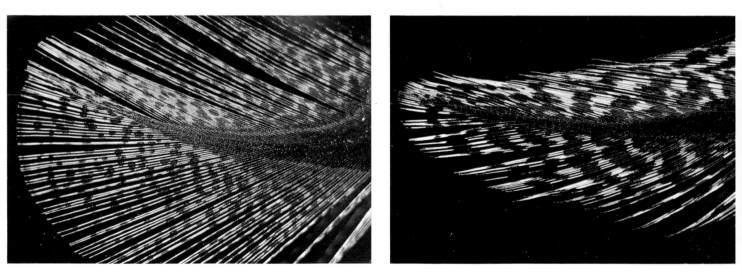

Flor de Escoba

Longareto

Natural Encounters

The Insect and the Plant

...uatic plants took place on the Wil-
...southern England. It was a bright,
...ohn Goddard and I hunted hard for
...the bank, John pointed to it—fine
... river. It meant nothing to me, but
...ance, John suggested that we move
...aid nothing, not wishing to expose
...cance to silk weed riding the swirls.
...n, and there, at a weak bend in the
... for shrimp. John knew that shrimp
...that trout aggressively rooted the
...ed adrift. Here was applied knowl-

...ade more complete by the study of
...re are about 1, 300 species of aquatic
...and 65 families. However, not all
...e angler. Those plants that harbor
... are of greatest value. These are the
...e currents, offer security from pre-
...support the periphyton slime—the
...gae and protozoa.

...s, are highly selective in their habitat
...be possible, at times, to determine
...plant community. Plants may select
...vaters, low or high aeration. Others
...ottom, or stone matrix. Some shun
...nt for photosynthesis and germina-
...y even have a direct relationship to
...e Fly-Fisher's Plants (1973), D. Macer
...the relationship between reed smut
...ercup (Ranunculus). He writes: "By
...developed specimens concentrated
...towards the apical ends of the ..., with the younger ones in the rear.
The latter presumably need less food and less oxygen than the former, and
their simpler needs would be met in the lower oxygen area near the plant
base." This "natural dispensation" allows the younger, upstream larvae

to avoid food competition by inhabiting a different flow line than their elder relations.

Briefly seen, the relationship between the crustacean or the insect, and the plant can be a complex one. And it is only recently that this relationship has received notice by anglers. If there was an established relationship between the silk weed and the shrimp, perhaps it was possible that there might be a consistent relationship between other plants and their creature tenants. The pursuit of plants is as interesting and challenging as is the pursuit of selective trout.

Trout use aquatic plants directly and indirectly. Plants provide cover for trout, and plants provide the habitat for aquatic insects that live all or part of their lives among the plants. To trout, the plant mass is a larder filled with food. Plants are necessary in order for a water system to carry the maximum amount of animal tissue, so the propagation of plants is essential for the production of insects and trout. The following ecological factors encourage aquatic plant growth, reproduction, and distribution:

1. Sunlight necessary for photosynthesis and germination
2. Absorption of gases for growth and maturation
3. Available nutrients and essential minerals
4. Physical disturbance of currents that constantly rearrange the plant mass
5. Distribution by current dispersal of seeds or plant fragmentation

Plant zonation, where particular plants occupy particular water zones, is especially evident in still waters and is determined by the plants' limited ability to adjust. A zone may be determined by several factors; however, water depth clearly demonstrates a plant's limited community zone. The water buttercup (*Ranunculus flabellaris*) inhabits the shallow shore zone of six inches to two feet. Water buttercup (*Ranunculus circinatus*) and Canadian waterweed (*Anacharis canadensis*) occupy the shallow, three- to seven-foot zone. In deeper water, the ten- to twelve-foot zone, will be the yellow water lily (*Nuphar advena*). Because certain insects have a preference for certain plants, this knowledge can help place the angler in the right place with the right fly. Prescott's *How to Know the Aquatic Plants* (1969) classifies over seventy plant species according to the various "living-zones."

America does not farm or groom aquatic plants as is done in England. There, the husbandry of aquatic plants is done primarily for flood control and secondarily for the maximum biotic potential of insect, trout, and angler. The rich English chalkstreams, those slow-moving meadow streams similar to our western spring creeks, possess optimum plant growth, due to their clear water and stable temperatures. Aquatic weed cutting on the English chalkstreams is controlled by regional water authorities and regulations. The weed cutting, usually done by a weed boat if the water allows, enhances the waterway for selective plants. Weed cutting may also be done by other methods, such as with the pole scythe, the smaller hand scythe, or the shackle-bladed chain scythe. Hand cutting is slow and difficult, but more discriminate. Depending upon the particular purpose, weed beds are cut in various checkerboard, bar, or run patterns. Only a specific amount of weed bed is cut and then only for specific purposes. Some weed beds, such as those at a bend, may be allowed to lodge permanently to prevent bank erosion.

The rooting and erosion process of plants constantly changes. When a drifting shoot takes root in the streambed, it causes a localized reduction of current. This leads to deposition on the downstream side, which eventually builds up a silt bank. This diverts the current up and along the sides, which increases the channelization of the river between plant clumps. The growth of the plant hummock, the elevated base and the plant mass, eventually back-erodes and undermines the whole structure. Consequently, the result of the process leads to plant isolation and constant plant redistribution on the stream bed. A stream is always alive and always changing. It slowly gnaws a different channel in a different direction. Plants compress and spread the currents. They help the river do its job of devouring and depositing. Rivers always run, and in the running is continuous change.

Plants serve the angler in diverse ways. Too many plants clog flow and favor only those creatures that survive in slow water. Too few plants generate scant oxygen and sparse habitat for plant-dwelling insects. From an angler's point of view, a plant has several purposes. Plants maintain adequate water levels by holding water back. Plants bring oxygen into the water. Like the bankside plants, aquatic plants provide cover for trout. Plants provide habitat for the various foods trout feed upon. Furthermore, plants prevent erosion if appropriately situated. Long-stemmed grasses and the bushes bind the bank together and create fish cover. Certain plants and certain amounts of plants encourage a productive habitat. Plants offer food, oxygen, and moderate temperatures. And, esthetically, they make a waterway attractive and varied. The quality and quantity of plant life along the stream are significant factors in the habitat quality. Heavily forested banks can canopy the stream and impede photosynthesis, thereby limiting a stream's productivity. Plants can kill as well as protect. In balance, trees and riparian plants cool a water system, preventing calefaction, the warming of the waters. This is most evident in the West where wanton clearcutting has raised water temperatures of exposed drainages to seventy-five degrees or more.

It is impossible to say what percentage of water surface should be devoted to plant life. This depends upon various factors. On the English chalkstreams, about one-fourth to two-fifths has been estimated. The weeds are cut periodically to regulate water flow; this is, unfortunately, more for water control than for the propagation of certain insects. Cutting also prevents an excessive buildup of mud. A few centimeters of mud, a microhabitat for some insects, is all that is required to create insect habitat and plant nourishment in most chalkstreams or spring creeks. Mud can be either detrimental or beneficial to a river system, and much depends upon the amount and the location of the mud. Mud must be managed along with the plants.

The study of aquatic plants, especially for the layman, is difficult. Many aquatic plants are "plastic" and mold themselves to a variety of environmental niches, while others do not. But because of the uniformity of water temperature, water chemistry, and nutrients, aquatic plant species are more widely distributed throughout the world than are terrestrial species. Compared to terrestrial plants, the water habitat is often less subject to temperature and water supply; however, water quality—the dissolved salts and nutrients, the turbidity and chemical properties, and the substrata mosaic—is subject to significant variations. Certain species of aquatic plants, moreover, require an exacting environmental niche. Their distribution may be limited by the chemical properties of the water, by the temperature, by the flow, by the depth, and by the physical properties of the stream bottom. Aquatic plants, like terrestrial plants, may be cosmopolitan, living anywhere, or highly restricted, living only in limited areas. It is these "restricted" plants that offer more to the angler because the interconnection of flora and fauna is consistent. To know the water and the plants is, in some measure, to know the insects.

Metaphorically, an aquatic plant is a high-rise, tenanted by a variety of creatures who seek, in the various parts of the plant, their particular needs. Wright describes this concept of fauna dispersal: "In water celery, *Apium nodiflorum*, we have one of the fly fisher's most valuable plants. Its roots are mostly in slack water, but its foliage frequently extends into the current, and as the leaves are relatively large they offer a considerable surface area for grazing fauna. Thus on its slack water portions the plant supports species needing shelter, and on its extended portions those needing flowing water." Wright further describes the fauna-bearing properties of the plant: high shrimp count may be found, along with snails in the basal area, and reed smut larvae and mayfly nymphs in the freely washed sections. Thus, each plant part may be a microhabitat for particular insects and crustaceans. One must add, as Wright does, that the surface area of any plant is not merely determined by leaf size. The finely divided leaf threads of a *Ranunculus*, in comparable plant weight, has a greater total surface than does a broad-leafed plant such as water celery. The ability to house fauna, the animal tissue that trout consume, is based upon the total surface area of a plant.

Aquatic plant identification, at least for the angler, is best accomplished by the leaf shape, stem, and flower formation. More complex taxonomies include the identification by the stipules, sheaths, flowers, and seed structure, and the shape, margin, and arrangement of leaves. For the layman and angler, the simplest method of identification might be a dichotomous taxonomy, where two choices are compared toward a final selection. Exhaustive analysis is not necessary; plant genera rather than species is all that is normally required for the angler. Classification to the species level may be especially difficult when the seed, often minute and available only during certain times, is the determining factor. However, there is seldom an angling necessity for such specificity.

The study of aquatic plants is further complicated by other factors. Some aquatic plants do not grow exclusively under or on the water. Some are submerged as seedlings which will later produce either floating or emerging leaves. And the submerged leaf shape may differ radically from the emergent leaf shape. Leaf shape, even on the same plant, may be significantly varied. The leaves of many aquatic plants will collapse into a characterless clump when they are taken out of the water. It is best, therefore, to examine the leaves in a shallow dish of water, moving the plant to achieve its natural spread.

The following discussion of plants is for the average fly fisher and makes no attempt to be technically complete. There are aquatic plant taxonomies listed in the bibliography for further study. With modest student background, the Prescott dichotomous key listed in the bibliography should prove adequate. The dimensions of this book preclude a more extended investigation of the flora-fauna connection.

Plant collection may be done with a raking tool or plant hook. The specimens are safely transported in plastic bags that have water added to cushion the movement. Most aquatic plants, those without thick or rigid stems, may be washed, spread into a natural position, dried with paper towels and placed in a flower press. The thick stems of some plants must be split and divided before pressing. Herbarium paper is sometimes used for submerged plants or those with fragile filamentous leaves.

The purpose of this field investigation is the examination of the relationship between the plants and the trout diet. The field work is best done only on slow-moving or spring-creek systems with selective trout. In freestone waters plant life is not abundant: slow spring creeks foster heavy plant growth and wise trout. Furthermore, not all plants require research. Only the common plants will be dealt with here, and only a general introduction to the plant-insect relation is possible. The "basic" plants under consideration are Canadian waterweed, milfoil, muskgrass, starwort, water buttercup, water cress, and water parsnip. Other plants that are indigenous to your home waters may be approached in the same manner.

CANADIAN WATERWEED (*Anacharis canadensis*). Canadian waterweed has long flexible stems bearing small elliptical dark green leaves mounted, usually, three to a whorl. Toward the stem tip, leaves may be in opposing pairs. There is no leaf stalk. The leaves do not emerge, but rest directly beneath the water. It is an excellent oxygenator, has rapid growth, and does not die down in winter. It has a notorious reputation, stemming in part from its devastation in England about 1860 when, with its profuse and troublesome growth, it became a threat to canal transportation. *Baetis* nymphs, *Chironomid* pupae, caddis, flies and smuts all inhabit waterweed. In fact, it will carry a rather varied gathering of most fauna, including dragonfly and damselfly nymphs. It can be, in terms of its density, either productive or troublesome. But, if controlled, it can carry numerous creatures and provide valuable oxygen. In some waters, where there is poor insect propagation, it may be a sparse larder at best. The plant is often cursed, but Wright points out that waterweeds "are good plants to have in a trout fishery." In contrast, other writers merely note that it is slightly better than no plant at all. Only close examination will determine its true value in your home waters.

WATER MILFOIL (*Myriophyllum*). The stems are long and narrow, bearing alternate or whorled feathery leaves with threadlike divisions. This genus forms dense, rooted, or free-floating beds. It is an oxygenator and is used by moose and muskrat for food. Various birds consume the seeds. Nine species are widely distributed throughout America. The emergent stem tip, which bears the inconspicuous red or brown flowers, rises from one to three inches above the water. On stems up to nine feet in length, the dark green herringbone leaves usually cluster or whorl in fours. Many milfoils grow in a tangle of extended, horizontal stems. The leaves may vary significantly from oval or linear leaves to whorled, threadlike strands. Wright makes no comment concerning the insect inhabitants of milfoil. They are, as might be expected, similar to waterweed. Milfoil can be bed and board to a remarkable variety of creatures or it can be sparsely inhabited. Unless it grows in well-oxygenated, chalky waters, it usually favors

Canadian pondweed.

Milfoil.

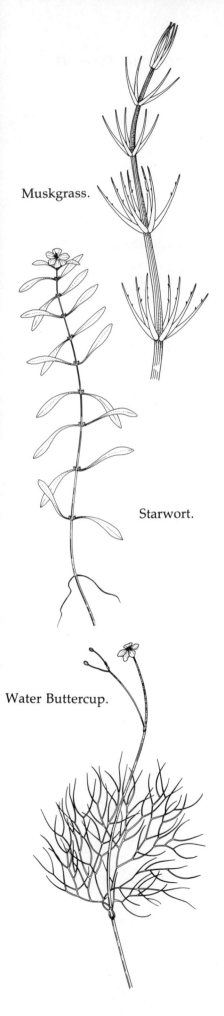

Muskgrass.

Starwort.

Water Buttercup.

those insects with low oxygen requirements—snails, shrimp, and some caddisfly larvae. Those insects that require flowing water, such as reed smuts, will avoid milfoil when it grows in calm water.

MUSKGRASS OR STONEWORT (*Chara*). This brittle gray-green plant is usually covered with gritty calcium carbonate deposits. It has a distinct skunky odor. There are whorled, prickly-looking shoots or "leaves" the same length and at regular intervals on a central "stem." Muskgrass is really a highly developed algae. The average height of the plant is about twelve inches. The animals found on the muskgrass are similar to those found on water-weed: caddis larvae, reed smuts, *Baetis* nymphs, *Chironomids*, snails, and others. Their fauna-carrying capacity appears very good at times, both in species mixture and quantity. The plants usually occupy only hard, fresh, or brackish waters and are widely distributed.

WATER STARWORT (*Callitriche*). Starwort, which grows in static and lotic waters, has thin threadlike submerged stems up to a yard long. The leaves are linear. The emergent sections appear as small "rosettes" of leaves slightly above the water, hence the name "starwort." The plant, which remains in leaf year long, makes up small, dense mats often interspersed among other plants. When the plant grows in flowing water, a high *Baetis* count is normally present. D. Macer Wright indicates that such current as the starwort can tolerate evidently does not produce enough oxygen for many larvae. Wright's *Fly Fisher's Plants* identifies starwort as a "principal home of shrimps." Those creatures that demand less oxygen—shrimp, dragonfly nymphs, and some caddis—will occupy the plant. The tender plants are used as food by aquatic birds. *C. heterophylla* and *C. palustris* are widely distributed species in America. Starwort, because of its water resistance and mass shape, can create excessive silt accumulations.

WATER BUTTERCUP OR CROWFOOT (*Ranunculus*). The submerged stems carry finely divided, threadlike, flexible leaves that are variously shaped depending upon species. Even the same plant may have different leaf shapes. The white or yellow flower, which is held within an inch or so of the surface, occurs one per stalk. The degree of the variable leaf bunching depends upon the species. *Ranunculus* harbors flies and trout well. It holds mayflies, which require high amounts of oxygen. The leaves harbor *Baetis* and the thick base area nurtures various *Chironomids* and plant-living caddis. Shrimp will occupy the areas at the base where the current is gentle. Some species, such as *aquatilis*, *cymbalaria*, and *circinatus*, are widely distributed from the Pacific to the Atlantic rim. Water buttercup is food for moose and aquatic birds.

WATER CRESS (*Nasturtium officinale*). Water cress, a sprawling and erect aquatic, is a valued trout plant. It loves rich marl bottoms and thrives in clear, cold, shallow water. When growing in well-aerated flowing water it harbors a high count of mayfly nymphs and in denser stands supports colonies of shrimp and snails. In springs and small feeder streams it can be so abundant that it reduces water flow and can be a nuisance. The plant was introduced from Europe and is naturalized throughout America. The leaves are compound and the terminal leaf is more heart shaped than the lateral, elliptical leaves. The leaves are dark green with the pungent flavor of cultivated water cress. Speciation is determined generally by leaf form and size. Water cress is an excellent home for mayfly nymphs because it grows in flowing, well-oxygenated waters.

WATER PARSNIP (*Sium suave*). The widely distributed water parsnip plays an important role as oxygenator. The leaflets have no stem. They occupy meadow waters, and may be rooted in the quiet under-banks with the submerged leaves trailing into margin currents. The plant becomes a "high-rise" for various dwellers, based upon their habitat needs. Shrimp, which require less oxygen than most mayfly nymphs, will house in the basement. The penthouse is occupied by those animals that require more oxygen and current—mayfly nymphs and reed smut larvae. Wright calls the water parsnip "a basic food plant for a trout fishery." It supports a high shrimp population as does starwort. Wright also points out that certain plants will foster dry-fly fishing. To some extent, he laments a total subsurface fare for trout and hopes that the fat, shrimping trout might one day rise to his dry Orange Quill. One might add that opulent dry hatches are products of subsurface activity. Dry-fly fishing is usually a index for good wet fishing; however, good wet fishing does not always mean good dry-fly fishing. In nature's system, the delicate Blue-Winged Olive is not innately superior to the lowly shrimp. The day may come when we will plant plants and their insects as well as trout.

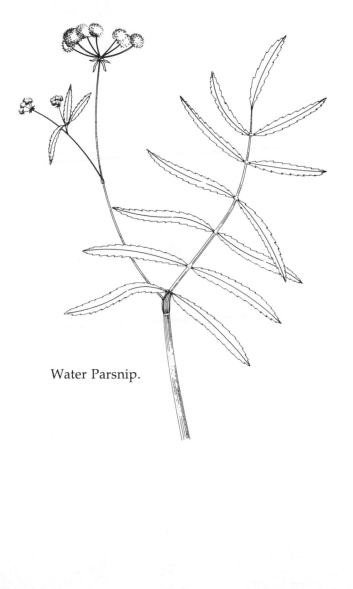

Water Cress.

Water Parsnip.

Water Parsnip—a submerged leaf section (after Muenscher, 1939).

Plant populations will vary from season to season and from year to year. However, knowing what particular fauna enjoy what particular plant increases angling knowledge. To recognize that starwort usually has a high *Baetis* count in a certain stream section at a certain season and then to observe trout immediately below starwort take countless emerging nymphs is a fair indication that a *Baetis* nymph pattern may be appropriate. A trout working a particular plant mass will usually be taking those creatures "great and small" that inhabit the plant. Knowledge of plant leads to knowledge of insect and, consequently, to knowledge of trout. Such a system is not infallible and sometimes there are more variables than constants, but an angler does gain pleasure and information in the pursuit of plants. As Ralph Waldo Emerson once wrote, "A weed is a plant whose virtues have not yet been discovered." There truly is a tale, if it can be read, in drifting silk weed.

CHAPTER 7

The Naturals

The following section contains the essentials of insect identification and habits. Aquatic insect venation, regardless of the species, consists of the basic pattern of six longitudinal veins—the costa (C), the subcosta (Sc), the radius (R), the media (M), the cubitus (Cu), and the anal (A). When these veins are repeated in a wing structure, they are subnumbered from front to rear. The cross veins connect the six primary veins in complex tracery. It should be noted that cross veins may vary even within a species. Wing venation has been greatly simplified in the text to illustrate only particular aspects. For greater specificity, please consult the entomological references listed in the bibliography. Insect classification is usually done with the mature male insect. Taxonomy and nomenclature in this text is usually complete enough for imitative tying. The modern angler, whether or not he believes it important, must tolerate a certain amount of insect information. And fly tying, to a significant extent, is imitating the shape, size, and color of insects. It is to be hoped that the discussion and illustrations will lessen the burden and make the object of imitation, the insect, a fascinating facet of tying.

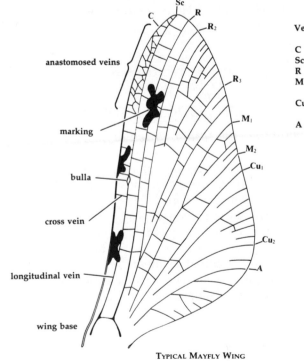

Venation Code

C	costa
Sc	subcosta
R	radius
M	median or MA medius anterior and MP medius posterior
Cu	cubitus (branch vein) or CA (cubitus anterior) and CuP (cubitus posterior)
A	anal

TYPICAL MAYFLY WING

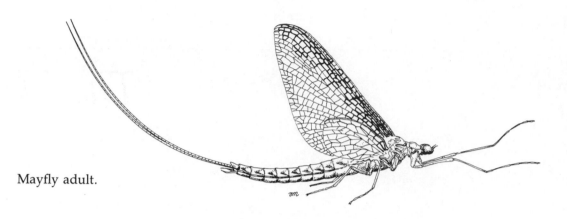

Mayfly adult.

THE MAYFLY (Ephemeroptera)

This introduction to the mayfly is a simplified and condensed overview of the western mayfly. Knowledge of when and where a hatch or spinner fall will occur erases much of the mystique of the mayfly. Furthermore, despite our homage to England and New England tradition, some of the traditional Wheatley labels do not match the compartment contents of the western fly fisher. The name Pale Morning Dun, for example, is given to both the *E. infrequens* and the *E. inermis* by Swisher and Richards. Schwiebert saves the name only for the *infrequens*, and calls the *inermis* the Pale Morning Olive. Arbona calls both the *infrequens* and *inermis* the Pale Morning Dun, listing the *infrequens* under the more widely distributed *inermis*. For the sake of clarity and accuracy, I have called only the *infrequens* the Pale Morning Dun. Swisher and Richards have given the name popularity and authority. I have called the diminutive olive-yellow *inermis* the Pale Morning Sulphur. In any case, neither of these sulphurs, the *infrequens* or *inermis*, should be called, as still others have done, merely western variations of the olive-brown Hendrickson.

CHARACTERISTICS OF THE MAYFLY

Nymph (the junior to senior instars)

1. Three distinct body divisions—the head, thorax, and abdomen
2. Three tails, except for one genus, the two-tailed *Epeorus*, and one species, the *Baetis bicaudatus*
3. Two short antennae
4. One pair of wing pads
5. Platelike or leaflike gills on the top or side of the abdominal segments
6. Ten abdominal segments
7. Six legs, each with a single claw
8. May vary significantly in size and shape

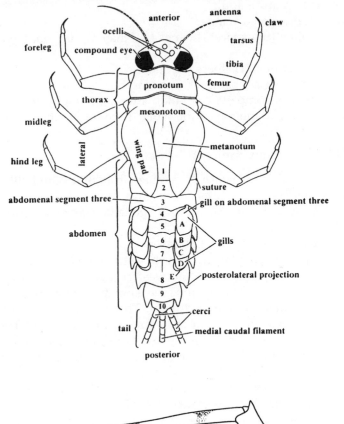

Typical mayfly nymph.

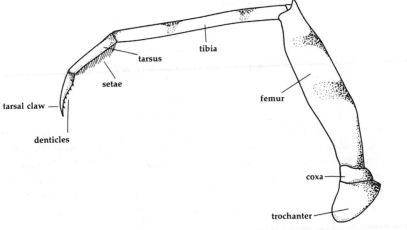

Typical mayfly leg.

Dun (the subimago)

1. Gray or gray-brown wings with or without markings
2. Lack of mature coloration of body and wings
3. Two or three threadlike tails
4. A sexually immature adult that will "bush hatch" in twelve to forty-eight hours
5. Large, triangular front wings, held erect or sail-like, and absent or vestigial hind wings reduced and rounded
6. Small bristlelike antennae

Spinner (the imago)

1. The sexually mature adult
2. Often with elongated wings
3. Glassy, hyaline (transparent) wings that may or may not have contrasting marks
4. Males have terminal claspers for mating
5. Male tails may be almost their dun length
6. Development of complete coloration after six to eight hours
7. The only insect to molt after the wings become functional

BAETIDAE (small swimmers)

Insects and Patterns: Western Iron Blue, Iron Blue Quill, Blue-Winged Olive (*B. insignificans*, *B. tricaudatus*), Gray-Winged Olive (*B. piscatoris*, *B. adonis*, *B. heimalis*, *B. parvus*), Western Spotted *Callibaetis* (Speckled Winged Quill, *C. nigritus*)

Genera: Baetis, Pseudocloeons, Callibaetis

Identification and Habits: The nymphs have three heavily fringed tails with the midtail distinctly shorter. Some western species have only two tails with a vestigial midtail. The nymphs have an abdominal margin free from spines and a slender, streamlined body. The legs of the nymph are long while the single oval gills appear on segments one to seven. The nymphs have a unique darting swim that is the result of violent flicks of the abdomen and filamentous tails. The adult male's eyes are stalked and shaped like an inverted cone (turbinated). The spinners have hyaline wings and gray, brown, or olive bodies. Their underdeveloped hind wing has three longitudinal veins. *Note*: The important *Callibaetis* has a teardrop-design double gill. The secondary gill is minute. And unlike the *Baetis* in general, who prefer riffle water, the *Callibaetis* are found primarily in static or slow water. The nymph has three tails of equal length and often a dark terminal tail band. The adults are speckled on forewings and body. The *Callibaetis* is evident on eastern Washington lakes. The adults have, beside the reduced hind wing, two tails. Their multigenerations season makes them important. Hatching takes place from midday to evening, from February to November. *B. insignificans* has only local importance; however, the *B. tricaudatus* has wide western distribution. The western *B. parvus* also has angling significance, while the *B. piscatoris* and *B. adonis* appear only in the Southwest. The *B. hiemalis* is found in the central states. *Pseudocloeon edmundsi* produces some excellent hatches on western waters. In time, *Pseudocloeons* may achieve genera status rather than species designation in the *Baetis* group. Field entomologists have identified the *Pseudocloeon* by the adult's lack of hind wings. This is not conclusive, because Idaho species have been collected that have hind wings in the males, but not the females.

CAENIDAE (micromay sprawlers)

Insects and Patterns: Angler's Curse, Snowflake Mayfly

Genera: Caenis, Brachycercus

Identification and Habits: Smaller even than the Tricos, the *Caenis* nymphs have a rectangular second gill, and their coloration is toward the light brown and tan. They usually inhabit the slower silt waters and back pools.

The adults have a single pair of hyaline wings that are significantly wide (two-thirds of the length) and with few cross veins. They are sporadic evening emergers, often with remarkable density; yet, they generally do not form significant western hatches. The slender *Brachycercus* nymph has rounded gill covers and three cone tubercles on the head. They produce only minor hatches that are nothing like the surface tapestry of the *Tricorythodes* duns. It may be of interest that the *Brachycercus* nymph will display its tails in a scorpionlike attitude when captured.

TRICORYTHIDAE (micromay sprawlers)

Insects and Patterns: Trico, Black and White

Genera: *Tricorythodes*

Identification and Habits: The diminutive *Tricorythodes* nymph, like the *Caenis* and *Brachycercus*, has an enlarged second gill. The Trico second gill is triangular or oval and does not meet medially. It forms a protective shield that prevents silting of the functional gills beneath abdominal sections three to six. The eggs hatch in spring, and there are usually two peak periods of hatching, midsummer and early fall. The nymphs prefer the marl-rich silt of alkaline waters or the calm mirror waters near a rip flow where they consume the periphyton slime and algae. The adult (imago) has three tails that are longer than the body (at least three times as long), a pair of roundish wings, and a blunt pair of tubercles at the rear of the head. The adult is usually about three to six millimeters in length and best imitated in hook sizes 20 to 28. The Trico adult female has short forelegs and a stout body. The wings of both sexes are about one millimeter longer than the body. Fred Arbona, in *Mayflies, the Angler, and the Trout* (1980), indicates that the males emerge throughout the night while females emerge during the early morning. By midmorning, both will be spinners and mating takes place soon thereafter. For some species, both the male and female emerge in the morning. During this time the blizzard hatches can produce remarkable trout feeding. The imago may carry the dun body case a distance, hence the so-called "flight-hatch" of the Trico. Hatching usually takes place from about 4:00 A.M. to 11:00 A.M., from late June through October. Spinner transformation takes a few minutes to two hours. The *T. minutes*, with light brown femurs, and the *T. fallax*, with red-brown femurs and a purple-brown body, are common western hatches. Some females may have a gray body in contrast to the black-bodied male. In *The Mayflies of North and Central America* (1978), the authors state that the *fallax* differ from the *minutes* only in color. "At most, *T. fallax* and *T. minutes* seem worthy of subspecific rank, but we believe that these will best be regarded as mere clinical variants and hereby designate *fallax* as a synonym of *minutes*." They classify them as one species with color differences due to geographical distribution.

Identification of the Trico is relatively simple. The nymph has the dominant triangular second gill and compound eyes similar in size to the ocelli (simple eyes). They have three tails in all stages and, as adults, lack hind wings. The imago has a heavy thoracic section, a turned down CuP, the IMP and MP extend less than three-fourths the distance of MP. The MA has a symmetrical fork. Their appearance is generally one of a small black insect with white wings.

EPHEMERELLIDAE (sprawlers)

Insects and Patterns: Western Blue-Winged Olive (*Attenella margarita*), Small Western Green Drake (*Drunella flavilinea*), Western Green Drake (*Drunella doddsi, Drunella grandis*), Blue-Winged Olive (*E. cornuta, E. lata*), Slate-Winged Olive (*Drunella coloradensis*), Pale Morning Sulphur (*E. inermis*), Pale Morning Dun (*E. infrequens*)

Genera: Ephemerella

Identification and Habits: The *Ephemerella* constitute the most important western hatch. Some subimagoes emerge from the nymphal husk a distance below the surface, others, at or just beneath the surface film. Once on the surface, they require significant "flutter time" before flight. I have watched the *E. infrequens* float several yards into the mouths of waiting trout. The nymphal bodies may have conspicuous lateral spines, and may be smooth or hairy. The nymphs have small platelike gills on the dorsal side of segments three to seven, except the *A. margarita*, which has gills on abdominal segments four to seven, and three equal tails that are retained in the imago. The gills have a distinct sequential undulation and the nymphs swim in a whipping wiggle. The hind wing often has a costal hook, technically termed *projection* or *angulation*, and the adults appear, like the *Tricorythodes*, sexually separate in the water. Most subimagoes are olive or brown and require twenty-four hours to "bush-hatch" into spinners. The female imagoes have an errant dip as they penetrate the surface film to release the egg sac. They hatch from April to August, from midday to evening.

EPHEMERIDAE (burrowers)

Insects and Patterns: Great Lead-Winged Drake (*H. limbata*), Brown Drake (*E. simulans*)

Genera: Hexagenia, Ephemera

Identification and Habits: This family is not prolific in the West, but it does form some significant hatches in the marl-bottomed and siltaceous streams of the Rocky Mountains. These rather large tusk-bearing mayflies burrow in the bottom. The nymphs have flanged forelegs, shovel-shaped heads, and three heavily fringed tails. The feathered branchlike gills undulate with wavy motion. The nymphs must periodically come out of the eclipse or horseshoe burrows to molt; thus, they are available to trout even during the winter. Although some species appear to have instant emergence, others may have significant flutter time prior to flight. The adult wings are well veined and the hind wings are prominent. Emergence is normally in the evening from June through August.

HEPTAGENIIDAE (clingers)

Insects and Patterns: March Brown (western variations), Western Quill (*E. longimanus*), Dark Western Quill (*R. morrisoni*)

Genera: Heptagenia, Epeorus, Rhithrogenia, Stenonema (eastern)

Identification and Habits: Generally speaking, the nymphs inhabit the swift, steep rivers of the West. A few species may even inhabit waters typical of the Ephemeridae. Many have the overlapping gills (the circular "suction-cupped" system), which allow them to adhere to rocks and deflect the current pressures of heavy water. They have saucer heads and, except for the *Epeorus*, which has two tails, most have three tails. The head is as wide as the thorax with the eyes on the lateral, dorsal edge. Gills are platelike and are often highly modified. The two-tailed adults have five movable tarsi in the hind leg with four cubital intercalary veins on the fore wing. Adult wings are usually heavily barred with cross veins. They hatch nearly vertically from riffle water, having escaped the nymphal husk while ascending. Hatching usually takes place at midday and the perpendicular nuptial dance is in the evening over the riffles. Some authorities advocate the Hare's Ear for the *Epeorus* nymph. However, a reddish brown dubbing would prove more effective. Not only does it match nymphal coloration better, but, in the quick waters usually associated with the *Epeorus*, it appears to attract trout more effectively. I have found *E. longimanus* numerous in the Cascade streams where they hatched sporadically but quickly from the midday waters. I have found them most abundant about mid-July to mid-August in the small, quick streams.

MAYFLY WING VENATION

The venation of the following wings has been greatly reduced and simplified to illustrate only particular aspects of spinner venation at the family or genus level. Most aquatic insects have membranous wings supported by rigid, thickened veins. These veins, which look like leading in Gothic glass, indicate identity. Knowing what to read makes the insects familiar friends. With limited work, every student of the fly can identify the stage and the family of the major insects. Writers such as Fred Arbona, Al Caucci, Bob Nastasi, Carl Richards, and Doug Swisher have converted many anglers into field naturalists. Angling students truly wish to read nature, to decipher the insects, and to enjoy the fullness that knowledge brings. The following venation is based on the male spinner. For greater specificity consult the entomological references listed in the bibliography.

MAYFLY FAMILY CLASSIFICATION
BASED ON WING VENATION

FAMILY BAETIDAE

Baetidae forewings show basally detached double (or single in some species such as the *Cloeon*) marginal intercalaries present in the interspace; note also lack of costal, basal cross veins. Forewing veins MA_2 and MP_2 are not basally attached. The hind wings are reduced, veinless, or absent. Male eyes are turbinate. Two tails are present. The genus *Callibaetis* has unique pale venation on a dark gray field, a reduced hind wing, and dark blotches on the glassy spinner wing.

FAMILY CAENIDAE

Forewing vein MA_2 attaches to MA_1 with a near-right-angled cross vein. Forewing vein MP_2 is almost as long as MP_1. Caenidae adults have three tails and no hind wings. They are minute adults, two to four milimeters in body length, and are usually a creamy yellow.

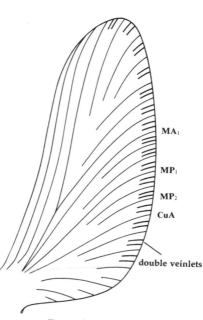

Baetidae forewing.

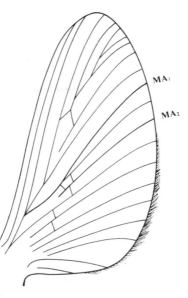

Caenidae forewing (after McCafferty).

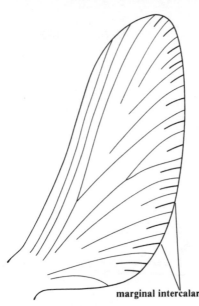

FAMILY EPHEMERELLIDAE

The Ephemerellidae forewing has short, basally detached marginal intercalary veinlets present along the entire outer margin. Dun and spinner have three tails.

Ephemerellidae forewing.

marginal intercalary veinlets

FAMILY EPHEMERIDAE

Ephemeridae forewing has veins MP_2 and CuA_1 basally divergent away from MP_1. Vein A_1 attaches to hind margin by two or more veinlets (McCafferty).

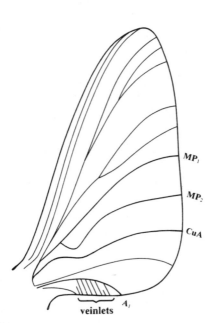

MP_1

MP_2

CuA

Ephemeridae forewing.

A_1

veinlets

FAMILY HEPTAGENIIDAE

Heptageniidae forewing has cubital intercalaries in two parallel pairs alternating long and short. Dun and spinners have two tails. *Epeorus* forewing has up-slanted basal costal cross veins (Caucci and Nastasi).

Heptageniidae forewing.

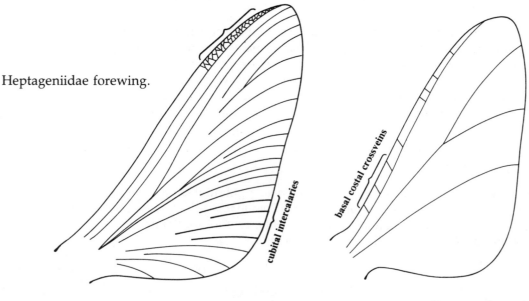

cubital intercalaries

basal costal crossveins

Epeorus forewing.

FAMILY TRICORYTHIDAE

Forewing veins MA_1 and MA_2 fork symmetrically. Forewing vein CuP recurves (Arbona). Male hind wings are reduced or with long costal projections. The blackish adult Trico has three tails and a stout thorax. Dun and spinner have three tails. *Tricorythodes* was previously classified under the Family Caenidae.

CLASSIFICATION OF THE BASIC MAYFLY NYMPHS

There is parsimony in nature. Nature simplifies or eliminates what it cannot use. It should not surprise us, then, that in the insect world form follows function. The shape of an insect comments on its habits and habitat. Nature's economy, the simplicity expressed in the shape of a nymph, actually allows us to classify mayfly nymphs according to the six basic families: Baetidae, Caenidae, Ephemerellidae, Ephemeridae, Heptageniidae, and Tricorythidae. The family level of classification centers on the easily understood "architecture" of the insect: the size, shape, and structures of the mature nymph, the nymph with darkened and developed wing pads. My own classes have consistently succeeded with the following family key. With limited technical knowledge, anyone can classify the important mayfly nymphs according to their basic families. This is the easiest introduction to taxonomy that I have encountered. It is based on distinct nymphal structures: body shape, gill shape and placement, head size, antenna length, tusk size, tail length, leg shape and, to a lesser extent, size and color.

Before beginning, make certain that the specimen under consideration is a mayfly nymph. Mayfly nymphs have abdominal gills, single claws, and two or three tails. The alderfly larva has only one tail. The damselfly nymph has three tails ("plume" tails called lamellae), large eyes, and no abdominal gills. The stonefly nymph has double claws and no abdominal gills. This is not a complete key. More detailed and scholarly works are listed in the bibliography. But even with limited time and knowledge, anyone can find success with the following basic key to mayfly families. It is, in fact, unnecessary to make a detailed study of the mayflies in order to be proficient in family identification. A small nymph net and an 8X hand lens is all that is required. For field and classroom work, I highly recommend the *Instant Mayfly Identification Guide* by Al Caucci and Bob Nastasi; it is clear, complete, and compact. The parenthetical numbers indicate the principal features of each family.

BAETIDAE (small swimmers)

(1.) Mature nymph length, excluding tails, three to twelve milimeters
(2.) Oval or elongated oval gills on abdominal segments 1–7 or 2–7
(3.) Three fringed tails with fine, interlocking hairs; a few have two tails
(4.) Long antennae, more than three times the head width (Merritt and Cummins)
5. This nymph family is transcontinental with varied habitat, including still to fast water
6. Emergence from mid-May to mid-October
7. Body colors vary from pale tan to cream to olive to dark olive-brown

Tricorythidae forewing.

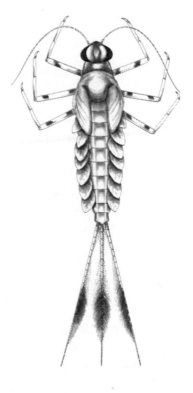

Baetidae nymph.

8. Lateral eyes
9. Genus *Callibaetis*:
   a. Small, recurved flap gills on abdominal segments 1–4 or 1–7
   b. Three, fringed tails of equal length, with interlocking hairs ("paddle tail")
   c. Mature nymph length, excluding tails, six to twelve millimeters
   d. Body colors include tan, gray, green, and grayish brown
   e. Abundant in western lakes
10. Genus *Baetis*:
   a. Middle tail shorter than outer two
   b. Some species, such as *Baetis bicaudatus*, have only two tails
   c. Single gill plates on abdominal segments 1–7
   d. Long antennae, often two or more times longer than head width (Hafele and Hughes)
   e. Streamlined with long, slender legs
   f. Body colors include tan, gray, green, and grayish brown

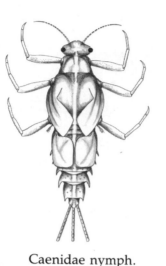

Caenidae nymph.

CAENIDAE (micromay sprawlers)

(1.) The smallest of the mayflies; mature nymph length, excluding tails, two to eight millimeters
(2.) The second gill is enlarged (operculate) and squared. The operculate gills are visibly separate (Caucci and Nastasi)
(3.) The head and pronota are narrower than the mesonota (Schwiebert)
(4.) Three tails
5. Hind-wing pads are usually absent
6. The body may have lateral spines or fine hairs for silt camouflage
7. The claws are often slender and curved
8. Emergence from June through September
9. Genus *Brachycercus*:
   a. Rounded operculate gills on abdomenal segment 2 that cover segments 4, 5, and 6
   b. Head has three prominent tubercles (knoblike projections)
   c. Operculate gills overlap (Caucci and Nastasi)

EPHEMERELLIDAE (spiny sprawlers)

(1.) Mature nymph length, excluding tails, five to fifteen millimeters
(2.) Postero-lateral abdominal spines
(3.) No gills present on abdominal segment 2
(4.) Wholly dorsal gills that slightly overlap on abdominal segments 3–7 or 4–7; gill shapes are variable: small plates held against the body, long forked or trailing gills and operculate gills roofing other gills
(5.) Three, body-length tails, often hairy
(6.) Sequential undulation of gills
7. Diverse and specialized body shapes: streamlined, ventral flattening, humped thorax, flat femora, smooth, haired, or spined bodies; body cross section is usually either flattened or cylindrical; the nymph is often identified by default by not belonging to any other family
8. Only one North American genus, *Ephemerella*, usually divided into seven subgenera

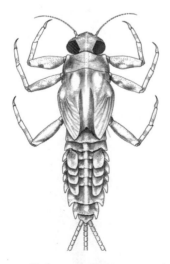

Ephemerellidae nymph.

9. Includes many famous hatches: Hendrickson, Pale Evening Dun, Blue-Winged Olive, and Western Green Drake (*E. grandis*); the popular Gold-Ribbed Hare's Ear often used as an imitation for the nymph
10. When disturbed, the nymph often raises its tail in a scorpionlike stance
11. Prolific, widespread, and important
12. Head and body often with spines or tubercles (knoblike projections)

EPHEMERIDAE (burrowers)

(1.) The largest mayfly nymphs; mature nymph length up to thirty-seven millimeters
(2.) Large tusks (mandibles)
(3.) Flanged, turned-out front legs for burrowing
(4.) Long plumelike gills arched over the abdomen
(5.) Three fringed tails with nonoverlapping hairs
6. Bodies long and slender, only slightly tapered
7. Live in horseshoe tunnels in silt and mud
8. Prefer lakes and moderate currents
9. Genus *Hexagenia*:
   a. *Hexagenia limbata* (Western Yellow Mayfly)
     1. Conical, rounded, or truncated frontal process
     2. Mature nymph length, excluding tails, up to thirty-seven millimeters
     3. Usually body is a pale yellow brown
     4. Gills on abdominal segment 1, rudimentary and forked; long, fringed gills on abdominal segments 2–7
11. Genus *Ephemera*:
   a. *Ephemera similans* (Brown Drake)
     1. Forked frontal process, widest at apex
     2. Mature nymph length, excluding tails, twelve to twenty millimeters
     3. Usually body is a light brown with dark brown markings
     4. Gills on abdominal segment 1, rudimentary and forked; long, fringed gills on abdominal segments 2–7

Ephemeridae nymph.

HEPTAGENIIDAE (clingers)

(1.) Mature nymph length, excluding tails, five to twenty millimeters
(2.) Wholly dorsal eyes on lateral edge of horizontal head
(3.) Flattened head as wide as or wider than thorax
(4.) Gills, usually with basal tufts, on abdominal segments 1–7; modified "friction-disk" gills for ventral attachment
5. Antennae mounted dorsally
6. Genus *Epeorus*:
   a. Two tails
   b. Prefers medium to fast water
   c. Overlapping suction gills
   d. Mature nymph length, excluding tails, seven to eleven millimeters
7. Genus *Heptagenia*:
   a. Three tails approximately body length
   b. Gill plates on all abdominal segments, gill 7 may be slightly smaller, but similiar to gills 1–6; gill plates do not extend beneath the body

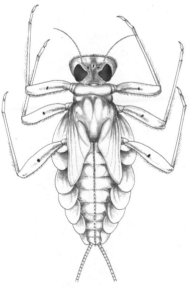

Heptageniidae nymph.

    c. Prefers slow water (Arbona)
    d. Mature nymph length, excluding tails, four to twelve millimeters
    e. Labrum width is ½ to ¾ head width
  8. Genus *Rithrogenia*:
    a. First and last gills enlarged and meet beneath the abdomen
    b. Center notch in head front
    c. Three tails body length or shorter
    d. Mature nymph length, excluding tails, five to twelve millimeters
    e. Abundant in the West

TRICORYTHIDAE (micromay sprawlers)

(1.) Mature nymph length, excluding tails, three to ten millimeters; commonly about four millimeters (Caucci and Nastasi)
(2.) Enlarged triangular or oval gills (operculate) on abdominal segment 2 that cover gills 3 through 6
(3.) Three relatively long tails, as long as or longer than the abdomen; center tail may be longer than outer tails
4. Stout thorax
5. Common throughout North America
6. Emergence from July through October
7. Some species live interstitially in silt
8. Previously classified in the Caenidae family

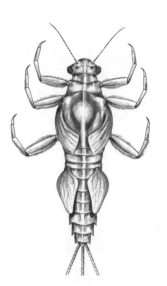

Tricorythidea nymph.

THE CADDISFLY (TRICHOPTERA)

The tailless adult caddisfly is dressed in dull motley. It has four membranous wings, with the forewings slightly longer than the hind wings. These tent wings, which completely cover the body of the insect when at rest, are usually covered with minute hairs or scales. The order name, Trichoptera, means "hair-wings." They have a flopping, fluttering flight. The adults feed upon liquid foods—moisture is the most important factor for insect longevity—and will live about one month. They may be found in static waters (these may be reared in the home aquarium) as well as lotic waters. The larva is called, in the promiscuous angler's argot, such names as rockworm, caseworm, and periwinkle. They have a complete metamorphosis and the aquatic larva, after a year, will pupate. In a manner of speaking, the caddisfly or sedge is an aquatic silk-worm moth.

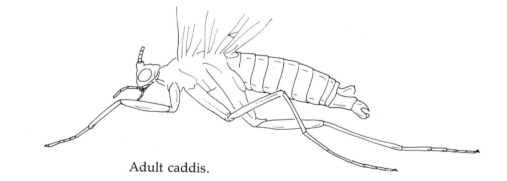

Adult caddis.

CHARACTERISTICS OF THE CADDISFLY

Larva

1. Minute antennae
2. Caterpillarlike without wing pads
3. Filamentous gills, if present, only on abdominal segments
4. Anal hook on the last abdominal segment
5. Cased (mineral or plant sheltered) and uncased (campodeiform) species

Pupa

1. Subsurface emergence upon pupation
2. Antennae nearly body length
3. No anal hook or tail
4. Immediately prior to emergence, housed in a silk cocoon usually encased in mineral or plant debris

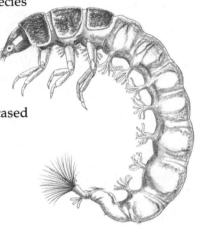

Adult

1. Four wings covered with fine hairs or scales
2. Wings swept back and held rooflike over the abdomen
3. Antennae body length or longer
4. A fluttering, floppy flier

Caddis larva
(*Hydropsychidae interruptrus*).

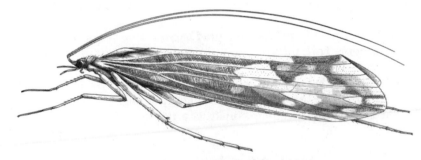

Adult caddis (Limnephilidae).

Pupation lasts about two weeks after the insect seals the case, allowing water entry. The pharate adult (the adult immediately prior to emergence and still enclosed in the pupal husk) then cuts the case open with mandibles and swims to the surface (in swift water), or crawls out on objects (in calm water), to emerge. The midlegs, or mesotarsus, of the pharate adult are free and formed for subsurface emergence.

The ova are usually laid en masse in the water or on objects; some species enter the water to deposit the eggs. The larval cases, which are cemented with a sticky silklike saliva, possess a slight negative suspension that helps the larva pull its case along the bottom as it grazes upon algae and plant debris. The heavier case construction, of course, occurs in flowing water, while the lighter construction occurs in calm water. The majority of caddisfly larvae consume various plant life and perform a significant act in the biosystem by producing protein from plants. While it appears that most species hatch during early or late hours of the day, a few species evidently are purely nocturnal in their emergence.

Most adults have slate brown wings and antennae that are two or three times the body length. It is important to note that some species are transformed immediately into fliers as soon as they surface. Others swim and struggle a considerable distance before flight. The struggle of an emerging caddis is perhaps due to the difficulty in breaking the pupal cuticle or increasing wing strength. It is not the act of wing drying. As Dave Ruetz, an aquatic biologist, indicates, the fine hairs or scales make caddisfly wings water repellant, thereby eliminating the need for drying prior to flight. On still waters this flight struggle is quite evident and encourages trout feeding.

Much has been written concerning the caddisfly's toleration for adverse water conditions and pollution. Ruetz places it into perspective. He notes that, instead of the importance of pollution toleration of particular insects, rather a change in habitat, such as the degradation of a stream, may favor the needs of one insect over another. Conditions that do not favor one insect may favor another. One insect may thrive even to the exclusion of another. A typical trout stream contains a diverse aquatic fauna consisting of Ephemeroptera, Plecoptera, Trichoptera, and Diptera. If water enrichment occurs, the algae increase may favor the existence of the net-spinning caddisfly, which feeds on drifting algae in the water column. Since productive space is limited, other insects may decrease, thereby drastically altering or decreasing the fauna.

General classification includes the following five categories:

1. Casebuilders: This includes the majority of caddis; they are herbaceous and, based upon case construction, are called either "carpenters" or "masons."
2. Campodeiform: This includes the predaceous "free livers" or "hunters."
3. Net spinners: This includes the silk-tube makers or the herbaceous "weavers."
4. Purse-makers: These larvae are extremely small and free living until the final instar, when they make a portable purse case.
5. Saddle-makers: These larvae construct a portable "saddle" case.

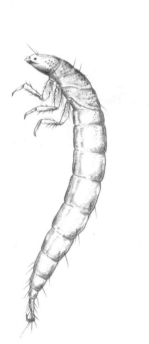

Caddis larva (psychomyiidae).

MIDGES (Chironomidae)

The Chironomidae, by sheer volume and distribution, are important inhabitants of streams and lakes. They prefer slow streams with heavy plant growth and soft silt, but they can survive in a wide span of temperatures and habitats. It is said that 50 percent of all standing waters contain midges, and, in those waters that do, there will be more than fifty different species. The active larva is wormlike, and many are under five millimeters in length. The larva, both predaceous and herbaceous, is slender, with thoracic sections swollen and fine-haired. The last abdominal segment has a conspicuous tuft of hairs on the dorsal apex. The larva is usually olive or bright red, the so-called "blood worm." Pupation occurs in the last larval skin, although some species pupate in a silk cocoon or gelatinous purse. Prior to emergence, the pupa hangs vertically in the surface film. Emergence differs in species: there is usually a spring and summer maxima, the period of greatest hatching, in March or April and later about July. Otherwise, they will emerge sporadically throughout the year. Winter midging can be excellent due to the multibrooded midge and the lack of competing hatches.

CHARACTERISTICS OF THE MIDGE

Larvae

1. Segmented maggotlike body with no distinctive thorax or abdomen
2. No distinctive gills, legs, or wing pads
3. Usually a soft body with eleven or twelve segments
4. Distinct, sclerotized head capsule or retracted head capsule
5. Some species have fine scattered body hairs or individual tufts or fringes
6. Small fleshy projections, called tubercles, may be present on one or more body segments
7. In many species, the tubercles may form prolegs with crotchets (small curved hooks)

Pupae

1. Pupae are obtect (the appendages are sealed to the body surface) or coarctate (the pupal state is passed in the puparium or last larval skin)
2. Head, thorax, and wings concentrated and clustered together
3. May have filamentous gills on top of thorax
4. No tails

Adult

1. No tails
2. One pair of wings with simple venation
3. One pair of halteres (vestigial wings or balancing knobs) located behind the wings
4. Sucking mouth parts
5. Enlarged thorax
6. Long, slender legs
7. Mating forceps and feathered antennae on the male

Midge larva (*Chironomus tentans*).

Imitative patterns of the pupa, the stage normally fished, are tied in sizes 14 to 22. This is one of the few insects to emerge in abundance from the deepest areas of lakes. However, some species may be found in the shallow and moderate shore areas of the lakes.

In general, the olive larva indicates high oxygenation, while the red larva shows low oxygenation. John Goddard, in his classic text, *Trout Flies of Still Water* (1966), states that the red coloration is hemoglobin that assists the blood by storing oxygen and providing it when required. Thus the insect is able to live in low-oxygen waters. Also, in specimens he had studied, it appeared that the more mature the larva, the brighter or more dense the hemoglobin as pupation approached.

The adults are gnatlike with short, flat-lying wings shorter than the body. They have a thickened mesothorax and long, slender legs. The wings are either gray or hyaline, while the body is green-gray, green, or black. Neither sex have tails and the male has distinctive feathered antennae. They have minute balancing knobs or haltere in place of the rear wings.

Other species of Diptera may form, at times, a significant part of the trout's fare: reed smuts or black fly (*Simulium* spp.), black gnat, a most ubiquitous title to a myriad of insects including the black dance fly (*Hilara femorata*), Dixa midge (*Dixa minuta*), and many others both aquatic and terrestrial. Most Diptera emerge at dusk or dark, a few at dawn.

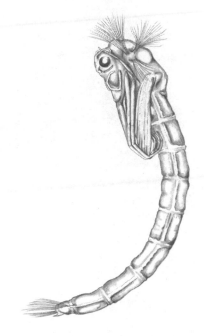

Midge pupa (*Chironomus tentans*).

DRAGONFLIES AND DAMSELFLIES (Odonata)

Western lakes contain a remarkable variety of insects, and one of the most significant is the dragonfly nymph. The renaissance in still-water fly fishing has allowed dragonfly imitations recognition and a place in the fly wallet. The aquatic nymphs, sometimes called naiads, are easily recognized by the fly fisher. They have large eyes like the adult, insignificant wing pods, and a corpulent body usually ovoid or trigonal in cross section. The nymphs appear primarily in slow waters and, while not abundant in comparison to such major insects as the mayfly, they can attain a length of over thirty millimeters before emergence. Their size alone is enough to support large trout. The order Odonata, which the dragonfly shares with the delicate damselfly, refers to the toothed labium or lower lip that extends nearly one-third the body length and functions as a capture lobe. They are predaceous in their nymphal stages, particularly in the stages near emergence (the senior instars), and devour nymphs, larvae, and even small fish. The suborder designation Anisoptera refers to the adult wings being held at right angles to the body while in flight or repose. When ready for transformation to the adult stage, the nymph usually crawls out of the water onto rocks or plant stems for the final molt. Once out of the final nymphal husk, the newly hatched (teneral) adult is soft and a pale yellow for the first day or two. The adult will expand its wings to full size in about half an hour. Male and female adults are usually similar in color, although the male may be brighter.

CHARACTERISTICS OF THE DRAGONFLY

Nymph

1. Large compound eyes
2. Inconspicuous bristlelike antennae
3. Extendible labium
4. Internal rectal gills
5. Usually a compact, corpulent body, often oval or triangular in cross section
6. Locomotion by rectal expulsion of water
7. Six clustered legs moved forward on the thorax
8. Modified and extendible capture lobes (the labium)

A clinger dragonfly nymph (*Aeschnidae*).

Adult

1. Large compound eyes
2. Inconspicuous bristlelike antennae
3. No tail
4. Two pair of large wings held horizontally, often tilted up or down, when at rest
5. The eyes are never separated by more than their own width
6. Superb fliers that capture insects with their "net" legs during flight
7. Unusual sexual organ (penis vesicle) on the ventral surface of the second abdominal segment

Unlike the fabled dragons, the dragonfly nymph "breathes" water. Movement is the result of the rapid expelling of water from their anal cavity that functions, because of the thin-walled lower intestine, as a rectal gill.

This anal respiration produces an unusual swimming pattern. In order to determine the movement pattern of the dragonfly nymphs, I have filmed the swimming sequence in slow motion. My cinematographic experiments, although inconclusive because of limited research and the abnormal environment of the filming tank, are suggestive and of value. The dragonfly nymphs averaged twenty-two millimeters in length and seven millimeters in abdominal width. The common expulsive attitude consisted of a slightly arched body with the legs relaxed and folded beneath the thorax. The abdomen dilated and contracted both in length and diameter during propulsion. It was a fast-slow sequence and the nymphs sank momentarily before another expulsion of water propelled them up and forward. It is unlikely that they travel long distances through open water; they live a furtive existence among the plants and debris. It must be noted that this research is not extensive enough for permanent conclusions. The length of the glide may depend upon speciation and maturation of the nymphs.

For the fly fisher, the dragonfly nymphs may be classified according to two habitat types: the plant clingers (such as the Aeshnidae), which actively pursue their prey, and the burrowers or silters (such as the Libellulidae and the western riffle-dwelling Gomphidae), which either camouflage themselves with silt and algae or burrow into the marl and mud. The more predaceous clingers usually have an ovoid cross section. There are, naturally, distinctions between the burrowers and silters, but for practical purposes both may be considered bottom dwellers. The silters have minute hairs or horns that assist in camouflage, while the burrowers have somewhat flattened or shovel-shaped body parts for digging. The burrowers and silters normally strike only when their prey is within labium range. Both the burrowers and clingers inhabit the marginal epilimnion of the lake. Their general coloration tends toward the mottled deep olives, bright greens, and dark browns, with often intricate, cryptic stippling and delicate runic etchings along the abdominal plates. The nymphs that conceal themselves in the silt and mud appear, for the most part, dull and mottled, while the olive and brown nymphs usually inhabit the plant mats.

CHARACTERISTICS OF THE DAMSELFLY

Nymph

1. Three featherlike "tails" (actually caudal gill lamellae)
2. Large eyes
3. Modified and extendible capture lobes (the labium)
4. Long and slender body
5. Two pair of wing pads
6. Swims with whipping body undulations
7. Inconspicuous bristlelike antennae

A common *Coenagrionidae* damselfly nymph.

Adult

1. Four wings "yoked" or narrow at base
2. When at rest, the wings are held together, often edge up, and extended above and parallel to the body
3. Large eyes, separated by more than their own width
4. Inconspicuous bristlelike antennae
5. Unusual sexual organ (penis vesicle) on the ventral surface of the second abdominal segment

The gills of the damselfly, suborder Zygoptera, are in the form of three feathered paddles at the end of a slender abdomen. These nymphs swim by body undulations, the gills functioning much like sculling oars. The damsel nymph is able to travel in a whipping, rhythmic motion. Most damselfly nymphs are pale yellow, tan, olive, or brown. Immediately prior to hatching (usually in June or July), the damselfly nymphs will migrate toward shore in number. Such migrations during the morning hours will boil the water with slashing and rolling trout as they feed on the struggling nymphs. The wings of the adult damselfly when at rest are folded parallel on top of the body with the edge up. The base width of the forewing and hind wing is nearly the same; the hind wings of the adult dragonfly are wider than the forewings.

Based upon the nymphal habits of the Odonata, the dragonfly and damselfly nymphs have their own nymphing techniques. The dragonfly burrower and silter nymph patterns are cast and worked much like a streamer or wet fly. The burrower is twitched rhythmically just beyond the plant ledge in deeper water. A hand-strip retrieve of the line should accompany rod-tip movement. This will place steady pressure on the nymph at all times and telegraph any takes. The hand-twist retrieve, which loops line into the palm, is best used on shallow nymphs like the dragonfly clinger and the damselfly. The hand-twist method can impart a rapid, staccato movement similar to the anal expulsion of the natural. And the method can accommodate the rapid, serpentining damselfly movement if combined with rod-tip movement. The damselfly movement, like the natural, should incorporate a periodic pause of the shallow-running floating line.

It is difficult to work a deep nymph with the distinct, short spurts of the dragonfly burrowers. The short-strip method, in which the stripping hand draws the line energetically through the rod-hand forefinger, can be used on dragonfly and damselfly patterns. However, it is virtually impossible to keep the strips under fifteen centimeters as the angler attempts to imitate the dragonfly movement. The short-strip method will produce movement two or three times the length of the dragonfly glide. Try to keep the dragonfly strips short and varied. A floating line is usually used for the clinging dragonfly and the damselfly patterns; a wet tip or wet head is used for the burrower patterns. Obviously, it is easier to impart a distinct twitch to a shallow-running nymph rather than to a deep-running nymph. Hence, by necessity, the burrower pattern cannot imitate the explosive bursts of the deep-running burrower dragonfly nymph. And when casting to ringing trout, it is best to place the fly well beyond and to one side of the ring. This avoids placing line or leader directly over the trout.

Angling literature usually laments that only minor research has been done on the nymphal habits of the Odonata, and that only a few effective patterns have been developed. But the development of effective patterns should not be separated from the nymphal habits, nymphal movements, or even the nymphal habitat itself. And there is one aspect of the lake environment that may play an important part in the life of the Odonata.

In the rich alkaline lakes, the phenomenon of photosynthesis may actually affect nymphal activity. This is an aspect of lake nymphing that is all but totally ignored. In nymphing, the angler is concerned with a concealed world—a world of depth. And what happens within a lake is as important as what happens on a lake. Aquatic plants, especially the common *Anacharis* and the Chlorophyta, undergo photosynthetic respiration. After several hours of penetrating sunlight through clean water, the free-floating and stemmed plants rise toward the surface. The flotation of the plant population is the result of miniscule oxygen bubbles adhering to the plant mass. Photosynthesis produces abundant oxygen in these fertile lakes, more, in fact, than the lakes may readily dissolve, and this excess oxygen creates plant flotation. Even the free-floating filamentous algae, commonly miscalled moss, will rise toward the surface. At the surface the plants slowly pass the excess oxygen to the atmosphere. The lake "breathes." After sunset, when photosynthesis ceases, oxygen is no longer available for plant flotation. The continual process of cellular respiration of carbon dioxide does occur, of course. But carbon dioxide dissolves readily into water and consequently does not support the plant mass. Lacking the undissolved gases, the plants slowly sink during the night.

This "breathing" rhythm of a lake can methodically disturb and displace plant-clinging nymphs, such as some species of dragonfly and damselfly nymphs, thereby initiating trout-feeding patterns. Nymphing is more productive during the midmorning periods and from deep dusk to solid night. This phenomenon may, in part, account for the systematic feeding patterns in alkaline lakes. And the ascending-descending plant mass is more evident during the heat of summer and the early fall. It is general knowledge that trout-feeding patterns are related to the insect rhythms of emergence and hatching. Perhaps feeding patterns are also related, under certain conditions, to plant rhythms. And a fly angler might be well aware of the "breathing" pattern of his particular lakes.

STONEFLY (Plecoptera)

Patterns: Sofa Pillow, Yellow Sally, Bird's Stone, Montana Nymph

Insect Identification and Habits: Structurally, the Plecoptera or "folded wing" fly has a head and thorax whose combined length nearly equals that of the abdomen. The abdomen has ten segments, with nine clearly discernable. Each thoracic section has a pair of legs terminating in a two-clawed tarsus. A pair of wings is rooted in each of the two rear thoracic sections. The ventral thoracic area carries the filamentous gills. The placement of the hair gills is one index to speciation. The nymphs have two whiplike tails, segmented and slightly shorter than the abdomen. However, in some genera, the tails are noticeably longer than the abdomen.

The nymphs are primarily herbivorous, living on riparian plants; but, depending upon species and available food, predaceous activity is found among some senior instars, the nymphs immediately prior to emergence. The nymphs are easily distinguished by the absence of abdominal gills. Only the two-inch *Pteronarcys* will have minor strand gilling on the first few abdominal segments. The nymphs usually have one subaquatic year; however, the larger species, like the *Pteronarcys californica*, may have three. The nymphs crawl and clamber among the rocks. Their swimming ability is minimal; they are best imitated with an upstream tension drift or a teasing dead drift.

The classic hatch of the salmon fly (*P. californica*) on the Madison River in Montana begins about the end of the first week in June at Three Forks and moves upstream. The hatch arrives about the fourth of July at Ennis, appears about the fourteenth of July at McAtee Bridge and finishes during the last week of the month at Slide Inn. The three-year-old *P. californica* develops rapidly in the warm waters of spring and migrates to the slack shallows where it crawls out on rocks and other objects. The cranial suture splits and the adult emerges. The nymphs will emerge for a couple of days on any particular stream location as the hatch slowly moves upstream. Such mass hatching provokes active rises from Madison trout.

CHARACTERISTICS OF THE STONEFLY

Nymph

1. A distinct head, thorax, and abdomen
2. Six legs, each terminated by two claws
3. Two distinct and separated whiplike tails
4. Distinct, segmented antennae
5. Gills absent, or filamentous gills beneath the thorax and between the legs
6. Ten distinct abdominal segments, usually oval or circular in cross section
7. Inferior swimmers that either arch the body or assume the fetal position when adrift
8. Instars vary from twenty-two to thirty-three in number with a nymphal period from one to three years
9. Two pairs of wing pads

Adult

1. The general appearance of a squat "aquatic cockroach" with wings tight and flat above the abdomen
2. Four equal-length wings
3. When airborn, a near-vertical body attitude and a heavy, fluttering flight
4. Three tarsal segments

The Sofa Pillow, originated by Pat Barnes of West Yellowstone, is one of the many successful patterns for the large stonefly nymph. Besides his floating nymph for the egg-laying adult stonefly, Dave Whitlock, in *The Second Fly-Tyer's Almanac* (1978), has produced a soft stonefly nymph that imitates the nymphs immediately after their periodic ecdysis or molting.

The Perlidae (gills on the three thoracic sections), Nemouridae (diverging wing pods), Capniidae (wide metathoracic pods), and Pteronarcidae (abdomenal segments one to two or thirteen-branch gilled, Cummins and Merritt) are common on Washington's Yakima River. The Perlidae, one of the largest stonefly families, are predominately carnivorous. The Pteronarcidae begin to emerge in April, but not in the numbers associated with the Madison. The Western Sally (*Isoperla* spp. and similar) is common in the Northwest and comparable to its English namesake on the riffle waters of Shropshire. In *Rough Stream Flies* (1976) by Taff Price, there is a Welsh border pattern for the Yellow Sally that is as effective as it is simple: pale yellow wool body and pale ginger hackle on a size 14. Other dusty yellow nymph patterns can prove effective for these smaller stoneflies.

PART THREE

THE WAY
of a
FLY

The Way of a Fly: A Preface to a Theory of Tying

Then round his hook the chosen fur he winds,
And on the back a speckled feather binds;
So just the colours shine through ev'ry part,
That Nature seems to live again in art.
                                        —JOHN GAY

In the mixed currents of fly fishing, when so much has been written concerning the esthetics of trout taking, it is odd that so few pages have been granted to the esthetics of fly tying. F. M. Halford, in *Floating Flies and How to Dress Them* (1886), defined dry-fly fishing as "presenting to the rising fish the best possible imitation of the insect on which he is feeding in its natural position." Such a definition, which is laden with ambiguities, does center on two significant aspects of fly fishing: presentation and imitation. Fundamentally, there should be no contention between these two aspects. A natural presentation may even be considered a form of imitation. Perhaps, at times, a natural presentation of a generic fly pattern may be more effective than an imitative or realistic pattern cast casually, yet surely the solution for difficult trout is an imitative pattern presented naturally. Of course, this will raise the issue of what is meant by "imitative pattern."

Another English angler—who, like Halford, would cast a long line across the currents of time—was G. E. M. Skues. In *The Way of a Trout With a Fly* (1921), Skues wrote that "imitation may mean imitation of life, of activity, of colour, and size. . . . And these things are equally true of the artificial fly that is a representation or a suggestion of the natural fly." Surely, such terms as "imitation" and "suggestion" require further discussion. And, without wishing to bring to net the classic controversies of the ancients versus the moderns, the dry fly versus the wet fly, realism versus impressionism, a brief examination of the terms and the quotes by Halford and Skues may enrich the fly wallet. And certainly, there should be space enough in our fly wallets for various and divergent theories.

It is questionable whether or not realistic imitation excludes self expression, since we view reality through a temperament and we comment on it through symbolized methods. The insect that we attempt to imitate is a fairy form, cryptically constructed. Only with power of observation and creative intensity are we able to imitate an insect on any level. The act of imitation is remarkably complex. There is more than a single reality in nature. What reality does the tyer wish to imitate? In order to imitate nature, it may be necessary to sacrifice appearance in order to save truth. A tyer, for example, may hinge the body of a damselfly pattern in order to achieve, he believes, a more realistic action in the water. Thus, to produce greater realism of movement, the tyer has sacrificed a degree of realism in appearance. It is really an antique assumption that what the artist sees in nature is what he produces. All of reality is not condensed in appearance—nature is always hidden and always hatching. An imitative theory based on nature as a process or activity must, by necessity, yield various viewpoints. But the problem of fly-pattern classification based upon the term "imitation" still remains: when is a pattern imitative rather than suggestive of the natural?

To give some insight into what is meant by imitation, fly patterns may be classified according to the following categories: impressionism, expressionism, and realism. These three terms, like all abstract terms, are prone to vagueness and misuse. And seldom, if ever, will a particular pattern be a complete expression of a single category. Tyers have a tendency to emphasize certain aspects of a pattern. And it is often those elements of exaggeration that excite the rise and prove to be a better pattern. Nevertheless, the three categories are serviceable with respect to specific esthetic aims.

Impressionism is a manner of tying with the purpose of rendering the sensation rather than the strict appearance of reality. This type of tying takes into account that movement and light play a significant part in the seductive qualities of a pattern. While often neglecting form, impressionism attempts to imitate what is transitory. Insects are seen as fragments of flashing color that are unified by the trout's vision. The basic premise involved here is that truth is in perception, rather than in a specific, clinical portrayal of the natural insect. The more an angler knows about trout perception, the more he knows about impressionistic imitation. The problem, naturally, is to determine the appropriate, but fugitive, sensations that give the insect life and shape. Often, with highly selective detail based upon light theory, the tyer attempts to capture in his vise the fleeting vision of insect life. All tying is, to some extent, impressionistic.

It might be added that traditional tying during the last century is, essentially, impressionistic tying. Perhaps it was no coincidence that the nineteenth century produced both the blurred landscapes of Claude Monet and the Quill Gordon. Many traditional patterns give only a brief sensation of the insect through color and size. And often, color has become the most important element. Even the somber shades of a wet fly or the autumnal tones of a steelhead pattern can flash with impressionism, with the light of life. For the impressionist, insect detail and texture need not be imitated. Gary LaFontaine's Emergent Caddis incorporates an impressionistic blending of furs and sparkle yarn for a variegated vibrancy of color. And the hard body parts of the insect can be imitated with fluffy dubbing; and the wings, when compared to the natural, need not be placed at the precise thoracic point. A Quill Gordon by Art Flick has a music of its own, a fine sense of color tonality, body proportion, and hackle symmetry that gives the impression of *Epeorus pleuralis*. Tonality, proportion, and symmetry are often to an historic ideal rather than precise imitation. Tying such patterns, which is generally prescriptive and formal, does give the tyer a sense of ritual and historic continuity.

The theory of trout perception has been an angling companion since Chapter 1 of Alfred Ronald's *The Fly-Fisher's Entomology* (1836). The concern for light properties would produce within forty years the term "impressionism" and a bitter controversy over the paintings of Monet. The discussion of the merits of what would be called Impressionism, however, had already begun in 1863. Angling writing was merely an expression of the contemporary scientific discussions of light and optics. Theories of light and optics would be shared by such diverse fields as art and angling. Perhaps it was only natural that such theories would be applied by the lay scientist to the quiet recreation of angling. In any case, it was Vincent Marinaro's *In the Ring of the Rise* (1976) that drew the American angler's attention to the refraction theory. Marinaro's text is afloat with brilliant photographs of trout rises and slant-box visions. The watertight slant-box photography, limited by the principles of physics and optics, attempts to reproduce the trout's window. Marinaro's insights into the trout's window became the bases for two tying codes—"the artificial dun pattern must be kept above the surface film," and "anything that breaks through the surface film is no longer obscured by the oblique rays or the diffusion above the film." A tyer must not expose his patterns unnecessarily to trout scrutiny.

The Trout and the Fly (1980), an excellent text by Brian Clarke and John Goddard, attempts to modernize our knowledge of trout perception and, like Marinaro, create patterns based upon the trout's impression of the natural. For example, the authors emphasize two sensations produced by the dun that they believe are key trigger points for the rise: "the star-burst of dimples created by the feet of the naturals," and the wings' penetration of the trout's ring of vision. In the case of the spinner, the authors advocate pockmarked polyethylene wings that "come close to transmitting the correct light pattern below the surface." Only time and trout will tell whether or not these new patterns based upon trout perception will become future traditions.

Expressionism, the second category, produces patterns that exist neither in nature nor in the smeared impressions of nature. They are products of the imagination. Such patterns are often original and extravagant blends of method and material. Some of the exotic and esoteric salmon patterns, as well as some New Zealand and Canadian wet flies, may be stuck in the expressionistic wallet. Surely, not all salmon flies and wet flies are expressionistic; some do have their obscure counterparts in nature. But such patterns as the Jock Scott and Durham Ranger, and other feathered mosaics, are only vague simulations of reality. They are stained glass windows that pull the angler and the trout beyond reality. They are more the result of imagination than the imitation of nature. If this is an application of "the fallacy of misplaced reality," then the tying table is only the richer for it.

Realistic tying, the final category, is, in the broadest sense, fidelity to the appearance of objective reality. Realistic tying centers on the object imitated and seeks something close to a one-to-one correspondence between the imitation and the natural insect. Obviously, an absolute correspondence is impossible. Realistic imitation is not only based on size, color, and form, but also on texture. It concentrates on the detailed imitation of the hard and soft insect body parts through the creative use of materials.

The realistic tyer, armed with a plethora of pages on insect nomenclature and taxonomy, searches for his recipes beneath the rocks and among the plants. In this regard, realistic tying is the imitation of the actual insect. And, although the difficulties of realistic tying increase with knowledge, realism may excite a more intense power of observation and specific imitation. But how far should realistic tying be carried? Perhaps few would maintain that a fly should be an exact copy of nature (a nature which is remarkably subtle and cryptic in the insect world), and few, perhaps only the extreme expressionists, would say that a pattern should have no recognizable relation with nature. Ultrarealistic tying, which may be akin to model building, can be esthetically satisfying to some. So much care may be devoted to each step the tyer takes that the procedure itself may engross his attention. The means, in fact, may become the end. But then all tying is not simply to catch trout. All tying is not utilitarian. A well-wrought fly is a joy to behold. And collectors and connoisseurs of the craft would agree on the intrinsic value of a fine fly. A fly delicately done can possess value apart from its ability to take trout.

We can only see a limited amount with the naked eye. Most "representational" tyers force the eye to complete the reading of clues the pattern implies; they halt the tying process somewhat short of the natural. The eye is both microscope and telescope. But microscopic reality cannot be rendered with fur and feather. Total reality is untyable. It is untyable because it is infinite. All tying, even realistic tying, is only approximation. But realistic tying usually does include more detail and more parts. Below a certain scale the approximations turn into code, into suggestion, which, it is hoped, the trout completes. Even realistic tying is not so much in the degree of realism as it may be in the backing away from reality through approximation. Realistic tying may be selective realism, as in the waving marabou tendrils that create the appearance of life. Although the term realism is often used, it is one of the most difficult to define.

Although there have always been attempts at realistic patterns, the recent decades have seen a revival in realism. Bob Boyle's Grass Shrimp is an excellent example of realistic tying that imitates the texture as well as the structure of the natural. Also, Ted Niemeyer's Caddis and Stripped Quill Stonefly are examples of textural and structural imitation. Moreover, a tyer may often imitate only one particular aspect of a pattern in a realistic manner. For example, Dave Whitlock's Sculpin is a venture into realistic silhouette and the mottled coloration of the natural. In this pattern, the barred prairie hen feathers imitate effectively the flared pectoral fins of the sculpin. In a more functional manner Doug Swisher and Carl Richards, with their No-Hackle duns, have taken a traditional tie and modified it to achieve a more realistic float angle. One thing that has helped realistic tying is the increase in the use of synthetics and the more realistic use of natural materials. Never before has the tyer had such a worldwide range of materials, and never before has there been such an interest in creative techniques. Heated pliers flatten and shape nylon nymph legs. Plastic strips wrap nymphal forms. And latex sheets stretch into shrimp. Wool from the ram's scrotum built Tup's Indispensible. Urine-stained vixen hair was spun into Art Flick's Hendrickson. It seems, at times, that the only items lacking are unicorn underfur, natal dragon down, and bronze Minotaur dubbing.

The   three   artistic   categories—impressionism,   expressionism   and realism—explain both the tyer's attitude and the artificial's approach toward nature. These categories, like all general and abstract terms, are susceptible to ambiguity. Nevertheless, they are serviceable with respect to purpose. But, there will be overlapping, mixing, and border problems. Even some comment made in one category may, at times, be made in another. And most tyers, despite their category, will claim that their patterns are realistic. This is especially true for the impressionists who assert that true reality is equal to the image of it. So perfect consistency in the categories is unattainable and perhaps not even desirable. In any case, the categories do not explain the factors that constitute the pattern as a pattern. One possible method of understanding the fly in terms of its own properties may be found in the shadowed waters of ancient thought.

Skues's comment that "imitation may mean imitation of life" recalls an esthetic theory some twenty-four centuries old. Aristotle, the classical Greek philosopher, viewed art as an imitation of the action that constantly occurs in nature. And Aristotle described the four "causes" that explain the existence of any art form: the material cause, the efficient cause, the formal cause, and the telic cause. But it should be remembered that Aristotle did not apply his comprehensive theories to the art of fly tying: fly tying would emerge, as we know it, much later in time. Nevertheless, Aristotle's theories have such universal application that they can be applied to tying, and they can reveal significant aspects of our craft.

The material cause is the substance "out of which" the object is made. In a manner of speaking, fly tying may be defined as dimensional sculpture accomplished principally by the aggregation of materials along the backbone of a hook. Yet, the mere accumulation of materials on a hook frame is not fly tying. A tyer should know the craft possibilities of materials and techniques, and he should constantly experiment with both. Ted Niemeyer's Stonefly Nymph is an excellent example of material use. The stripped goose quill is a fine imitation of the chitinous body plates of the Plecoptera. The knotted "undershaft" feather produces a realistic leg. But, no matter what materials are used, whether synthetic or natural, the properties of the materials should be used effectively. A variety of materials may be used for wings: calf tail, hackle tips, deer hair, wood-duck breast feathers and others. The problem centers on material selection: what material will produce the most effective imitation for a particular pattern? Tying is a constant compromise between materials and methods. Surely material selection and use is a prime skill for the creative tyer. Fly-tying methods and materials offer a wide range of possibilities. Natural and synthetic materials, for example, have a variety of characteristics from which to select:

1. color range
2. opacity and translucency
3. floating or sinking properties
4. durability
5. availability
6. variety and ease of application
7. reflection or refraction of light
8. texture range
9. pattern tradition
10. movement

11. air entrapment
12. blending and dying properties
13. beauty
14. imitative qualities (which might include shape and structure as well as the various characteristics themselves)

The selection of materials, the selection of tying properties and the selection of methods all weave their magic in a well-executed fly. The nuance of color and form, the imitation of length and width, the texture and translucency, and the effects of the angling technique upon the pattern all evolve as part of the creative process. Some of this is intuitive, some is learned, some is merely imitated, and some is often ignored.

The individual tyer's skills and techniques constitute what Aristotle would call the efficient cause. A fly usually shows the hand of its maker, and when it is a master maker, the hallmark is cleanly pressed. It may be the delicate tapered body by Art Flick, the swift, bold tie by Lee Wulff, or the pensive patterns of Al Caucci and Bob Nastasi. No matter who the tyer, some feature betrays him. It may be the cock of the wing, the taper of the body, the twist of the hackle, or the piling of the head. The unique woven hackle and fast taper clearly express the stylistic Stonefly Creeper in the hands of George Grant. A sparse and clean, even "crisp," Catskill style comes from Larry Duckwall. And there is the muted combination of synthetic and natural materials found in a Dave Tait nymph. Every tyer brings his personality and artistry to his tying vise.

The formal cause is the form or shape the tyer attempts to imitate. The form may be a natural insect or a historic ideal. Through the selective use of hard and soft body parts—the hard parts for shape and the soft parts for movement—the tyer attempts to imitate the spatial dimensions of the natural. The tyer wishes to imitate a particular form, or the appearance of a particular form, in space. No matter from what angle Dave Whitlock's Grasshopper is viewed, it appears to be a grasshopper. This is the most accepted, although perhaps least understood, aspect of tying. After all, tying is dimensional sculpture.

The purpose for which something is created is the telic cause. The term "telic" means tending toward an end. Of course, the explicit purpose for most tying is the taking of trout. However, flies may be modified for secondary or supplemental purposes. As mentioned earlier, a tyer may hinge the body of a damsel pattern to achieve a more realistic action in the water. Thus the fly is modified for the purpose of imitating the sculling motion of the insect. Another example of modified purpose may be seen in John Goddard's Suspender patterns. The *Chironomid* pattern incorporates a small nylon sack of ethafoam so that the fly will be vertically suspended in the surface film like the natural. A light tug on the line pulls the suspender horizontally, which closely imitates the natural's attempt to penetrate the surface film in order to emerge. Thus the ethafoam pod, which resembles the wing case and the feathered antennae of the males, also serves the function of flotation and imitative movement.

John Goddard's Suspender is an interesting example of the blending of causes: the material cause (the special properties of ethafoam), the formal cause (the imitation of wing pad and feathered antennae), and the telic cause (the dancing, imitative movement). The various causes imitate the natural in different ways. It is a marriage of materials, technique, form, and purpose. Creative tying will always imitate nature at more than one level. And creative tying will usually incorporate some elements of the categories—impressionism, expressionism and realism—as well as the effective use of Aristotelian causes. Patterns will become more effective as they possess a detail of reality, a flash of life, and a touch of the tyer. Here is Halford's "best possible imitation" and Skues's "imitation of life." As the trout becomes more critical and selective, so does the tyer.

The perfect fly has yet to be tied. But perhaps through the categories and causes, the tyer comes closer to wrapping perfection and recognizing the condensed complexity of his craft. The tyer may come closer to understanding his heritage and developing a language to express it. And no tyer can afford to ignore his heritage. Only through knowledge of the past can the tyer conserve his energy so that he can surpass the present. Every tyer should not have to reinvent the Royal Coachman.

In conclusion, one might add that tying is a fascination with the possibilities of imitation. There are many methods of imitation. And there are many realities to imitate. And certainly, there are many reasons why we imitate. Perhaps man is, as Aristotle asserts, an imitative animal. Perhaps it is the challenge and intensity of creation. Perhaps it is the liquid beauty of melting colors and fairy forms. Or perhaps we may finally come to believe that the artificial fly, imperfect as its creator, is a threshold symbol to the living waters.

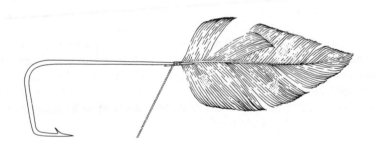

Art of the Fly

No field has a finer art than angling with a fly. We draw that which we admire. So it has been from the beginning. Since the first printed English commentary on trouting, *Treatyse of Fysshynge wyth an Angle* (1496), art has been an important part of angling. From the rough-hewed hooks printed in the *Treatise* to the hand-colored copper plate engravings in Alfred Ronalds's *The Fly Fisher's Entomology*, there has been a marriage of esthetics and science. After Ronalds, the colorist and engraver kept pace with the writer and scientist. Excellent examples of hand-colored engravings can be found in F. M. Halford's *Floating Flies and How to Dress Them* (1886). With a printed hook length of only nine millimeters, the patterns are rendered with remarkable color subtlety and purity. Under mild magnification, the color tints of the patterns seem to flow along the engraved hackle line or to swell throughout a dun's wing. And often, the single-hair-brush technique casts its own delicate line.

Drawing fly patterns allows the tyer and angler to create or record the basic form of the fly pattern as well as the methods and materials required for construction. Art is a way of seeing and recording. The drawings may be done in color to grace the leaves of a trout diary or to record tying data. And for those difficult tying procedures of favorite patterns, drawing can create sequential pattern sketches. Simple lettering may indicate the appropriate material mounting order. With a modicum of talent, any tyer can create simple sketches of patterns and processes. A brief introduction to the standard techniques of pencil, pen, and paint should show the angler more pleasure of tying and trouting.

THE PENCIL

The pencil is a most versatile tool—it can draw a fine line or produce a broad, graded tone. Drawing, while simple and inexpensive, is a natural form of expression and an excellent method of recording and preserving information. Drawing may also sharpen the skills of observation and recollection. There are numerous sketching styles that are appropriate for fly patterns. It is important to develop an individual style. Imitate the methods, not the art. Remember that fly-pattern sketches, apart from the esthetic consideration, may be object studies for the purpose of detailed and accurate information. Yet such a statement need not be inconsistent with artistic expression.

Most freehand drawing is done with the following leads: 6B, 5B, 4B, 3B, 2B, B, and HB. Drawing can be done, however, with only three leads—H (hard lead for light, fine lines), HB (medium-hard lead for sketching), and 3B (soft, dark lead for shading). Drawing leads are made of graphite with clay (kaolin) in varying amounts to make different drawing grades. The smaller the diameter of the lead, the harder the grade; the larger the diameter, the softer the grade. Hence, the relative degree of hardness can be judged merely by the diameter of the lead. Sometimes a more complete range of leads may be used. The medium sketching grades are 3H, 2H, H, F, HB, and B. The shading grades are 2B, 3B, 4B, 5B, 6B, and 7B. The softer grades like 6B and 7B smudge easily, and their intensity makes them difficult to erase. On humid days afield, when the paper absorbs more moisture, it may then be necessary to select a softer sketching lead. Specially formulated plastic-based leads are available. But usually they do not have the quiet patina of the pencil. A pencil line is never true black. It will have a soft, pewtery luster that is pleasing in itself.

A small pencil sharpener with a dust cover should be used to prevent errant graphite particles. And wipe the pencil point before drawing; this removes particles that could explode into paper spots. Use a combination of strong and soft lines, and work quickly to take advantage of the strength and spontaneity of drawing. A continuous, heavy line will only flatten the drawing. Nature never has a ring around it. Use a bold line to advance an edge and a soft line to recede an edge. Also remember that excessive shading will give the appearance of dun wool rather than the precise anatomy of a fly pattern. Work quickly with few strokes, and shade only those fly parts that require depth or texture.

The contour is the primary structure of a fly pattern. Details are built on the foundation of the contour. And the contour expresses the proportion and harmony of the parts. One method of viewing the "abstracted essence," the essential structure void of all detail, is to squint at the pattern. The eyelashes sift out the detail and reduce the pattern to its fundamental lights and darks. The structural essence emerges. All color and detail are dependent on the structural contour. There is always some pattern, some texture, some rhythm or repetition in a fly pattern. When the pattern is complex, such as a fully dressed salmon pattern, it may be best to squint and then rough sketch the general contour. This will maintain the correct proportion of parts and the subordination of color and detail in the final rendering.

In order to produce truthful tones, it is necessary to shade the fly pattern correctly. Areas of mass should have clearly defined light and shade. All shapes have boundaries wherein the tones meet and create volume. Try to think in terms of tones rather than lines. Translate the colors into their corresponding tones. The tones in nature are numerous. Even though a paper may be white, in subdued light it will appear to be darker. Establish a particular light source. Some artists find the upper left hand corner of the paper as the best established light source. No matter where the source is established, it is important that it be consistent throughout the rendering. Some artists will begin with the darkest tones and work toward the lightest;

Shading by scrumbling (6B lead).

Oak turkey wing
(H, HB, and 3B leads).

others will begin with the lightest and work toward the darkest. Usually, from the lightest to the darkest is more practical. It is easier to add dark than light.

A gradual transition from light to dark will give the pattern a sense of spatial dimension and life. Tonal effects may be achieved by smudging or rubbing a line. A stump—a tightly rolled and pointed paper tube—can be used to soften a line or evaporate a tone. The finger or a gum eraser can also phase out a tone. Cross hatching may be smudged with a cloth or stump to soften and blush an area. Even a dirty eraser can add depth by shadowing. Or a clean-eraser streak can shine and highlight metal or lacquer. The variations in line spacing change the density and produce a modeling effect. And remember that nature is rarely straight or symmetrical. It is often the odd fiber flair that gives life to a fly sketch.

Details give authenticity and texture, but the artist must determine how much detail is required for the integrity of the drawing. Detail requires selective interpretation. Too many details can confuse the sketch, making it busy or troubled. Remember too that the integrity of a drawing, pencil or ink, often depends on what is left out rather than put in. Suggestion may do more for a drawing than a solid line.

Guide lines may be lightly drawn for pattern proportion. But try to avoid excessive erasing. Erasers, like pencil leads, are available in several degrees of hardness and abrasiveness. Artgum, a soft-grade eraser, should be used to erase large areas and to remove pencil guide lines from an ink drawing. Artgum should not be used as a substitute for the regular eraser. An Artgum eraser leaves a dusty residue that can be hazardous to the drawing. A kneaded eraser, such as the Eberhard Faber 1225, is essential. A kneaded eraser leaves no residue and can be shaped to fit the purpose. Staedler Mars-Plastic or Faber-Castell vinyl erasers for paper and film are excellent basic erasers. The eraser should be cleaned periodically by wiping it on a piece of rough paper. Erasers may even be cut into triangles in order to give a sharp highlight.

There are the fine architectural lines and pastels of a fly pattern drawn by Ernest Schwiebert. Spontaneity and line strength exemplify the work of Dave Whitlock. Donald Downs, the English artist, does some visual explosions of difficult tying problems. And Donald Overfield, also of England, renders delicate miniatures. All of these different styles communicate effectively. Each drawing is a particular expression of technique, skill, and personality. Imitate the technique; never imitate the style. Try to develop your own signature of expression.

Dave Whitlock, nationally recognized angler, artist, and conservationist, draws with mechanical pencils (seven, five, and three millimeter) in HB, 2B, and 3B leads. The mechanical pencil is most convenient because it eliminates the need for resharpening. To achieve greater line density, he will draw the line and then spray it with a fast-drying acrylic fix. After it is dry, he will retrace the line or reshade an area and add more fix. In this manner, he constructs the drawing by piling line on line. The following drawing illustrates this technique as well as his authority of line.

Notice the variety of textures in Whitlock's drawing: the spun deer-hair head, the smooth mottled overwing, the flared hair collar, and the graceful hook bend. The twisted body strands, the irregular ribbing, the wanton flair of fiber all add realism to the drawing. The minor shading establishes

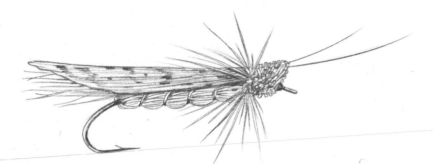

Dave's Stonefly—drawn
by Dave Whitlock.

solidarity and preserves the integrity of the drawing. The combinations of
hard and soft lines, of thin and wide lines, mold the pattern in space. Even
in the two-lined fibers of the flared collar, the close fibers are bold and
advance in space while the far soft fibers dissolve in the distance. The
consistent light source, in the upper left hand corner, shades the inside
hook bend and the underside of the ribbing. The shaded, tilted head and
antenna arc give the pattern a quiet curving rhythm. There is music in the
fly pattern's anatomy.

Whitlock's interplay of hard edges and soft edges, also called "found"
and "lost" edges, is an expressive tool for the artist. By playing the found
edges against the lost edges, a considerable amount of graphic information
can be presented. These hard and soft edges create the spatial depth and
trap the eye. The eye seeks the sharp edge. And the hard and soft edges
express the two different types of graphic presentation: the "wet" (or soft),
and the "dry" (or hard) techniques.

Tim England, whose work has appeared in many American publications,
uses the Rapidograph technical pen, size .30 with FW ink and a 6H sketching pencil. He traces the actual hook on Bristol board for most illustrations
and, after inking in, wipes away the completed penciled sketch with a
vinyl eraser. Many of his patterns are actually created on paper before they
are tied. His drawings, excellent combinations of controlled and free lines,
are then stored in a hardbound book for reference.

Donald Overfield, the English writer and artist, exhibits a fine sense of
light and detail. In his tying sequence of the Skues-style nymph, each
feather fiber is precisely etched. And each illustration clearly depicts the
tying process. A single light source, established in the northwest corner,
throws the nether side of hook and pattern into shade. The dubbing is in
brief single strokes that interwine and fall into shadow. And the body edge
fibers, the fibers in outline, are long, while the body side fibers are fore-
shortened crinkles. This creates a sense of shape and a sense of solidity.

In the tradition of a miniaturist, Overfield's drawings are about four
centimeters long. His hook template is carefully enlarged from an actual
hook. He uses only one lead—HB hi-polymer, size 0.3 millimeter—loaded
in a Rotring Fineliner automatic pencil. With variable finger pressure, he
produces the dark and light strokes of the tail, body, wing, and hackle.
He frequently adds a white watercolor gouache for highlight (Designers'

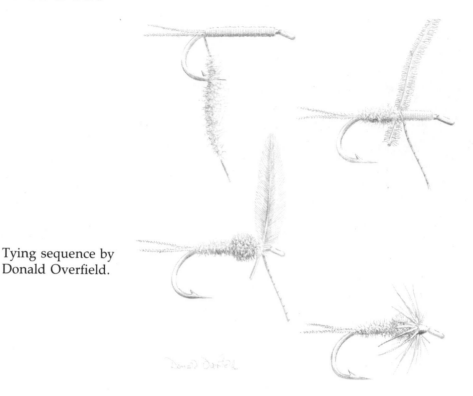

Tying sequence by
Donald Overfield.

Gouache Permanent White by Winsor & Newton, 522). The white gouache,
an opaque watercolor, gives lift and life to a feather barb. It can also create
a reflection smear along a hook bend.

His color technique is to use fine-tipped brushes, 000 and 00, as one
would a pencil. He usually avoids washes and wet-on-wet methods. The
wet-on-wet technique—where clear or colored water covers an area and
the added paint "swims" throughout to produce a soft wash—requires
large areas. Often, the dubbing fibers are applied, stroke by stroke, in
varying colors. The white gouache produces the highlight, and, in this
mixed-media method, pencil provides the shadow. The delicacy of the fly-
pattern portrait is further enhanced by reduction during the printing process.

Donald Downs, another English artist and author, produces some methodically detailed drawings of the tying process. He sketches with standard architectural pens and ordinary ink. His scraperboard technique
evaporates a line or polishes a highlight. This technique, also called "graffito," is simply cutting or scraping away the surface paint on a special art
board to reveal the white ground beneath. A craft blade can cut a fine line
to suggest light catching the heel of the hook or a bead of light on a
lacquered head. Always experiment first on the paper and take care to
avoid damage to it. Graffito should always be a well-controlled method.
Do not scrape too deeply. It should be a light, delicate scratch. And, in all
cases, the point must be sharp to prevent gouging the paper. Shading is
usually suggested by a variance in line width. Exaggeration and unique
perspective often illustrate a point or make a process clear, but the drawings
are usually within normal dimensions. Tracing overlays create accurate
repetition of procedural drawings, drawings that are repeated to demon-

strate a tying process. Finally, to show an element beneath another, intermittent lines outline the buried item. These techniques are excellent for pattern sequence.

Recording color is an excellent adjunct to preserving fly patterns, and it may be done in at least two ways—with watercolor or colored pencils. Colored pencil sets, such as Prismacolor (Berol) and Spectracolor (Venus), come in a wide selection of colors. And side pencil scumbling—where the pencil lead is held on its side—is a useful technique for blending colored leads. Generally speaking, however, colored pencils do not have the range and subtlety of watercolors. Monochromatic washes, such as sepia or diluted India ink, may also be used and, although they will give depth to a sketch, they will not convey pattern colors to the tying table.

THE PEN

For ink work, a good-quality pen is essential. Some steel "crow quills," or dip pens, produce extremely fine lines unless point pressure is applied, when they will flex into remarkably wide lines. Such pen points, which require constant dipping, are less convenient and are more naturally suited to smooth plate papers. The fountain pen is especially of value for sketch work where an open ink bottle is inconvenient. However, an art-grade fountain pen can be expensive and usually the points are not as fine as those available in dip pens. The Mont Blanc fountain pen, a German pen of exceptional quality with a stainless steel nib, produces a medium-fine line appropriate for most work. A gold nib, although not nearly the fine-line maker as the stiffer stainless steel, is more flexible and smoother in sketching. A greater variety of line widths may be made by the gold nib. A technical drawing pen, such as the Refograph by Reform, and the Rapidograph by Koh-I-noor, has a tube and needle point suitable for freehand drawing. The pen is available with interchangeable points for various line widths and only requires an occasional filling. The Tombo PGS technical pen offers a line quality nearly identical to that of a standard technical pen; however, it does not require shaking to load the point with ink, and it may

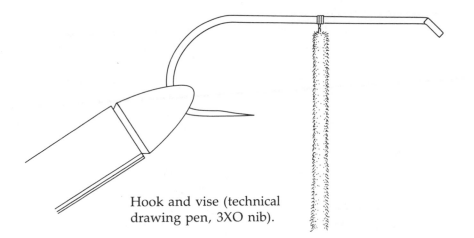

Hook and vise (technical drawing pen, 3XO nib).

be held at any sketch angle. The technical drawing pen has only one straight unvarying voice. A flexible nib has a thousand tongues for texture and life.

No matter what kind of pen is used, make certain to charge it with the correct ink. Artists often use Artpen India Ink (Koh-I-noor Rapidograph, 3083–F), Pelikan's Drawing Ink A (17 Black), or FW (Steig Products), all of which are nonclogging waterproof inks that dry to a matte black. Care must be taken to prevent flakes drying and clogging the feed or nib. Long storage while filled with ink can damage the pen's feed system and point. Such damage may require replacement parts. All art pens that use India ink deserve periodic cleansing.

The Osmiroid sketch pen for India ink is designed especially for sketching with waterproof India ink. For cleaning, the ink feed system must be removed with a special tool. Another pen, the Koh-I-noor artpen, manufactured by Rapidograph, is a technical drawing pen with a fountain nib. Both the Osmiroid sketch pen and the Koh-I-noor artpen have a medium flexible point for freehand artwork. Artpen India ink is recommended for these pens: it flows smoothly.

The Pelikan Graphos drawing pen, from Koh-I-noor Rapidograph, is a technical and freehand fountain pen that features four flexible sketch nibs (Type S): soft (B), medium hard (HB), hard (H), and extra hard (K). There are also over fifty different nibs of a predetermined width that are not affected by varying point pressure. The steel nibs, which include ruling, drawing, lettering, sketch, and slant nibs, are easily changed. Each nib has an ink cover that pivots for cleaning. The Graphos uses India ink. There are also three ink feeds to control inking speeds: sparse flow (1), medium flow (2), and free flow (3). The ink feed must first be removed before filling the ink reservoir.

The Rotring sketching Art Pen, based on the classic "crow quill" design, has two flexible stainless steel nibs—fine and extra fine—that produce variable line widths with hand pressure. The Rotring Art Pen, produced by the parent company of Koh-I-noor, comes with prefilled cartridges or an optional piston-fill converter. On the same design are Rotring's lettering and calligraphy pens. The lettering pen is excellent for cross hatching and shading. The Rotring sketching pen is a universal standard for freehand rendering.

Ink shading may be done by stippling (dotting), hatching (fine parallel or cross lines), or by varying the line width. As in the Whitlock drawing, shading should be done with a single, imaginary light source in mind. This will give dimension to the sketch. The main proportions can be blocked in with a few light pencil strokes. Determine the hard and soft parts of the pattern, the regular and irregular edges, the dark and light tones. Place the pattern next to the sketch for a direct comparison if necessary. And keep in mind the four considerations when drawing a fly pattern:

1. the imitation of shape and volume
2. the suggestion of light and shadow
3. the indication of texture
4. the addition and interpretation of color

Ink is a strong medium; there is a high contrast between the ink and the paper. All drawings should express the four considerations without being

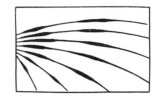

Density by line width and line spacing (crow quill nib).

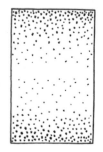

Shading by stippling (crow quill nib for variable size stipple and spacing).

Quill wing (crow quill nib for variable line shading).

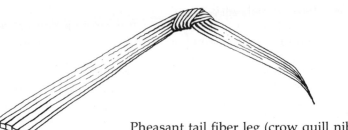

Pheasant tail fiber leg (crow quill nib for variable line shading).

overworked. It is usually best to draw less and to do it quickly than to draw too much and belabor it. Always strive for strength and simplicity of expression.

THE TEMPLATE

A plastic template allows rapid and systematic sketching. It is especially useful when a number of drawings illustrate a single tying sequence. A template, however, is not as spontaneous or as natural as freehand. But a template does allow for continuous smooth inking with limited stops. Draw freehand whenever possible to give life to the fly pattern. Templates, for various hook designs, wing styles, body tapers, and the like, can be cut from plastic, such as styrene sheet stock available in .015, .020 and .030 at most craft shops. The desired shape, penciled in the negative, can be cut with a fine swivel-tipped craft knife. When drawing, the pencil or pen is contained in the area defined by the cutout. The drawing edge should be smoothly sanded with a fine, 600 or 400 grit, finishing paper.

There are various ways to make a hook template. The hook can be drawn freehand and then transferred to the plastic stock. A swivel-point knife is best for following the hook bend; otherwise, a fixed blade or dual cutter can be used. Another method of creating different hook types and hook positions is through photography. The microphotographed hooks can be custom enlarged to template dimensions. The hook is then cut from the photograph and the shape is directly transferred to the plastic stock. Tail, wings, and body-taper templates may be made to the absolute proportions of the individual hook templates. With templates, drawings may be done quickly with accurate dimensions. When using a template with ink, it is important to elevate it with riser pads to prevent ink smears. Template lifts may be made from strips of tape along the underside of the template. Pressure-sensitive template lifts are commercially available, such as the Berol "Templift" (R–1016).

The drawing sequence does not necessarily follow the tying sequence. Pattern parts that appear over other parts must be drawn first. Moreover, pattern parts must have natural connections. The wings should grow out of the body, and the tail fibers should flow from the shank. Overlapping the parts further indicates the cohesiveness of a fly pattern. The following procedure illustrates a typical template sequence.

1. Before beginning, test the ink charge of the point on a piece of drawing paper. Draw with a smooth continuous stroke while keeping the point

perpendicular. Most angler-artists will find it easier to begin at a particular point. Be careful about starting and stopping—stop only at closed points such as the hook point or where one line intercepts another. Mild pressure against the template edge should be used when rounding sharp points or bends.

2. Draw, in correct proportion, the appropriate tail fibers. To sharpen the tail tips, merely slant the point on the return stroke. The second and consequent tail fibers begin at the intersecting tail line rather than at the body. This will produce a natural tail-to-tail connection where they bundle together.

3. Light stippling produces the soft texture of fine dubbing. It is at this point that overall hook length must be determined. Extended hooks may be drawn merely by placing the head and eye farther along the shank line.

4. The wings should appear as an integral part of the pattern—they should not float above the body. Compressed fibers are indicated by close lines at the base of the wing.

5. The freehand hackle strokes, done with a fine-nibbed pen, radiate from the fly body. The lessening pressure of the strokes makes them fine tipped, and the varying lengths of the strokes create the circularity of the hackle. Further shading molds the pattern in space.

Templates may be used with the obverse side up (the verso or backside up). If the flip is made on a horizontal axis, then the pattern will be pointing in the same direction, but upside down. If the flip is made on a vertical axis, the pattern will be pointing in the opposite direction, but right side up. Templates can be designed so that various placement combinations are useful. Many have an infinite number of pattern possibilities and should be used in creative ways.

To some extent different hooks can be made with a single hook template. Width differences are produced to create extra-fine dry-fly hooks or extra-heavy wet hooks. To vary the width or shape of a pattern, the drawing tool can be angled. If it is held in a vertical position, it will reproduce the original template pattern. However, by tilting the drawing tool, the pattern or part of the pattern can be made wider or narrower. To make a barbless hook, merely tape a piece of plastic stock over the barb. It may be necessary to shape the plastic to conform to the sweep of the point. Any template pattern may be modified in this manner for special methods.

To draw a far-side wing, merely shift the pattern slightly at the wing tip. To create long, curved fibers, a slight shift produces a delicate taper. A French curve, with its various progressive curves, creates a variety of lengths and spirals. A template pattern can be used to contain, rather than outline, a drawing. Free drawing within the pattern area creates different

Saddle hackle (drawn with technical pen, 3X0 nib).

fly parts. Specialized patterns parts, such as bass popper bodies, are easily produced with a simple template. Be careful to position and overlap the fly parts correctly. And often an edge is better indicated by discontinuous marks rather than by a solid running line. To make a template pattern short and narrow, merely draw a partial edge and then shift the template. This may be done with any pattern to modify the length and width.

THE BRUSH

In the eighteenth and nineteenth centuries, watercolor was used for scientific notation, landscape sketches, and depth in ink drawings. When rendering the details of plant and animal life, scientists preferred watercolor for its rapidity and accuracy. A compact and convenient watercolor kit accompanied many adventurers during the colonial expansion of the seventeenth century. The explorer Sir Walter Raleigh is said to have brought watercolors to the New World to record America's flora and fauna. With basic tools and modest skill, the amateur naturalist could achieve interesting and accurate results. These attributes still make watercolor appropriate for the angler-artist. With a few simple sketches, the watercolorist can record with subtle exactness the cryptic stippling of a spinner's body or the flush of a dun's wing. And water, the flowing matrix for watercolor, is also the angler's element. Even the water itself, whether from lake or stream, becomes part of the painting. Furthermore, the field kits—half tins of pan colors—are convenient to carry and are, already, part of the history of fly fishing.

Art is a tool for the tyer as well as the artist. An angler can use art as a recorder. Often the casual approach is more interesting and more valuable for a trouting document than as an expression of esthetic skill. The following suggestions may make watercolor a possible media for recording the elusive colors of fly patterns and insects.

1. Blend the colors before application; do not try to modify the color once it has been applied. Successive application of colors only destroys the original brilliancy. Work with light watercolor washes.

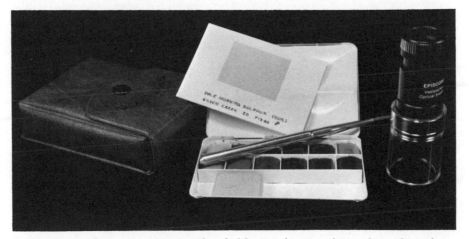

A Winsor and Newton watercolor field case for matching the color of the hatch—and a pocket Episcope for insect study.

2. Use two water containers: one for cleaning the brush and one for mixing the colors. Change water frequently to preserve color purity.

3. Paint quickly with a high-brush hold for broad work. This should prevent overpainting and increase natural expression.

4. When using lightweight papers, do not overwet the brush. Keep water content to a minimum for best results.

5. Paint from the light to the dark values, and preserve the white of the paper for highlight. Adding white to a color only decreases its vibrancy.

6. Keep shading to a minimum. The painting should communicate accurate color information for fly tying.

7. If possible, work in natural light. Natural light expresses a color more completely.

8. Most fly patterns possess a color harmony—there is the rich warm mahogany of a Coachman and the dry cool color of a Cahill. Capture the color harmony as well as the tying sequence.

The traditional approach for a watercolorist is to select a hard smooth paper. Cold-pressed watercolor paper, such as Arches of France, or a heavy Strathmore plate paper is appropriate. Rough, highly absorbent paper is usually not used for the delicate detailing required in a fly-pattern portrait. First, the fly pattern is lightly sketched with pencil. A hook and pattern template will give consistency and rapidity to the initial outline. A light pencil line may be ignored when watercoloring. Full attention must be granted to shading, proportion, and detail. Then the fly pattern colors are carefully matched. Either gouache or transparent watercolor may be used. Usually, the thicker gouache colors, which produce sharp lines and color control, are applied with an oil technique. Because of the limited area of a fly pattern, seldom is the wet-on-wet technique employed. However, if it is controlled, the wet-on-wet technique may be used to flush a dun wing or shade a body. Some artists even use gouache watercolor, transparent watercolor, and pencil in the same painting. Highlighting can be accomplished by gouache or the scraper-board technique, merely scratching off the color to expose the white underpaper. Many fine artists, with varying styles and methods, work in this traditional watercolor technique.

Watercolors should be mixed on a white porcelain or china ground. More accurate mixing will result if the ground color matches the watercolor paper. Every color has four aspects that must be matched: the hue (the color itself, such as red, yellow, or blue), the value (the light or dark of a color), the chroma (the purity or degree to which a color is free from any element of white), and the temperature (the purely esthetic distinction between warm and cool colors, such as brown and blue, respectively). The addition of any other small amount of color to another usually increases its subtlety; however, color mixing is always at the risk of making the colors duller. This is based on the theory that every additional color added to a mixture is one step toward black. Greens are made from a mixture of yellows or oranges with blues. Browns are oranges mixed with blue, green, or gray. Gray is the mixture of any three primary colors or any two secondary colors. Yellow should be darkened with brown, not black; it sullies easily.

Drawing fly patterns is an excellent method for creating or preserving patterns. And there are more reasons:

1. Art is a perfect tool for fly-tying instructors and tying classes. If the student must first sketch the pattern before tying, the tying process and proportions are usually much better. If the instructor uses sequence sheets for each pattern, the tying usually progresses better. I have found it of value to hand out pattern-sequence sheets without any written commentary. I then quickly go through the sheets as the students fill in the necessary instructions. In this manner, the students become part of the tying process even before they mount the thread. They gain a more complete understanding of the pattern parts and methods.

2. Pattern sketches add esthetic dimension to a fishing diary. Sketches record the pattern of the day for future reference. One of the most delightful angling diaries that I have seen was done by Ingo Karwath, the editor of the German fly-fishing magazine, *FliegenFischen*. It was graced with watercolors and sketches as well as actual objects, such as the first fly that he had tied. I have also received books that had hidden within their leaves delicate pencil drawings and watercolor washes done by the authors. Such "remarqued" books immediately become more personal and more valuable.

3. The process analyses shown in sequential sketches clarify complex tying procedures. It allows tyers to share their ideas and methods. The requirement, of course, is to draw the pattern large enough to include necessary detail. All patterns and methods may be drawn—hairwings and quill wings, herl bodies and dubbed bodies, caddis hooks and low-water salmon irons, dry fly and wet fly, bass and bonefish patterns.

Watercolor studies of pools and riffles laced with light and alder arms have a permanent place in the history of angling. But the precise studies of fly patterns and insects, while works of art in their own right, offer technical value to the tyer and angler. Even a rapid, preliminary sketch can record a tying process or essential information. Moreover, the angler becomes more observant: he begins to see the relationship between the insect and the imitation. Fly pattern rationale depends on two abilities of the tyer 1) the ability to recognize the insects that form the trout's diet, and 2) the ability to formulate simple, but effective, imitations based on size, shape, color, and movement. Art allows the angler to see nature more critically and more completely. Looking is also a part of tying because the mind invents as it works. The pleasure of creation is discovery. If all tying were merely prescriptive, just tying trout-fly recipes, then fly tying would not capture the imagination as it does. Discovery and appreciation are basic tying tools.

Much of our angling pleasure is independent of taking trout. We return to the riparian world of ancient ooze where light creates life. We return to the river where fern fronds capture rain, where the ratcheting blackbird wakes the waters, where a water ouzel washes in sunlight, and where caddis dance in the dark. The angler's workshop, that special place where earth touches water, is pregnant with plants and animals. It is an edge of nature charged with changing life. The complete angler is finally a naturalist. With Sir Izaak Walton, we "will walk the meadows by some gliding stream and there contemplate the lillies that take no care, and those very many other various little living creatures. . . ."

Fly-Tying Proportions

There is always a discrepancy between concept and creation. Yet a skilled tyer can create fly patterns close to his ideal, and he can do it often. For most tyers, though, matching the hatch is not nearly as difficult as matching a concept. In the alchemy of tying, the base materials of fur and fluff are converted into a golden harmony of color, shape, and proportion. And no matter what materials are used, those materials must behave, must conform to design and proportion. There is an enchantment in taking these fragments of fur and feather and translating them into an ideal. Apart from the selection and manipulation of materials, fly tying is an act of proportioning.

Despite the proclamations of books, fly-tying proportions are not absolute. And it does not take long before the tyer is confronted with conflicting proportions. Proportions may be based upon insect dimensions, tradition, or the mechanics of the pattern. It is not difficult to produce, now and then, a tie of exquisite proportions. However, the problem arises when a tyer must replicate a dozen ties with the same proportions. A knowledge of historic proportions can engender consistency in tying. And there may be, at times, no reason why one proportion is better than another. A tyer should select a particular proportion and maintain it. And to further that end, it seems to me that the best proportion system is one based upon the actual measurement of materials in relationship to the particular hook used. Although the gap and shank length may vary among the major hook makers, the proportions are absolute as long as the hook is known. Before each material section is tied in, it is sized according to the hook. In this manner, proportion is tied into the pattern.

What happens if a proportion error is tied into the pattern? Fly tying is a "plastic" art much like oil painting. And, like the painter, the tyer can correct most errors as they arise. If an error is made, the thread is backed up and the correction is made before continuing. As a plastic art, the materials may be reformed or replaced during the tying process. An accomplished tyer will seldom allow a significant error to pass if it can be corrected. Perhaps this is the most important lesson that tying teaches. If proportion is not established and maintained, the pattern will lack that symmetry of parts so admired in fly tying.

The following pattern proportions include a variety of possibilities. A tyer should select one and maintain it. Some proportion rationale is presented; however, some dimensions appear to have no other rationale than tradition or fancy. While it is impossible for one drawing to depict all proportions and mounting points, the following drawings do illustrate most common or historic dimensions. A tyer should refer to these proportion "patterns" until they are known by the hands.

The collecting of pattern proportions can be as difficult as tying the perfect fly or raising a taciturn brown. Modern dimensions and dimension terminology often differ from the past. Contemporary proportions are sometimes closer to the insects they attempt to imitate. And one country's proportions may not be the same as another's. It is hoped that the following guide, collected and recorded over my tying years, will solve some of the mystery of proportions.

THE DRY FLY

1. Hackle-fiber tail equals 2½ hook gap or equals hook shank; it may also be 1 to 1½ hook shank (from rear of hook eye to where hook heel starts to bend).
2. Wing length equals twice the hook gap or equals hook shank. The maximum wing length is total hook length (from eye to heel). Quill-wing width may equal hook gap.
3. The tapered head should equal the length of eye for that particular hook.
4. Hackle equals 1½ to 2 times hook gap or three-fourths hook shank.
5. Body, slightly tapering to the rear, equals shank length excluding the head.

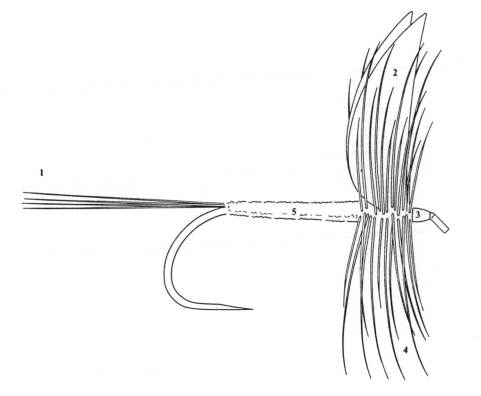

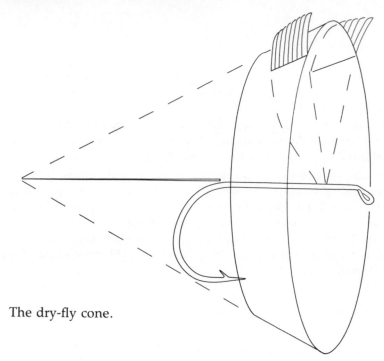

The dry-fly cone.

Note that the dry fly forms a cone with the tail tip as the cone apex and the hackle as the circular base. The hook heel and point act as a pendulum that rotates the pattern (on the tail tip and circular hackle) and "cocks" the wings. The hook should not quite touch the float line. Traditional hackling is three turns behind the wings and two turns in front. The wing mount point is at the front ⅕ point of the shank or the wingset point begins at the front ⅓ of the hook shank. Mount the dry-fly thoracic wing at the front ¼ point of the hook shank. Most mayfly naturals have the wing points ³⁄₁₀ from the head terminus. The body begins directly above the rear extension of the barb point. Usually, the head is not considered when determining the shank length.

THE PARACHUTE CADDIS

1. Downwing should extend one-fourth the shank length beyond the hook bend so as to completely hide the bend. Wing width should be from three-fourths to actual length of the hook gap. The folded tent-shaped wing should just cover the body sides.
2. Antennae, if present, should be hook length.
3. Thoracic section, if present, should occupy no more than ¼ body length.
4. Head equals hook eye.
5. As the full barb touches the water, barb length may be shorter than the typical dry fly. Barb length may be 1½ to full gap length.
6. Body ends directly above the rear of the barb and may dilate at the thorax to divide the folded wings.

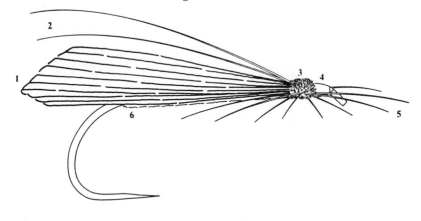

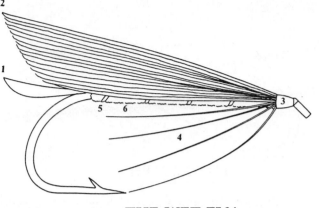

THE WET FLY

1. The tail equals one-half times the hook-shank length, or the tail tip extends to the rear extremity of the overwing. Some patterns have the tail length equal shank length.
2. The wing is 1 or 1¼ to 1½ total hook length. Wing length is variable, and historic patterns called for wing length "just proud of the hook length." Wet-fly wing width is three-fourths hook gap. Wing mount point, a head-length from the eye, is forward of the dry-fly wing mount point. The bottom edge of the wing may also be mounted as the top edge. The illustration depicts the "sedge" or caddis-type mount.
3. The head equals the hook eye.
4. The hackle length just touches the hook point, or the hackle length equals hook gap. Hackle length may also equal one-half body length.
5. The traditional ribbing on standard hook shanks is four turns. Ribbing turns may vary depending upon shank length, width of ribbing, and body material.
6. The body occupies the distance from the rear of the head to directly above the rear of the hook barb.

THE SOFT-HACKLED FLY

1. The body terminus begins directly over rear of barb, directly over hook point, or slightly short (one head space) of the hook point.
2. The thoracic section (slightly fuller than the body to give the hackle an open, pulsing movement) is one-third to one-fourth body length.
3. The hackle length is equal to the body length or equal to the rear extremity of the hook. Only 1½ to 2 hackle turns are used for a full hackle. A side-stripped hackle (one side of a soft body feather is stripped so that the remaining side may be wrapped on to create a sparse hackle) may be wrapped two to four times. When using a side-stripped hackle, make certain that the correct side is stripped; that is, strip the right convex side when the feather tip, which mounts first, points down. Because of the steep taper of most body feathers, the barb lengths will seldom match when wound.

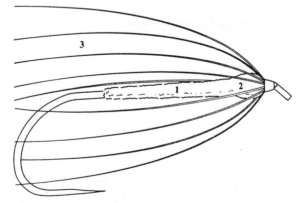

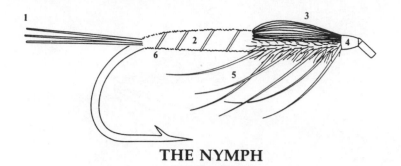

THE NYMPH

1. Tail equals one-half hook shank or abdomen length. More realistic patterns may require a tail length of one-third the hook shank.
2. Tapered abdomen equals one-half hook shank or two-thirds hook shank, depending upon insect imitated.
3. Thorax equals one-half hook shank. The extended immature wings of the natural nymph, as well as the head, are often counted as part of the thorax; hence, the thorax appears to occupy one-half the hook shank. This is especially true of the stonefly, whose thorax is closer to the "traditional" dicta of one-half the shank length. On some patterns, the thorax equals one-third body length.
4. Head equals hook eye.
5. Hackle legs equal hook gap, one-fourth shank, or thorax length.
6. Four ribbing spirals, often variable and depending upon shank length and ribbing width.

The dimensions of the recent realistic nymph pattern tend to follow the naturals—especially the stonefly and damselfly—rather than tradition.

THE HAIRWING FLY

1. Hair tail equals twice the hook gap or one-half hook shank.
2. Wing equals 1½ hook gap, ¾ body length, or shank length.
3. Hackle is two-thirds shank length or shank length, and is often doubled.
4. Head equals hook eye.
5. Body equals shank length and terminates directly over the rear of the barb.

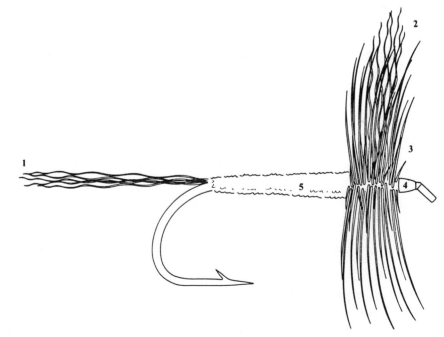

Note that the crimped-hair tail will often intercept the float line sooner than the straight hackle-fiber tail. Furthermore, the shank length the hackle occupies may be twice the shank length of the traditional dry fly. Western and rough-water patterns may have as many as four turns of hackle behind the wings and three turns in front. Often, such patterns as the Humpy are double hackled.

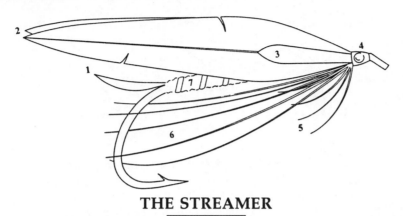

THE STREAMER

1. Tail, if present, is one-third shank length.
2. Wing length is 1½ to 2 times hook shank length or ⅓ longer than hook length.
3. Cheek (jungle cock) hackle about one-half shank length.
4. To accommodate the pattern eye, the head may be longer than the hook eye.
5. Throat hackle is one-third body length.
6. Hackle point just touches hook bend.
7. Body, which is usually divided or ribbed, equals shank length and terminates directly over the rear of barb. Ribbing turns variable depending upon shank length and ribbing width.

It is advisable to use a hook length about two-thirds the total length of the overwing. Shoulder hackle is about one-half shank length. The jungle-cock-eye length should be either one-third or one-half wing length.

THE SALMON FLY (COMPOSITE STANDARD)

1. Tag, the first dressed section, consists of two or three turns directly above the barb. The tag may be divided into two sections such as "silver twist and light blue silk" or "gold twist and light orange silk." The second section of the tag, which has been called the "tip," is equal to the length of the barb and directly above the barb. Tag materials include tinsel, wire, or floss.
2. Tail length is usually 1½ hook gap. Tail materials include golden pheasant crest, Indian crow, blue chatterer, blue kingfisher, teal, or wood duck.

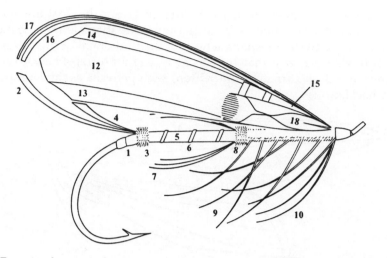

3. Butt is three or four wraps, depending upon the particular pattern. Butt materials include ostrich or peacock herl, yarn or dubbing.

4. Tail topping (sometimes called "tag") is one-half tail length. Compound tails have "either a feather laid above the topping or tied on each side of the topping, forming thereby cheeks to the tail" (Taverner, *Fly Tying for Salmon*, 1942). Tail toppings include hackle, floss, or herls.

5. Body length is dependent upon style: A) Standard length where tag is directly above the barb; B) Low-water, where the tag mounts at midshank, or the extended low-water where the tag mounts two-thirds down the shank from the hook eye. If the tag mounts in the middle, the tail and hackle length should be about three-fourths the hook gap. If the tag mounts two-thirds down the shank, then the tail and hackle should equal 1 hook gap. The wings tips always mount directly inside the tail tip. Body materials: flat and oval tinsel, dubbing, chenille, and herl.

6. Traditional ribbing is five shank spirals only. Some of the older patterns used three to four spirals for each body section. Poul Jorgensen advocates five turns for a complete shank length, and on bodies broken up by butts, from two to five turns depending upon the body-section length. Jorgensen also suggests a possible rationale for five turns. "If there were more than five turns of tinsel, the hackle would be too dense and thus adversely affect the performance of the fly" (*Salmon Flies*, 1978).

7. Trailers or joint trailers, usually the length between joints. Also called "veiling." Materials: Indian crow, toucan breast feathers, or floss.

8. Joint occurs directly at midshank point. Materials: same as butt.

9. Palmered-hackle length at mount point equals hook gap. Materials: various wet hackles.

10. Throat (beard) should be slightly longer than the front hackle barbs, or 1½ the particular hook gap. Materials: Body hackles from teal and guinea fowl.

11. Head space equals the eye of that particular hook.

12. Main wing is slightly short of the tail tip, and the width should be about ½ hook gap. Materials: various natural or dyed, strip or married feathers.

13. Under wing matches length or taper of main wing. The under wing is often composed of tippet strands, turkey sections, or jungle cock feathers.
14. Upper wing strip (the roof) matches the main wing length and is one-half the width of the outer wing. On some patterns, an outer wing sits on the outside and in the middle of the main wing. The outer wing is half the width of the main wing. Upper wing materials include brown mallard shoulder or bronze mallard.
15. Side feather, located on the outside of the main wing, is usually one-third to one-half main wing length and other feathers often longer. Sometimes called a shoulder feather. Side feathers include jungle cock, starling, teal, or black-barred wood duck.
16. Topping, which follows the outer perimeter, joins with the tail tip.
17. Horns, if present, normally extend to the end of the wing.
18. Cheek is usually one-half to one gap-width in length. It sits on the outside of the side feather: ". . . cheeks, that is, the last pair of feathers put on close to the head" (Taverner, 1942). Sometimes also called side or shoulder feather. Cheek feathers include Indian crow, blue chatterer, or jungle cock.

Feather selection and preparation are very important. Feathers must have the correct arc and length. Note also that the soft, sheathy fibers allow the various under colors to show through. Salmon-fly feather nomenclature is variable. Past and present writers often tangle the terms for side and cheek feathers or call one of them shoulder feathers. Perhaps the most modern and universal approach to terminology is offered in *Salmon Flies* (1978) by Poul Jorgensen. The wing structure may consist of three sections (strip, upper wing, and under wing) covered by three feathers (over wing, side, and cheek). Sometimes the over wing is omitted, and sometimes the width of the wings is regular (main wing is one-half hook gap, outer wing is one-half main wing width, and roof or upper wing is one-half the width of the outer wing).

Much of the grace of a salmon fly lies in its body and wing work. For example, a tinsel body should be mounted at the wing mount point and then spiraled to the rear without overlapping. The return wraps that form the finished body should also avoid overlapping. If ribbing is used, it too should be mounted first at the wing point and then tied in directly beneath the hook shank. The "working" ribbing extends from the tail mount point. By placing the ribbing mount point under the wings rather than at the tail mount point, a smooth body is produced. Fine, flat-nosed pliers can flatten oval ribbing laid along the shank. This too maintains a slender body. A thread cover will create a smooth base for a tinsel or dubbed body. Both methods of mounting tinsel and ribbing avoid the bulk created by mounting points along the shank. Wayne Luallen, a savant of the Atlantic salmon fly, uses flat, needle-nose pliers to flatten quills for veiling, toppings and body joints that are ready to accept veilings, as well as to aid the placement of body parts such as horns. Other master tyers have their own artful dodges. Bill Hunter advocates bending the low-water shanks slightly upward to grant a touch of "softness" to the curve and the finished fly. Lefty Kreh keeps thread bulk to a minimum with a flat thread that, by counter-spinning the bobbin, remains flat during tying.

THE LARVA

1. Tail fibers and feathered gills are short, about the length of the distance to the hook point. Often tail length is determined by the natural.
2. The body length is determined by shank length. Note that the shank length may vary according to the specific circular hook shape. Generally speaking, the body should end at least halfway down on the hook heel to take advantage of the circular bend.
3. Ribbing creates the segmented body of the larva; hence, five or more wraps are used.
4. Thorax equals about one-third or one-fourth shank length. The thorax may vary in length or not be present dependent upon the larva imitated.
5. Wing pad, if present, covers the top of the thorax. Some tyers, however, advocate that the wing pads cover the thoracic flanks as illustrated.
6. The leg length is short, often equal to the hook gap.

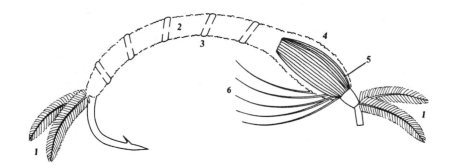

PART FOUR

Methods

Hook and Thread

MOUNTING THE HOOK

The vise jaws should hold the hook heel firmly as illustrated, and adequate hook surface should be anchored so that the hook does not move during the pressures of tying. A tyer must learn to wrap around the barb and point without catching or fraying the thread. The barb and point, which are highly tempered, may easily fracture if buried in the jaws. Often the fracture goes unnoticed. To facilitate working around the barb and point, keep a short working thread. Usually a two-inch (measured from the lip of the bobbin tube to the hook shank) working length of thread is preferred. Adjust the vise carefully to accept the particular diameter of hook wire. Depending upon the vise type and cam angle, the vise handle position may vary. With a standard Thompson A, some tyers prefer the handle to be at the seven or eight o'clock position when "locked in" to the hook. The hook shank should be horizontal.

MOUNTING THE THREAD

First, the thread, under tension, is folded over the hook shank as illustrated. The taut thread end, held in the left hand, is nearly vertical.

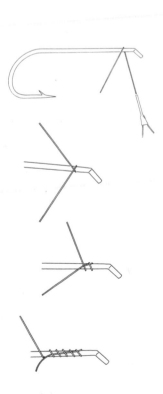

The thread wraps clockwise (when the hook is viewed from the eye to the bend) around the shank to overlap the first wrap.

Continue to spiral down the shank with open wraps. The wraps and the space between the wraps offer an irregular foundation for building a pattern. A few patterns and methods, however, may require a smooth, continuous foundation.

Continue to spiral the thread down the shank, thereby locking the loose end. The excess under thread should be trimmed. The working thread continues down the shank to the tail mounting point.

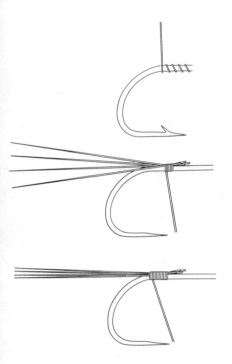

Stop spiraling directly above the rear of the barb. This is the body boundary and tail mounting point.

THE TAIL MOUNT

Soft, natural tail fibers may require firm wraps to hold and gentle wraps to bundle. Firm wraps at the end of the mounting point can cause some fibers to flare. Knowing where to be firm and where to be gentle often determines the management of the tail.

Tight thread wraps should anchor the tail fibers immediately in front of the tail mounting point.

Then, gentle gathering wraps, or slack wraps, bundle the fibers into a united tail.

THREAD TACTICS

Precise thread handling marks a master tyer. Precise thread work is smooth, sparse, and accurate. Dave Hughes once wrote that "if a hook is the backbone of a fly and the materials its flesh, then thread is the tendons that hold it together." The pressure and placement of the thread tendons are the most significant skill required in tying. Proper thread tactics allow material to be planted, rotated, or even slipped. In other words, material may be held by the thread, moved by the thread, or allowed to slip along the thread. All three skills must be mastered and used when necessary. If thread skills are poor, the pattern suffers. There are several factors that determine thread-work skills:

1. Constant thread tension must be maintained by taking advantage of the natural stretch of the thread and by working immediately below the breaking strength of the thread. An exercise comes from Dave Hughes: Mount the thread, pull the bobbin away, and hold the thread in the tying hand. Now, slowly pull down until the thread breaks. Repeat this several times until the hand knows the breaking point of a particular thread. A tyer should develop a sense of the maximum thread pressure possible and work slightly below it. Establishing and maintaining the correct tying pressure encourages polite, behaved materials. A tyer often has a choice: either he will control the material or the material will work its will. Therefore, it is essential to develop accurate thread tension and placement. To conceal the starts and stops, some tyers mount and whip-off most body materials directly beneath the shank. In the vise of a skilled tyer, even heavy moose mane becomes compliant.

2. Always use a minimum of thread wraps when tying. Seldom are more than three wraps ever required to control material. In most cases, one or two wraps will do. If one wrap will do, do not use two. Minimum wraps create slender, delicate patterns. I have watched some tyers actually count the number of wraps for particular patterns. Although I do not advocate tying by the numbers, minimal wraps usually mean that our feathered

confections are slender and delicate. The total number of wraps on a pattern does not significantly increase the thread length or pattern weight. However, depending on where the extra wraps are placed, it can produce a bulky pattern. A typical Light Cahill, tied on a size 14 Mustad 94842 with a maximum of three wraps for materials, and with a hackle tail, dubbed body, rolled and split wings, dry hackle, and tapered head, consumes 11.75 times the total hook length in thread. In contrast, the same pattern, freely using excess wraps, expends 13.25 the total hook length in thread. The extra wraps use only 1.5 times the total hook length more. Thus, there is approximately ten percent more thread consumption with excessive wraps; it is enough to create bulk, but not weight. Always practice the minimum-wrap method. The popular wisdom is that more wraps with a finer thread are stronger than fewer wraps with a heavier thread. In order to achieve that delicate tie, resort to the finest thread possible and restrict the wraps.

3. The soft-loop maneuver, which mounts material at a given point, also incorporates the pinch. There are times when relaxed tension, rather than indiscrete or random slack, aids in mounting materials. With a soft-loop, the material is placed directly on top of the hook shank. A proper soft-loop may be required to mount materials that are slick and stiff. With lateral pressure on the pinch, the thumb and index finger stack the material in the channel created by the finger tips. The thread transgresses between the thumb and the material, loops softly over the material, and then travels down between the material and the index finger. This is repeated, and, while still exerting lateral pressure on the material, the thread snugs down over the material. Further wraps are made in front of the snug point. An excellent practice maneuver, especially for beginning tyers, is to mount a 20-pound-test section of monofilament directly on the top of the shank. This slick, stiff material resists mounting. The required force and control teaches much about thread work. After short practice with the monofilament, natural materials will behave.

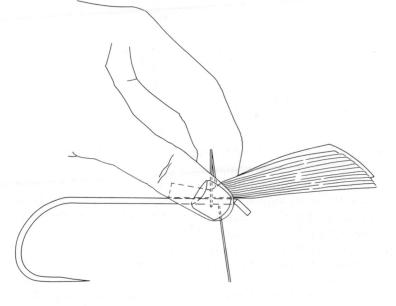

The soft loop.

4. The distributive spin, which creates a slow, controlled rotation of fibers, must be mastered for deer hair and stripped-barb spinning. Stripped-barb spinning is similiar to hair spinning, which will be discussed later. Hackle barbs are stripped and stacked. They are then positioned on the hook shank. A loop lightly traps the barbs so that they rotate around the shank as the thread is drawn taut. The fingers can encourage the distribution of the barbs. More barbs may be added to any vacancy. The distributive spin permits the tyer to use a variety of feathers and fibers, no matter what their length, that may otherwise be discarded.

5. The bobbin-loop method is a unique strategy for stacking material that defies vertical stacking. The method mounts the wings directly on the shank without wing twist. After a thread foundation is laid down, align and "proportion" the wings in place. Next, while squeezing the sides of the wings with the thumb and forefinger of the left hand, make a complete thread loop and place the bobbin tube in the loop as illustrated. Notice that if the shank thread descends immediately into the lower loop and then over the wings for a single wrap, the thread pressure on each side of the wings is precisely matched. In any case, pull the loop straight down with the bobbin tube. This places equal thread pressure on each side of the wings so that the fibers compress vertically without twisting. The fingers hold the wings at the mounting point during tightening, and the thread feeds freely from the bobbin. Once the thread has compressed the wing, the bobbin tube slips out and continues to tighten the loop. To complete, continue to wrap the wings in the conventional manner. Practice makes the motion smooth and strong.

The bobbin loop.

Winging requires special thread tactics. The following standard maneuvers control and adjust composite wings. Adjusting the pliant bundles of woodduck fibers is not difficult although a heavy hand may flick the thread through the wing bundle rather than capture and control. However, these wraps are useful, if not necessary, for the stiff and stubborn calf-tail wings as well as for the soft, flaring deer and elk wings. These "corrective" wraps are used only when required; they are never used to cover poor tying. With minimal wraps, these methods achieve the standard thirty-degree spread between wing bundles and the ninety-degree cock to the shank.

1. The Figure-Eight Wrap. This wrap opens and divides the wings. The thread crosses between the wings and to the opposite shank side. It then passes beneath the shank and comes up the opposite shank side to cross

the thread laid down between the wings. It is easily visualized as a figure-eight wrap with the shank passing through the loops of the eight. To avoid bulk do not figure-eight beneath the wings.

2. The Cross-Wrap. The cross-wrap consolidates, aligns, and erects the wings. The thread, which never drops under the shank, passes between the wings and around the wing bases to cross over the thread laid down between the wings. It then passes around the base of the opposite wing and returns to cross over between the wings. This wrap is best visualized as a figure-eight with each wing section passing through a loop of the eight. As the thread is pulled taut, the wing sections align and consolidate.

3. The Double-Base Wrap. The double-base wrap consolidates, erects, and aligns the wing bundles together. The thread merely passes around the base of both wing sections. This wrap is similar to the cross-wrap except that the thread does not cross between the wings.

4. The Post Wrap. The single base wrap, often called the post wrap, consolidates and positions a *particular wing bundle*. Posting is especially useful for adjusting heavy hair wings. The thread wraps around a single wing base and then anchors the wing. If the thread comes from the outside of the wing to anchor as illustrated, then the wing bundles draw together. If the thread comes from between the wings and anchors at the opposite shank side, then the wings are divided and pulled back. The particular wing problem determines the direction of posting and anchoring.

The post wrap.

Dubbing Methods

The term dubbing refers to fibers, either natural or synthetic, and the method of mounting the fibers. Thus, it is a term for the material as well as the method used with the material. Dubbing is a popular method to achieve shape, volume, and color while preserving texture and translucence. Almost every degree of coarseness or fineness is available, from silky-soft Muskox underfur to spiky, stiff seal guard hairs. Dubbing is durable and can imitate a variety of creatures. It also allows light and air to work their wonders. The translucent fibers that trap air prisms shatter and scatter the light much like the natural emergers shrouded in air. In dry patterns, the captured air increases flotation; in wet patterns, dubbing absorbs water for good water entry and sink. Dubbing is one of the oldest and, with the marriage of natural and synthetic fibers, one of the most modern tying materials.

In the *Catskill Flytier* (1977), Harry Darbee points out that "when spinning dubbing onto the thread, a counterclockwise spin will tighten when wound and give a segmented effect. A clockwise spin will tend to loosen when wound, giving a soft, smooth look to the body." There is a reason for this. When the fibers are twisted counterclockwise on the thread (as viewed from beneath the bobbin), the thread twist is the same direction as the wrapping twist. The dubbing fibers should be mounted on the thread in a single direction, not by merely scarfing the fibers back and forth. Twisting the fibers in a single direction will bind them to the thread as well as to each other. Then the dubbed strand is wrapped on the shank in such a manner that the hand comes from behind the hook with the palm facing the tyer. When the hand is nearly beneath the shank, the hand rotates slowly in a counterclockwise action so that the back of the hand faces the tyer as it wraps over the shank. This action increases the counterclockwise twist on the thread and encourages the fibers to twist together and mount the thread during the dubbing process. Note that the static wraps (a non-twisting wrap), which occur as the dubbing is mounted on the top of the shank and down on the far side, merely maintain the binding action. The hand cannot continue to twist counterclockwise as it orbits down the hook shank. The cording effect is determined by several factors:

1. The fiber length (the longer fibers increase cling)
2. The fiber softness (the softer fibers increase cling)

3. The fiber crinkle or wave (the crinkled or waved fibers increase cling)
4. The fiber texture (some fibers, especially natural fibers, have scales or structures that increase cling)
5. The fiber diameter (the finer fibers increase cling)

Effective dubbing methods usually take into account the following elements:

1. Use fully waxed thread.
2. Mount the dubbing to the thread with a counterclockwise movement. At times a clockwise mount may be just as effective; however, as the thread is rotated on its axis in a counterclockwise direction during the shank wraps, greater twist will be imparted to the thread and the dubbing. Do not merely rub the dubbing back and forth on the thread. Spin the dubbing on in a single direction while maintaining the twist. Hold the spun strand during the shank wraps. If you hold only the bobbin, much of the twist will be lost. Do not allow the thread to unwind and loosen once the dubbing has been twisted on.
3. Use a spinning loop to create the full spiky bodies appropriate for some patterns.
4. Add the correct amount of dubbing to the thread. This usually means a small amount of fiber is distributed evenly over the correct thread length. If a full body is required, it is usually best to wrap the body with more dubbed wraps rather than to add more dubbing to the thread.
5. Use carders or blenders to mix the materials thoroughly to achieve complete blending.

THE DUBBING METHODS

LONG-FIBERED METHOD

This is the basic method for dubbing traditional patterns. Cut the fur close, remove guard hairs, and scarf or roll the fibers in a clockwise motion when mounting them on the waxed thread. Keep the long fibers parallel to the thread and gradually increase the amount of fibers to produce a tight, smooth body for dries and nymphs. The older patterns often were very sparsely dubbed so that the thread color showed through. Today, there is a distinct tendency to cover the thread so that it does not show. Perhaps the modern tyer has omitted the subtle color play between the dubbing and the thread. The long-fibered method is appropriate for the long, soft fibers found on fox, muskrat, and otter.

SHORT-FIBERED METHOD

This method employs a spinning loop. Make a thread loop, insert the correct amount of dubbing with guard hairs, make no attempt to adhere the fiber to the thread, clip hackle pliers to the loop end, and spin clockwise. This method converts the dubbing into a fur chenille that is then wound on the shank with the hackle pliers. This has been a standard method for fuzzy and spiked bodies such as the Gold-Ribbed Hare's Ear nymph.

SHORT-FIBERED FUR METHOD

This method also incorporates a spinning loop. Remove the guard hairs from the fur, scarf or palm roll the fur into a "cigar," and insert it in the loop. Spin the loop with hackle pliers. Wrap the fur rope evenly on the shank to produce the segmented body often found on natural nymphs.

HAND-FEED METHOD

This method is especially suited to the long, crimped synthetic dubbing available. Take a loose palm-ball of dubbing and mount a small finger-spun strand to the dubbing thread in a counterclockwise direction. Gently hold the dubbing ball in the palm. As you wrap over and away, the dubbing will feed naturally on the twisting thread. With practice, it is possible to control the amount of dubbing applied and the degree of twist. If the dubbing is fed quickly, the result is a fast-tapered segmented body; if it is fed slowly, the result is a smooth body with gentle taper. I saw this first done, and done with commercial quickness, by Dave Whitlock.

Long, soft, and crimped fibers swirl on the thread during dubbing. As the twisting and wrapping continues, there is an increase in the twist so that, finally, the last wraps show a distinct "cording" effect as illustrated in the photograph. Furthermore, as the dubbing is wrapped on the hook shank, more and more fibers are caught in the twist so that a natural, expanding taper results. The cord and taper are more appropriate for some patterns, such as grasshopper and stonefly bodies, than for others. The cord and taper may be modified (or eliminated) by hand skills, dubbing methods, and dubbing fibers.

THE DUBBING WHIRL METHOD

It is possible to "chenille" dubbing by whirling it between two threads with a weighted spinner. If the dubbing fibers are soft and long, the wrapped fly body will have a segmented, corded effect. If the dubbing is short and stiff, then the body will be bushy and spiky. Dubbing applied with the spinning loop will be stronger and somewhat bulkier than the single-thread method. With practice and the appropriate dubbing, it is possible to produce a specific dubbed effect. Based upon the principle of a spinning "whorl," a single spin will cord a long, dubbing loop. Because the thread loop embraces the fibers, preventing loss or misalignment, various materials such as polypropylene, marabou, peacock herl, zonker strips, and deer hair may be spun. However, some thick fibers, such as deer hair, must be mounted sparsely to avoid hair clusters and vacancies in the loop. When wrapping the hook shank with long fibers, make certain that you stroke them rearward to prevent them from being trapped during the wrapping process. Some long dense bodies may even be trimmed to create a variety of pattern shapes. The solid brass dubbing whirl by Dyna-King is illustrated.

Mounting the Dubbing Whirl

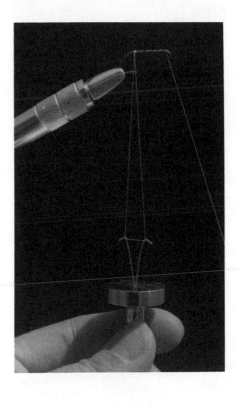

Wrap on the thread and make an appropriate-length dubbing loop.

Wrap the working thread around the loop base at the shank. This gathers the loop and allows it to twirl from a single point. Then, spiral the thread up the shank to the tie-off point. Notice that by pulling down on the whirl, the thread hooks come together to capture any material placed within the loop.

The Spun-Dubbing Method

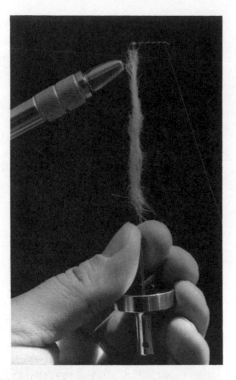

Place the appropriate amount of dubbing in the spinning loop and push the dubbing sliver to the shank. Pull down on the whirl to trap the dubbing. Some tyers find it easier to dub a single thread and then fold the thread back up to the shank to form the spinning loop. This will produce, of course, a tighter strand with greater "cording."

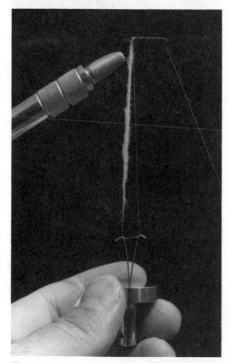

To create a smoother fly body, dub a single thread and then return it to the shank to form the spinning loop. Continue the process as indicated.

After the dubbing strand is spun, the body may be wrapped. During the body wrapping the whirl can be slowly rotated counterclockwise to increase the strand twist. At the tie-off point, merely wrap the working thread over the dubbed strand and tie off.

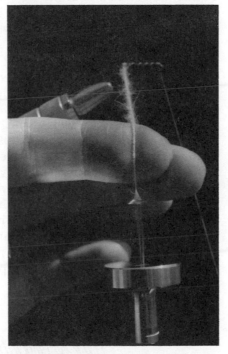

Then, while keeping the thread loop closed to trap the dubbing, drape the end of the dubbed loop over the left index finger and spin the whirl with a clockwise motion (as viewed from the top). By slowly moving the thread back and forth across the left index finger the spin is transferred to the dubbed loop.

The Hackling Methods

The radiating hackle imitates the legs, wings, or breathing appendages of insects and crustaceans. A hackle may be mounted to float a dry fly or to give movement to a sunken one. Different tyers have different hackling methods. But the three methods presented here may be regarded as standard. "Accurate" hackling comes from quality feathers and appropriate methods.

Hackle selection and preparation are essential. Select for absolute barb length, uniform barb length, and stem length. When mounting a dry hackle, avoid as much webbing as possible by trimming the hackle stem. A hackle may be tied in at the tip or at the trimmed stem. The tip method uses more of the stiffer tip barbs, but the thick stem may form a heavy head. The trimmed stem mount, while creating a smaller head due to the smaller stem at the tip, uses more of the soft barbs. Select a hackle with appropriate-length barbs. A dry fly usually requires a barb equal to three-fourths shank length. Do not allow the mounted stem to extend beyond the hook eye. Each tying movement should melt into the next with constant, but firm, stem tension. Use hackle pliers that have the finger ring set at a right angle to the jaw line. This allows the hackle to be wrapped without twist. Notice that the barbs on the shank side will fold over and become part of the radiating hackle. Hackle is spiraled behind the wings before passing in front. Despite advice in the older books, it is best not to wrap between the wings; this will only splay the hackle fore and aft. Keep the hackle stem at right angles while wrapping. Avoid overlapping the stem; this creates chaotic barbs. The well-wrapped hackle should stiffly radiate around the shank rather than resemble a windfall. After the hackle is wound, the thread is lapped over the hackle tip and the excess is trimmed before whip-finishing. During whip-finishing, fold the barbs back to prevent entrapment.

When wrapping a hackle, the first few barbs often flare to the rear. Some tyers use a following wrap to gather them in before advancing the hackle. Wrapping a hackle over a previous wrap, however, may interlace the barbs and secure the stem; but it often creates errant barbs. If the hackle stem is mounted parallel to the hook shank, the stem (which must abruptly bend at a right angle to cock the barbs) twists and splays the initial barbs. As a stem is wrapped around the shank, it eventually aligns itself and cocks the barbs correctly. But the first few barbs may strut in defiance. Of course, the splayed barbs may be trimmed. But to avoid this problem completely, one thing may be done. Mount the hackle stem (barbless for about a head space) directly beneath the shank or low on the shank side. If the stem is mounted low, it will have more space to twist into position before the barbs appear. If the hackle stem is mounted along the shank side or at the wing base, strip the stem base of the first few barbs directly beyond the mounting point. Furthermore, another barb flare may appear directly beneath the fly as the hackle is wound. In this case, the concavity of the hackle and the stem twist during hackling forces the barbs forward. These bottom barbs (which are essential for flotation) are easily trapped by ensuing hackle wraps. Usually, it is a simple matter to caress the barbs back as the hackle is wound so as not to snare the bottom barbs.

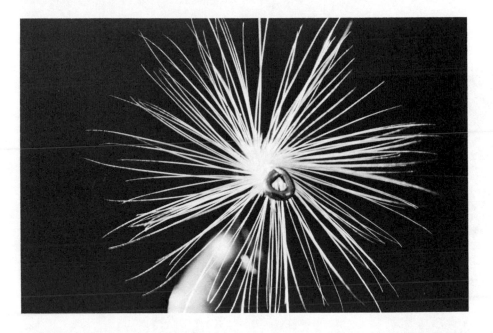

Notice that the radiating barbs vary in length and swerve slightly at the tips. Usually, premium genetic hackle will have more consistent barb length and minimal tip swerve.

THE PARALLEL-MOUNT METHOD

In this method the stripped stem is laid beneath the near wing and parallel to the shank. The hackle tip points toward the bend with the dull, concave side toward the tyer. Three or four wraps are taken to secure the stem. The thread is passed forward to the head position. The dull side of the hackle faces the tyer. The hackle is then bent into a vertical position so that the dull side may be wrapped toward the eye.

1

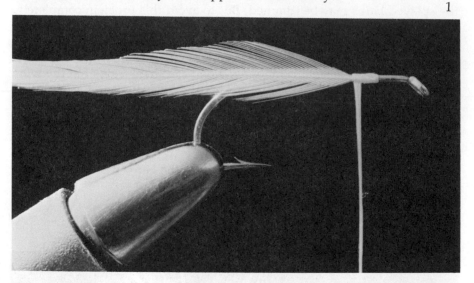

2

3

THE CROSS-MOUNT METHOD

In this method, the stripped stem is placed at a right angle across the shank. The first overwrap comes behind the stem on the tyer's side. Then figure eights lap the stem. Once the stem is secure, fold the projecting butt along the shank and secure it with wraps. The advantage of this mount is that the hackle begins without a bend or twist. The neater beginning produces a neater spiraling. The hackle is then wound, dull side toward the eye, in tight spirals toward the hook eye.

Cross-mount hackle with dull side toward hook eye.

THE REVERSE METHOD

In this English method, the stripped hackle stem lies along the shank so that the hackle tip points to the right. The tying thread binds the hackle stem throughout the hackle space—from the rear of the head space to the rear of the hackle space. Although many English tyers wrap the dull side of the hackle toward the rear, wrapping the dull side toward the hook eye cones the barbs forward for better balance. After mounting the hackle in this manner, add the tail and body. The body may cover the hackle stem or terminate at the rear hackle position. In any case, the working thread must finish at the rear hackle position. The mounted hackle is now wrapped rearward, clockwise, in the usual manner, to encounter the hanging thread. When hackling is complete, the thread secures the hackle tip and the excess is trimmed. Now the thread spirals forward and between the radiating barbs to lap the hackle stem. The thread coils completely through the hackle to whip the head. Wrapping through the hackle while avoiding the barbs is simpler than it sounds. The key comes from Stewart Canham, an excellent English tyer and raconteur of tying trivia. He says that the best method for wrapping the thread through the barbs is: 1) to spiral the thread at the barb angle, and 2) to wrap quickly, completely ignoring the barbs. If you attempt to "weave" through the barbs, there is a greater tendency to trap them beneath the thread. The spiraled overwraps secure the hackle stem, creating a strong tie. Most traditional patterns may be tied with this method.

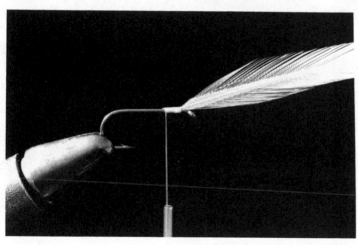

1

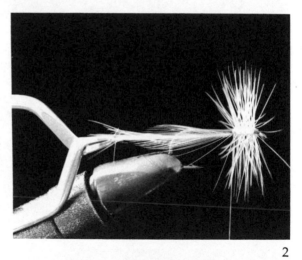

3

4

2

CHAPTER 14

The Head

Most tyers are indefatigable collectors—all those odd pieces of fur, feather, and floss find their way into the tying kit. But an observant tyer collects methods as well as materials. On one of my shelves is a stack of various methods for tying fly heads. The quality of the head knot, and indeed of the entire fly, will depend upon the perfection of the wraps and knots. After all, a neatly tapered head is a hallmark of craftsmanship. Fundamentally, a fly is wrapped, not tied. The initial friction wrap that acts as a foundation for the fly parts is, in fact, a pressure knot. The pressure knot or whip finish—the same knot used on the guides of a fly rod although the application is different—is merely a knot that overwraps the end with the thread itself. The pressure of the overwrap secures the knot. Other knots, such as the half hitch, may be used to finish the fly, but the most common is the whip-finish. Complete instructions for the various head methods may be found in books and the commentary that comes with tools. Before taking a closer look at the various head methods, a general commentary on tying might be appropriate.

A well-tied fly is under pressure. Depending upon the hook and thread, an average tyer places about ten ounces of pressure on the tying thread. Even a light hand will exert at least eight ounces of pressure on the thread. If the thread is cut on a well-wrought fly, it should unravel like a clock spring. During tying, the tension must be consistent and continuous. Otherwise, a shift in fly parts may result. Allow the pressure and elasticity of the thread to aid the tying process. Age and moisture may lessen the thread pressure, but the modern waxed threads are remarkably strong and impervious to time and the environment. The wax functions as a preservative, a matrix that bonds the fly parts and solidifies the wrappings. This pressure and elasticity of the thread is most evident when a tyer attempts to place material, such as a topping or wing, vertically on the shank. To erect the material vertically, place it about five degrees toward you off the vertical plane. As you wrap "over and away," the thread pressure and elasticity erects the material correctly. It is this same pressure and elasticity that makes the head knot secure.

The head knot has had various historical shapes. It may be anything from the small oval button, whipped to the gutted shanks, of the last century, to the classic teardrop design of the low-water salmon fly, or the modern tapered triangle. In any case, the head threads should be evenly wound so as to appear like the threads on a spool—crossovers, twisting and piling of threads, produce an unsightly head. In the past century, with the easily frayed silk thread, it was necessary to lacquer the head. But with the advent of synthetic threads, it is only necessary to lacquer the head for cosmetic reasons. The length of a head knot is traditionally the same length as the eye of the particular fly hook. No matter which head knot is used, a tyer should be aware of the following methods for finishing a fly.

One of the ancient head methods is the single-loop half hitch. This knot, which is also called a jam knot, may be accomplished by hand or by the half-hitch tube. The tube is wound on the thread near the eye in such a manner that when the tube is placed over the eye, the half hitches may be slid over the head and tightened. In the hand method, after the head has been formed, a loop is made and the end is pulled through the loop with hackle pliers, fingers, or tweezers. At least three half hitches should be used to secure the knot. Many tyers who use the half hitch also lacquer the head to make certain that no unraveling occurs.

Another method for the half hitch is to hold the head securely with a finger to prevent the head from unraveling, and then merely make a series of thread loops with the thumb and index finger. By rolling the thread between the fingers, the loop will rotate over the head. Notice that the half hitch makes a series of twisted loops; it is normally not a method for a fine head. A variation of the half hitch is the double hitch head knot. Instead of a single wrap over the half hitch tube, two or three are made and passed over the fly head and tightened. This, in effect, produces a mini-whip that holds far better than a single-loop hitch. After all, a half hitch is only a premature whip-finish. The double hitch is an efficient compromise between the full whip-finish and the single half hitch. The single half hitch method was, as a matter of fact, already considered before the turn of century as an older method that some thought should be abandoned. F. M. Halford wrote in *Floating Flies* (1886), "I cannot too strongly impress upon the professional as well as the amateurs the necessity of abandoning the old system of finishing off a fly with a series of half-hitches." Halford's replacement knot was the lay-by whip-finish.

In the lay-by method the end of the thread is held at the head by the thread loops formed. The loop thread is wrapped around the head several times and the end is pulled to tighten the whip formed. A dubbing needle is useful in controlling the loop while it is being pulled beneath the head wraps. This method is easily done on large flies, and it could be accomplished over the extended gut loop of nineteenth century flies.

A variation of the lay-by method is the two-fingered knot. The thread is wrapped around the index and middle fingers of the right hand. The lower section of the loop passes over the top section, which is placed parallel to the head. Several turns are made in this manner with the lower thread. The head is tightened by pulling the lower loop. In wrapping this knot, the fingers must retain continuous tension on the loop, and they must slide around in the loop in order to resume the initial position so that they may continue to rotate the thread around the head. This method, as in most whip methods, produces a twisted shank thread. The twisted shank thread, of course, is not seen beneath the overwraps. Again, it is best to control the thread loop with a dubbing needle while tightening the knot.

The whip-finish may be accomplished with just one finger. The thread loops over the end of the index finger and rotates in such a manner that the lower thread passes over the head several times and secures the end. During the wrapping, and like the two-finger method, the finger must rotate counterclockwise in order to continue the overwraps. The left hand may be required to maintain tension on the bobbin end so that the whip is pressed against the head. I often use this fast and efficient method for intermediary knots such as a tie-off before weaving.

Another method that produces a whip-finish is the loop method. The final head wraps pass over a thread loop and the end passes through the loop. The loop is then pulled and the end snakes beneath the head wraps. This method is simple and avoids shank-thread twist. It works best on large flies—salmon, bass, and saltwater flies. Small flies do not allow much working room, and often a wing or hackle barb becomes trapped in the drawn loop. But it is a method that is simple and easily taught. The loop tool may be made from carpet thread, rod-wrapping thread, fine monofilament, or wire whipped to a bamboo handle. Dental floss, which is strong, well waxed, and flattens under pressure, makes an excellent loop.

There are several other variations on the loop method, such as the needle whip and bodkin whip. In the needle whip, several wraps are made around the needle and head. The end is passed through the eye of the needle, which pulls it beneath the overwraps. This method is awkward and seldom produces uniform wraps. The bodkin method is equally awkward. A bodkin is placed parallel to the head while wraps are made over the head and needle. The end passes through the tunnel made between the shank and the needle. It is especially difficult to thread the tunnel on small flies. The whip is pulled taut by the end. Like the needle whip, this method seldom produces uniform wraps.

Few hand methods can match the ease and speed of mechanical whip-finishers—such as Thompson, Matarelli, and Veniard—once the procedure is learned. All the tools accomplish the same operation; they wrap one thread over another so that the underthread may eventually be tightened to produce a whip finish. Both the Thompson and the Veniard whip tools have a spring side hook that feeds and tightens the knot as the tool is rotated. Furthermore, both the tools may be operated some distance from the head itself. In contrast, the Thompson tool works better if the tip hook touches the head, yet the tip hook may be angled in such a manner that it pushes aside stray fibers as the knot is formed. The Matarelli and the Veniard have a near-full-circle tip hook. This allows the tools to operate some distance from the head and is useful in the accurate placement of thread between wings and nymph eyes. And the near-full-circle tip hook prevents accidental slippage of thread.

If the whip tool works with a spring lever side hook, it is important that there be a fairly long throw between the tip hook and the side hook, because this will be the working length of the thread used in forming the head. This is the primary disadvantage of small whip-finishers. It is possible to lengthen the working thread by pulling the tool away from the head; but once the overwrap tightens, it may be impossible to increase the working thread length. The working thread of the Matarelli is the thread spanned between the head and the tip hook. Because this length is varied by the distance of the tool from the head, the advantage of the tool is apparent.

The fundamental advantage to the mechanical whip-finisher is the rapidity and pressure during knotting. The head of a fly, like each tying step, should receive full esthetic attention. Always correct errors as they arise and always collect methods that make the next fly the best of all possible flies. Even the finishing knot can be an artistic act.

THE SINGLE-FINGER WHIP-FINISH

The single-finger whip is simple, fast, and perfect for those intermediate tying knots. An important element in this knot is the play of tension between the left hand (which becomes the bobbin hand) and the whip finger. Once mastered, it is a natural method.

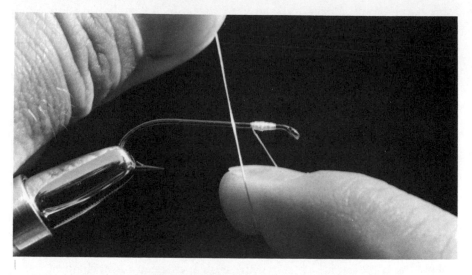

Loop the thread around the right index finger. Like the typical whip-finish, the knot is formed by several vertical wraps over a horizontal thread.

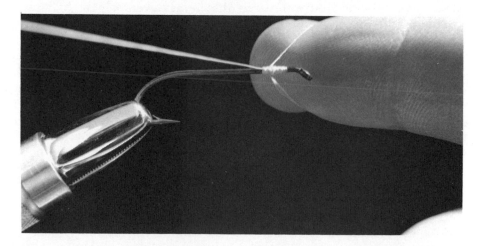

Holding the excess thread below the horizontal, orbit the whip finger and pass the hook eye through the formed loop. Note that pressure must be maintained on the underthread of the finger loop so that the overwraps are held tightly against the shank. The correct play of tension comes with practice. The finger is now in the whip position.

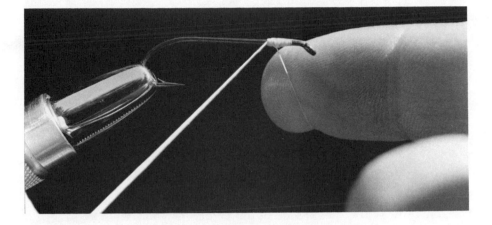

Drop the finger down and around the shank to finish at the near side. Continue to orbit the finger around the whip until the head is formed. During wrapping, the thread loop may be extended by pulling and rocking the whip finger. To finish, merely touch the knot with the middle finger to hold the wraps and draw the loop closed with the left hand. It is possible for the thumb and middle finger to close the loop before the index finger slips out. This avoids trapping any stray fibers in the closing loop.

THE HAND WHIP-FINISH

The hand whip is a standard method for finishing the fly head. Some tyers who use a whip-finisher tool also use this method for fast, intermediate knots. Because the hand whip is so standard, it has been included in this text. A new method of release has been added to prevent those errant fibers from being entangled in the drawn loop. Like all whip-finishing methods, the hand-whip method produces a smooth, tapered knot. The right-handed whip is illustrated.

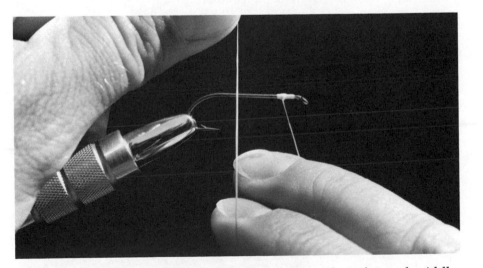

With the left hand holding the bobbin, place the right index and middle fingers together on the extended thread as shown.

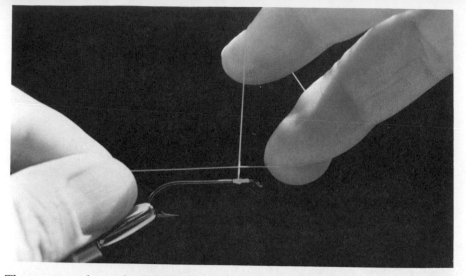

Then rotate the right hand clockwise to form the number "4" with the horizontal thread on the far side of the vertical thread.

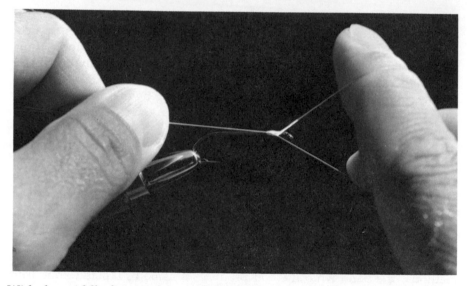

With the middle finger of the right hand, drop the horizontal thread down to the head area. This is the whip position.

With the hand in whip position, rotate the vertical thread around the hook shank so as to capture the hook eye in the enclosed triangle of the thread "4." Notice that the index finger correctly positions each thread wrap.

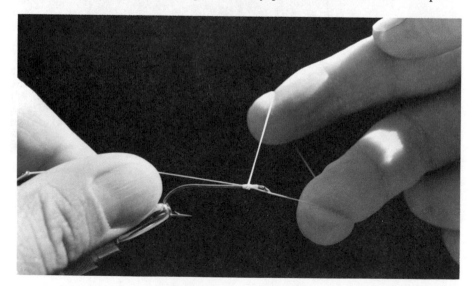

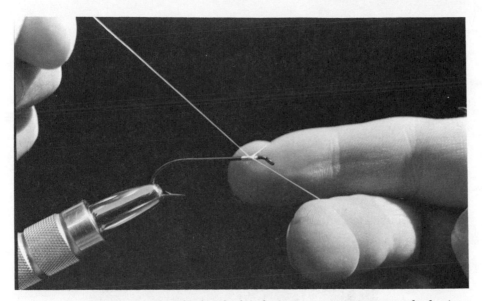

As the hand passes under the hook shank, it must rotate counterclockwise to resume the whip position illustrated above. Continue the hand-whip sequence until the correct taper and required wraps are made. At least five complete whips should be made.

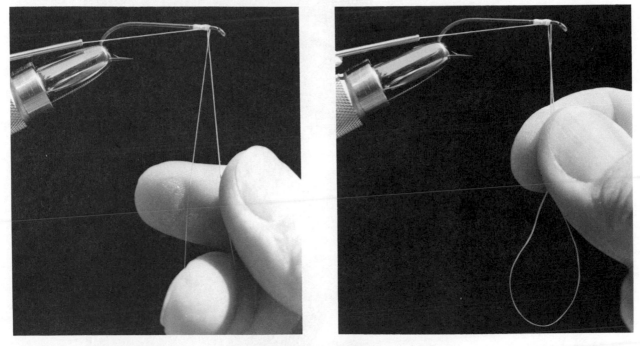

Because the hand whip requires a large loop, the completion of the knot is important. While maintaining mild pressure on the thread loop with the middle finger, slip the index finger out and place it across from the thumb, outside the thread loop.

The thumb and index finger will press the loop together so that hackles and wings are not trapped in the closing loop. Now, slip out the middle finger. Then, slowly pull the excess thread with the left hand while the lessening loop is controlled between the thumb and the index finger. The finger tips may feed the closing loop directly to the finished head. Trim the excess thread.

THOMPSON STANDARD WHIP-FINISHER

Thompson produces two whip-finishers, the standard right-hand model, and the new R/L model for either left or right hand use. During the whipping process, a side-spring hook maintains thread tension and an S-curve tip piles one thread over the other thread. Unlike the Matarelli whip-finisher, the tip S-curve should touch the head during whipping. It is possible to angle the tip of the S-curve so that the hackle barbs and wing fibers are pushed out of the way during the whipping process. The standard model is illustrated with multistrand Kevlar thread.

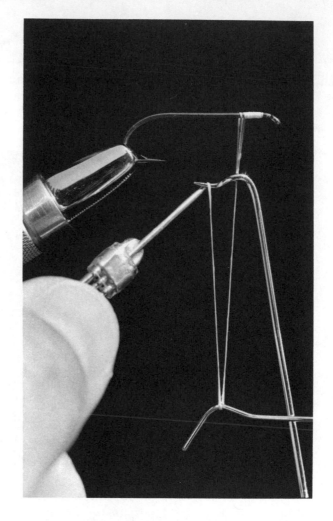

With tension on the tying thread, pass the thread through the inner S-curve (the curve nearest the stem) and the side-spring hook. Then loop the thread back up to engage the outer S-curve as illustrated.

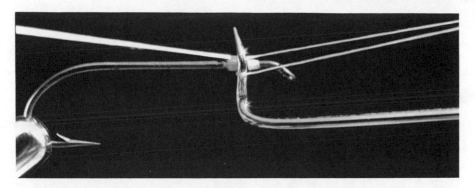

If the whip-finisher is held at a right angle to the thread, it can slide up the thread and into the whip-finishing position. Note that the hook shank is nestled in the bend of the outer S-curve. By rotating the handle, which is held parallel to the hook shank, the thread in the inner S-curve loop passes over the thread held by the outer S-curve loop. Continue to rotate the whip-finisher on its axis until the required wraps are accomplished.

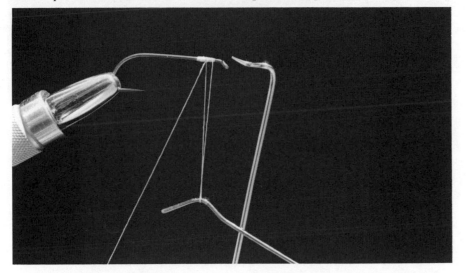

To remove the whip-finisher after the completed whip, drop it into a near-vertical position so that the hook eye is inside the thread loop. Then, drop the whip-finisher to a complete vertical position with slight tension against the spring hook, and disengage the tip S-curves.

While keeping the spring hook angled to prevent premature thread release, slowly pull the working thread until the spring hook touches the head wraps. Finally, with the spring hook against the head wraps, slip the side-spring hook out and pull the thread taut. Cut excess thread.

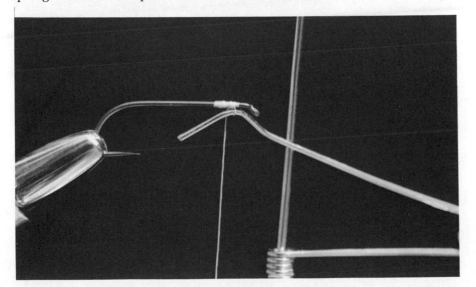

THE MATARELLI WHIP-FINISHER

The Matarelli whip-finisher, used either with the left or right hand, wraps any size fly. During the whipping process, it is possible to extend the thread for further wraps. And the Matarelli whip-finisher is held away from the wrapping point so that accurate thread placement is possible. With practice, tight wraps may be placed anywhere on the hook shank as well as in figure eights between bead eyes and base wraps around wings. The right hand sequence is illustrated, using multistrand Kevlar thread.

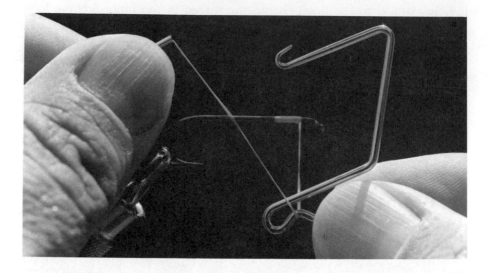

Prevent the whip-finisher from turning by placing the fingers over the base of the rotating hook. Loop the thread around the notch, as illustrated.

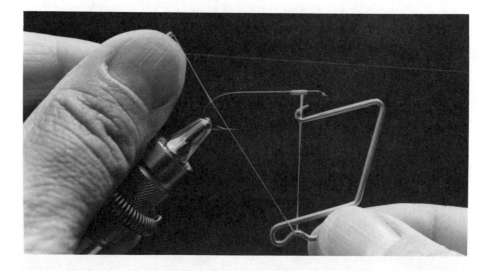

Connect the tip hook near the thread origin and bring thread up to form a tight thread angle.

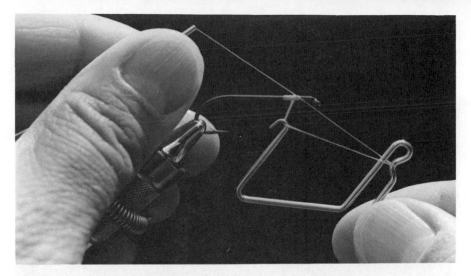

While maintaining thread tension, allow the whip-finisher to rotate as illustrated. The tool will position itself correctly when the handle is held parallel to the hook shank.

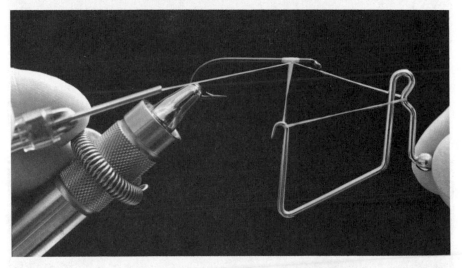

With the fingers only on the sleeve handle, orbit the tool around the head space until the required wraps are achieved. Notice that, prior to the wrapping process, the thread will form a number "4" when it is above the hook shank. The perpendicular thread section will wrap over the horizontal thread section with each revolution.

To feed more thread out, position the whip-finisher as illustrated and gently rock it while pulling away from the head. To prevent slippage, the tip hook and the thread notch must be approximately the same distance from the head.

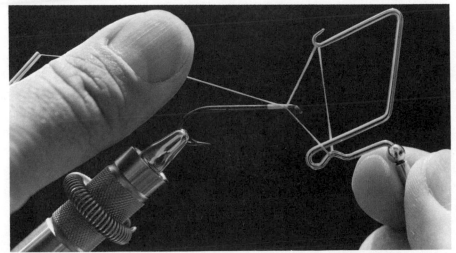

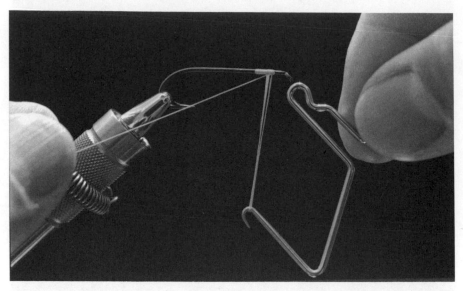

To remove the tool after the required wraps, disengage the notch while maintaining slight thread tension on the tip hook. With thread still engaged in the tip hook, pull excess thread away from the head with the left hand until the tip stops at the head wraps. Finally, disengage the tip hook and pull thread taut.

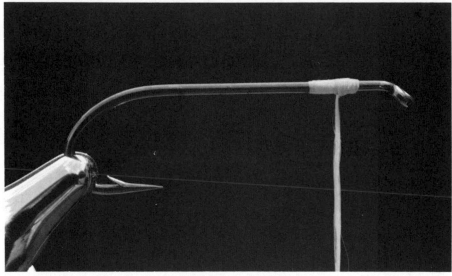

The tightness of the thread is determined by the pressure placed upon the whip-finisher during the whipping process. The result is a tight, tapered head with the excess thread extending from beneath the wraps. Cut excess thread.

CHAPTER 15

The Float Pod

Klaus V. Bredow's *Das Grosse Buch Vom Fliegenbinden* (1981) illustrates a simple method for making a float pod. The float pod is a tight ball of dubbing that traps air so that the pattern drifts on the surface. Most of the water that seeps into the pod is flushed during the backcast. Less absorbant dubbing, even a firm synthetic, is best. Float pods are normally mounted after the tail and body have been completed and before the legs or hackle are added. It is also possible to mount a parachute hackle around the compressed pod for greater flotation.

The appropriate amount of dubbing is tightly twisted on the thread in the usual manner. The dubbed thread must be kept taut during the process. The crotch of the scissors is angled so that the cutting edge does not touch the thread.

The blades and thread are then pressed down to form a tight ball. Notice that the thread passes harmlessly over the back of the blade while the dubbing is compressed.

The scissors are carefully removed while the ball is kept compressed. The compact ball is then secured with two wraps around the shank and the pattern is finished.

175

The Furled Body

A simple, flexible extended body for caddisfly, grasshopper, and stonefly patterns may be made merely by furling a length of dubbing or polypropylene.

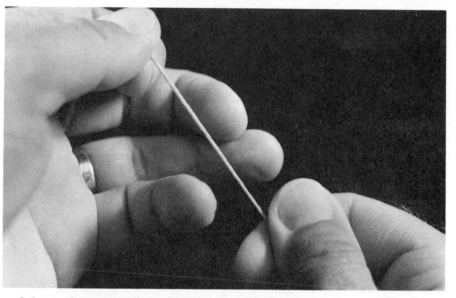

Select at least an eight-centimeter length of polypropylene. Grip one end with the thumb and index finger of the left hand. Spin the free end clockwise with the thumb and index finger of the right hand.

After the strand is spun once, grip the free end with the middle finger and ring finger of the left hand, while releasing it with the right hand. The free end is now held so that the hand may be repositioned for another spin. Continue to spin the strand in this manner until it is tightly furled.

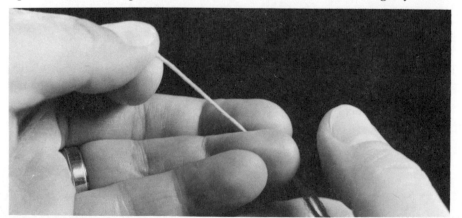

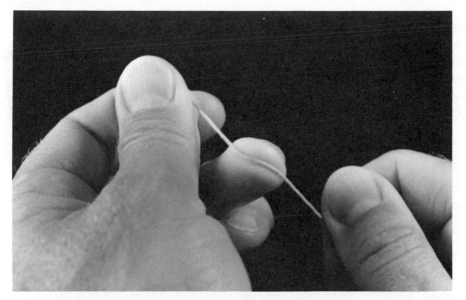

Once the strand is tightly furled, press the ring finger or middle finger in the center and relax the strand. This permits the strand to furl upon itself into a doubled cord.

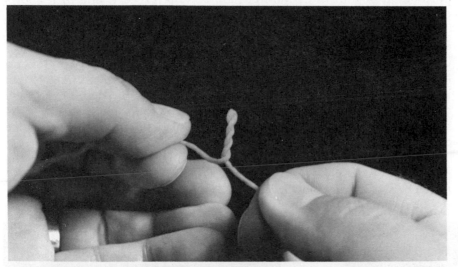

The furled strand folds upon itself to produce an extended segmented body that may be mounted in various positions.

Furled Body Caddis with Traun River Wings.

CHAPTER 17

The Langley Wing-Loop Method

This winging method, created by Ken Langley for English tying competition, and first explained in "The Fly Dressers Guild Newsletter" (Number 1, 1985), has several advantages over traditional methods: 1) it creates a thread loop for compressing or "stacking" the fibers vertically; 2) it permits positioning of the wings during the mounting process; and 3) it allows observation while placing and compressing the wings.

1. Langley wraps about twenty touching wraps immediately behind the eye. The position of the thread after the foundation determines the length of the head as all subsequent wraps pass forward (toward the eye) to form the head. After wrapping the thread foundation, a four-inch thread length is exposed between the shank and the bobbin. With the left index finger held 1½ inches above and parallel to the shank, loop the thread over the finger and down on the far side of the shank. Bobbin weight maintains thread tension.

2. Next, matched wing slips are positioned in the loop and held by the right hand directly on top of the shank. The wings and shank are held firmly between the thumb and the middle finger of the left hand, trapping the thread on the far side exactly opposite the thread on the near side.

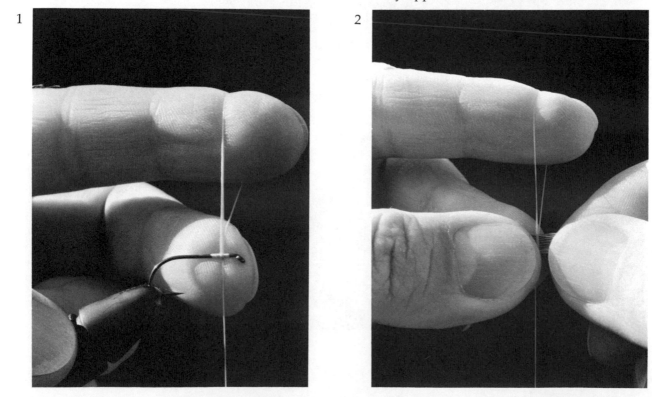

1　　　　　　　　　　　　2

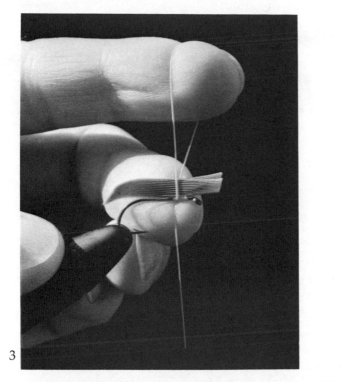

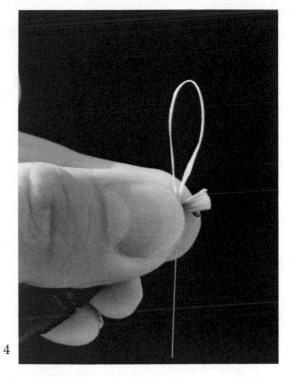

3

4

3. Accurately match and position the wing slips. To view the wing placement, drop the left thumb while trapping the wings in the tight "crotch" of the thread. Reposition the left thumb against the wing before continuing.

4. Now, slip the index finger out of the loop and release the wing butts with the right hand. The left thumb and index finger press laterally against the wing slips as the thread is drawn down, stacking the fibers directly on top of each other.

5. While the middle finger firmly presses against the hook, the left thumb drops down to reveal the initial compression of wing fibers. If splaying or shifting of the wing fibers occurs, the wings are corrected or removed. If no problems appear, then, with the left middle finger still against the wings, another loop is made over the index finger, directly in front of the previous wrap. Again, the far strand of the loop is positioned directly opposite the near strand. As before, hold the shank and wings, remove the left index finger from the loop, and draw the thread down over the wings. Follow with a third finger loop. After tightening the loop as mentioned, hold the wings firmly while the wing butts are trimmed. Finish the head wraps and whip to complete. This method, especially appropriate for traditional wet wings, plants the wings directly on top of the shank.

5

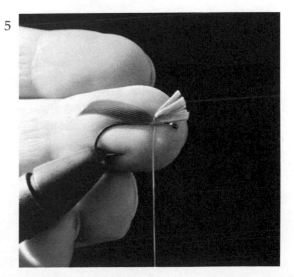

CHAPTER 18

The Needle-Body Method

The soft, hollow fibers of the deer and antelope families produce realistic floating bodies for the larger mayfly, grasshopper, and stonefly patterns. The following extended-body method avoids the ragged clipped butt so common in extended hair bodies.

1. Mount a fine needle with the point toward the right. Avoid heavy needles because they will only increase the looseness of the thread wraps and the diameter of the finished body.

2. Mount the tail fibers, if required. Extended grasshopper and caddis patterns are tied without tails. If a tail is present, it is important that the fiber butts extend far enough along the needle so that they are tied down when the body is mounted on the hook. To imitate the sutures that connect the body plates of an insect, a pale yellow thread may be used.

3. Select such compressible fibers as caribou, antelope, or reindeer. If a heavier hair is selected, such as deer or elk, usually fewer fibers are used. Next, trim the tips of the body hair to eliminate the fast-tapered fragile tips. Remove all underhair. The number of natural fibers used will, to some extent, depend on the diameter and softness of the fibers. For a size 12 hook, about twenty-five deer body fibers are used. Do not use an excessive number of fibers. Wrap the thread toward the butt as illustrated for the first few overwraps. Notice that the wrap area is only about four or five millimeters. At this point, for increased durability, a drop of penetrating cement may be placed on the initial wraps to solidify them.

4. Fold the fibers over the butt section and to the right. Now, bring the thread through the splayed fibers and wrap firmly around the body twice in the same place.

5. Then, holding the splayed fibers to the left, spiral the thread forward a short distance. The thread will now pass through the fibers for another double overwrap. In this manner, complete the body with tight, even segments. Of course, it is possible to spiral the thread forward over the body; however, the method described produces a remarkably neat and realistic body. The tail fibers appear to grow naturally out of the butt section.

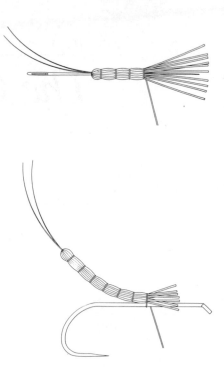

6. The tail body is then held near the butt and slipped off the needle. The completed body may be given a light Tuffilm spray or cement on the overwraps to make it more durable. The tail body assembly may now be tied in any position on a hook.

CHAPTER 19

The Olsson Parachute Method

There is a creative and simple method for making parachute patterns. The heat-saddle method that appeared in the Swedish magazine *Flugfiske i Norden* (February, 1983) was created by Tomas Olsson. The process begins by mounting a length of polypropylene yarn to a hook shank. The diameter of the yarn is determined by the pattern size. After the yarn is mounted, the tail and body are completed in the traditional manner. The hackle is tied in at the yarn base and "parachuted" around the base. The hackle is then secured and the head whip-finished. A heat shield or saddle passes over the hackle so that the yarn exits from the saddle hole. The yarn is then clipped so that about one-fourth inch extends. The flame of a butane lighter beads the extended poly, and a finger forms the warm bud into a button that secures the parachute hackle. All synthetic fibers that melt readily may be used. The saddle illustrated is modified to straddle the hook shank, unlike Olsson's original shield. The saddle folds down on both sides thereby freeing the hands. A flatter saddle may be best for smaller patterns when the button must be close to the shank.

With this method, a parachute hackle may be tied in any position on a hook—on the hook heel or beneath the shank. This method encourages unique pattern designs.

TYING THE OLSSON PARACHUTE

Example Pattern: The Floating Midge Pupa

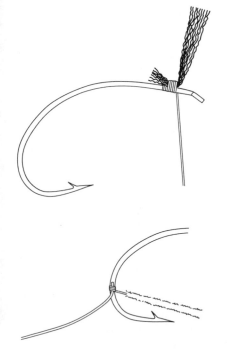

On a Partridge grub or sedge hook, mount a two-inch length of polypropylene yarn that matches the hackle color.

Next, add ribbing and dubbing.

Complete the body in the traditional manner.

At the yarn base mount a hackle, convex side toward the tyer.

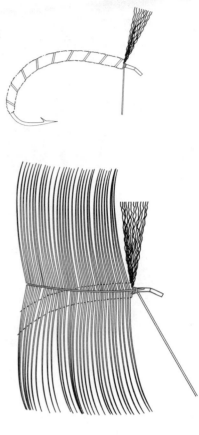

"Parachute" the hackle, concave side down, around the yarn base, wrap off the hackle, and whip-finish.

Slide the yarn down the saddle slot until it extends from the saddle hole. After the yarn has been trimmed to about one-fourth inch (actual length depends upon the amount of poly and the pattern size), flame the extended poly. Wait a moment until the melted ball is warm, and then press down to form a button. The saddle is removed by carefully sliding the poly down the saddle slot.

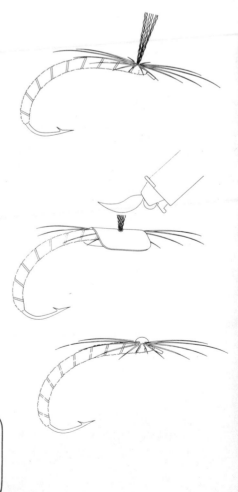

The completed pattern with the parachute saddle "buttoned" on.

Diagram of the heat saddle. The shield, made from light aluminum or brass plate, can be cut with shears. The saddle hole should be 1/16 inch or smaller. The fold is parallel to the saddle slot.

Wax Bath Method
For Stripped Peacock Herl

The stripped peacock herl, a classic wrap for well over a century, is the most delicate of the hard-body imitations. The stripped, double-colored peacock herl imitates the segmented abdomen of many insects. Although it is often claimed that the double-colored herls, actually a beige herl with black tracery, end near the yellow triangle at the eye base, strong double-colored herls may be found below the eye section. Herl from the eye section is sometimes too fine and fragile for tying. Select the plump, broad herls with stem color contrast immediately beneath the eye. These are the same full herls that are used for bodies.

The herl flue may be stripped off with the wax bath method. Select a dyed or undyed flued eye, including about three inches of herl beneath the eye. After slowly melting paraffin scrapings in a double boiler, dip the eye section in the paraffin. Dip according to the growth direction, from the base to the tip, of the herled stem. Cool the waxed eye by immersion in water. The flue along with the wax is then easily stripped off with the fingernail. The result is a flexible and glossy stem, and the wax will prevent water penetration and deterioration. Remember that wax will ignite if over-heated or exposed to an open flame. It is best to melt the wax slowly in a double boiler on the lowest possible heat; pure paraffin, such as Parowax, has a remarkably low flash point. Use extreme caution at all times. When wrapping a stripped herl body make certain that the contrasting colors are exposed. Some tyers will lacquer or even crosswrap fine wire over the body to increase durability.

The Weaves and Wraps

Various weaves and wraps achieve, for the fly tyer, the banded or variegated patterns so common in nature. Like other animals, insects may employ camouflage. Survival, as scientists since Darwin have argued, depends as much upon safety as upon available food. The fittest need not be the strongest, merely the stealthiest. Through their adaptation, insects demonstrate how camouflage, a function of form and color, offers some security. In nature, though, camouflage and concealment never grant total protection. It is only part of a larger system of skill and survival. Not all form and color is the act of concealment—all winter-emerging stoneflies are black. The black, according to H. B. N. Hynes, allows the winter stoneflies to absorb the maximum amount of radiant heat. Stream-dwelling caddis that build cases do so with large stones that make the cases less likely to be swept away. Yet color and form adaptation is likely to be part of a concealment mechanism as well. Most creatures inhabiting the stony substrata of riffle water are mottled. This is particularly conspicuous in the boldly mottled bottom-hugging sculpins. They blend into the background. One sculpin, the *Cottus cognatus*, can even adjust its color, dark or light, to match the habitat.

Perhaps fly tying itself is a form of camouflage, the art of concealing a hook buried in fur and feather. However, fly tying does not conceal the hook as much as it directs the trout's attention to an artificial disguised as a natural. In any case, weaving and wrapping methods allow tyers to imitate the different concealment systems employed by insects:

Color resemblance. This is the most common understanding of camouflage. An insect may repeat the color of its environment. Insects inhabiting monochromatic backgrounds find refuge in being almost solidly that color. Insects inhabiting a variegated environment often wear motley and printed attire. The Perlidae stoneflies—inhabiting the corrugated stone bottoms of young, quick streams—are often inscribed with brown and amber runic marks to match their world.

Form or pattern resemblance. An insect may repeat the natural forms of its environment. The elongated body of the water scorpion *(Nepidae)* mimics the twigs among which it dwells.

Material employment. Some insects, such as the burrowing dragonfly nymph, have body spines that collect debris for concealment. And some caddis larva construct cases of stones or twigs, thereby increasing their natural cover.

Shade and countershade (lightening). An insect may employ shade and countershade that destroy the appearance of the volume and depth of its form. Normally, with light coming from above, the back of an animal is lighter than the shaded underside. The light and shade create the solid shape that is quickly understood by a predator. However, if the prey's coloration is dark on top and light underneath, the reverse of sunlight, then the contrast becomes muted and the form more difficult to see. The countershading dissipates the animal's outline and makes it appear flat and inconspicuous. In animal life, predator and prey are usually indicated by a dark top and a pale bottom. This pattern destroys the recognition of the creature beneath it. If the predator is fooled for a moment, it may be an advantageous moment for the prey. The predator's perception is confused by deception. The zebra, in the hunting lights of dusk and dawn, is almost invisible. The stripes destroy the contour of the body; instead of a body made solid by natural shadows and lights, it appears shallow and lifeless. Countershading is found in the stripes, spots, and broken markings of many insects.

Disruptive patterning. Finally, an insect may use disruptive patterns. Disruptive patterns are marks of deception rather than concealment. Color patches or lines draw attention away from the underlying animal form. This type of disruptive, or "dazzle," camouflage leads the eye of the predator away from the recognizable animal or insect to the markings, the disruptive patterns, themselves. These color marks destroy the relationship of body parts. The prey is "fragmented" by the eye of the predator and, consequently, is less likely to be recognized. Unlike color resemblance or countershade, the disruptive pattern draws attention to itself and away from the animal hidden beneath. The dragonfly nymph with the electric green medial body segment divides its form and draws attention to the bright band and not its dimensions. The predator sees the part while losing the whole.

Of course, a tyer does not want to camouflage a pattern so that it floats or swims unseen. But it is essential to understand the underlying principles of color and form camouflage. The bright chromatic greens of the green darner dragonfly nymph (*Anax junius*) match the rich green plant mass. The riffle-burrowing *Gomphus* dragonfly nymph with its dark, mottled gray-browns matches the marl and trash substrata it inhabits. The strongly patterned Perlidae stonefly nymphs merge with their varied stone-strata haunts. The color and form of an insect can tell us much about the world from which it comes. And it is this color and form the various weaves and wraps attempt to capture.

Various materials may be woven—chenille, vernille, floss, monofilament, fly line, thread, yarn, horsehair, and others. Each material will have its unique characteristics when woven. Chenille and vernille are common weaving materials; the fine protruding fibers create a surface translucency that is similar to some naturals. And they absorb water well for fast-sinking patterns. In actual weaving, make tight bands, slightly snugged against each other and weave with continuous tension. Some weaves, such as the parallel weave, require removing the bobbin and weaving with continuous motion without exchanging hands. It is a simple matter to remount the thread when necessary. It may be required in some weaves to rotate the vise so that the hook eye faces away or toward you to maintain consistent strand tension and placement. The amount of strand tension will, in fact, assist the correct loop placement. Once weaving is accomplished, keep tension on the strands as you add the thread to continue the tying process.

Underbody preparation is very important for some weaves; it gives width so that the weave pattern is visible and it creates the shape of the natural. The underbody, the foundation for the various weaves and wraps, must be solid and smooth. An excellent underbody material is soft leather. Leather molds itself to the shank. The shape can even be modified by thread pressure and it will not rotate on the shank if correctly mounted. Furthermore, it absorbs water and has good water entry without awkward casting weight. For a size 6 dragonfly pattern, I use three-ounce soft-tanned leather. The two-millimeter-thick leather is cut to body shape. A thread foundation is built on the shank before the underbody is mounted. If the underbody consists of two parts, then each half may be firmly wrapped with the hook shank in the center. Also, an adequate length of core thread from the body strands must be stripped and firmly mounted so that the strands will not pull out while being woven.

Because weaving techniques can be applied to any pattern, no particular patterns are presented here. Tails, legs, hackles, and other parts can be added to produce a variety of patterns, both traditional and modern. With practice, the weaves are usually fast and simple. The weaves and wraps imitate the segmented and mottled body of many large nymphs. The color variety, soft volume, and translucent fibers produce effective imitations. Moreover, a variety of pattern effects can be achieved by changing and combining the weaves and wraps:

1. Different strand colors
2. Different strand materials and combinations of materials
3. Different combinations of weaves and wraps
4. Different underbody materials and shapes
5. Different shank placement of weaves and wraps

THE PARALLEL WEAVE

In the parallel or shuttle weave, one strand is shuttled back and forth over the top of the shank while the other strand comes from beneath and loops the top strand repetitively along the sides. The top strand never passes beneath the shank. This weave produces a strand looping along the shank sides and parallel bands along the top and bottom. Usually, because of the paler ventral sclerites of most insects, the lighter-colored strand is woven beneath the shank. This banded and mottled weave is excellent for such imitative patterns as the woven dragonfly nymph. Continuous tension must be maintained during the weaving process to correctly place the lateral wraps. The weave has been made popular by Dan Bailey's Mossback stonefly nymphs.

1. Add underbody and tie in two contrasting eight-inch lengths of Vernille at the shank bend. Rotate the vise so that the hook eye points away from you. Tie off the thread and remove the thread bobbin. Hold the black back strand in the left hand and the white belly strand in the right hand. Remember, there is no hand exchange during the weaving process.

2. With the hand held beneath the hook shank, pass the black strand over the shank, pointing to the right.

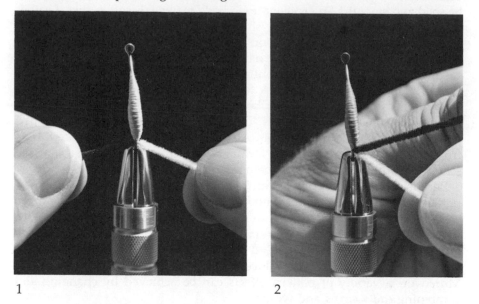

1   2

3. Then, take the white belly strand and come from behind and pass over the black back strand.

4. Pass the white strand over the black strand and under the shank, pointing to the left.

5. Next, move the black strand back across the top of the shank, pointing to the left.

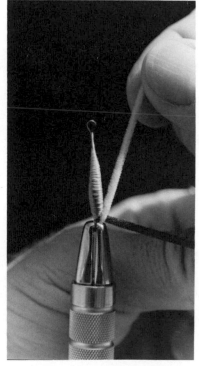

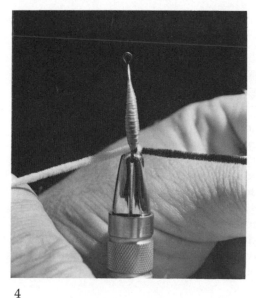

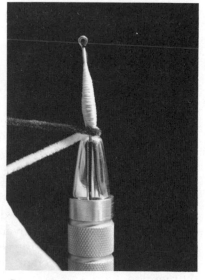

3   4   5

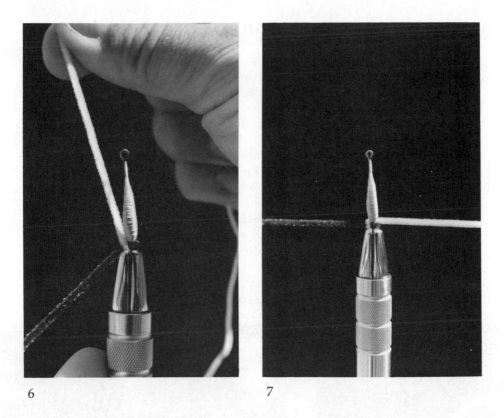

6   7

6. Bring the white strand up from behind and pass over the black strand.

7. The white strand now passes under the body, and tightly against the previous wraps. Notice that the original hand and strand position is resumed.

8. Continue this sequence until the weaving is completed. Then, while maintaining strand tension, remount the tying thread and wrap off the weaving strands. Notice that the finished weave appears as a solid back and belly color with alternating lateral colors.

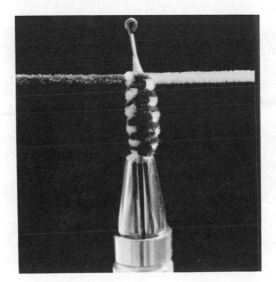

8

THE HALF HITCH WEAVE

This simple weave creates a series of contrasting interlaced bands with opposing lateral colors. It is easier to weave if the vise is rotated so that the hook eye points toward the tyer. If the underbody is mounted on a vertical plane with a dark strand used for the back, then this weave produces an excellent fry pattern with dark fingers flowing down to imitate the parr marks.

1. After removing the bobbin, take the white strand and make an encircling half hitch, as illustrated. The strand end may exit either from the top or the bottom of the loop; however, the exit should be consistent on both sides and throughout the weave. The encircling half hitch loop is snugged to the rear, against the black strand.

2. On the opposite side, the black strand makes another encircling half hitch that passes over the eye and down the shank and is snugged against the previous and opposite half hitch.

3. Repeat this weaving sequence until the body is formed. Reattach the bobbin to tie off the strands and to continue the tying process.

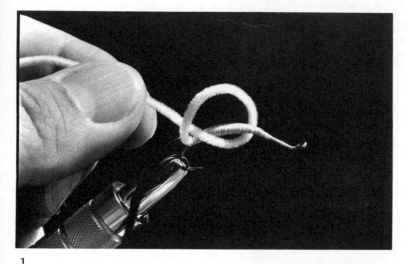

1

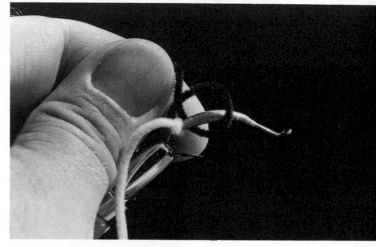

2

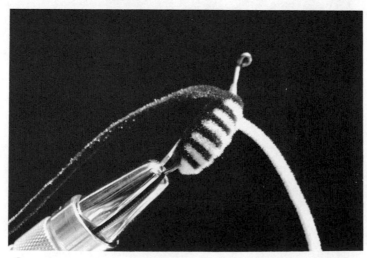

3

THE SPOTTED STRIP WRAP

This wrap produces running, intermittent spots. This wrap may be done on the back, as illustrated, or the belly and sides. This wrap may also be done with several strands so that side, belly, or back bands may be done together. The two-strand method is illustrated.

1. Two contrasting strands are mounted at the rear. One strand, in this case the white, will encircle the shank, while a black strand will alternately pass over and under the encircling body strand. The white body strand wraps around the shank while the black strand is lifted out of the way.

2. This time as the white body strand comes around, it passes over the black strand.

3. The next encircling wrap of the body strand passes under the black strand.

4. Continue this wrapping sequence until the body is formed. The two-strand wrap, as illustrated, produces a solid body interrupted by a spotted strip of contrasting color.

1

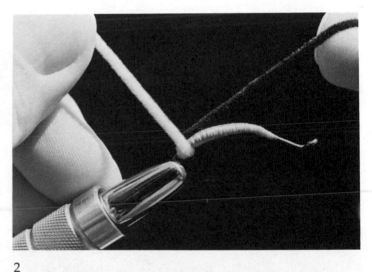

2

3

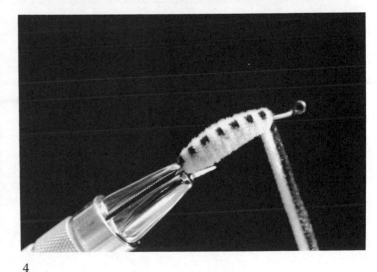

4

THE MOTTLED WRAP

This wrap, a dual spotted-strip wrap, creates a mottled checkerboard pattern. It is especially effective for the boldly mottled dragonfly nymph and sculpin patterns. Three strands, two of the same color, are mounted in the rear. The body strand, in this case a black strand, encircles the shank, alternately passing over and under two parallel strands. Each encircling body wrap will pass under the one previously passed over, and over the one previously passed under. In the sequence, the encircling body strand is black.

1. The black body strand is pulled up to encircle the body, passing over one white strand and under the other.

2. In the next encircling body wrap, the black strand reverses the over-under sequence of the white strands. The illustration shows the third wrap made by the black body strand. This wrap shows the opposing over-under sequence of the second wrap.

3. The succeeding body wraps will alternate between over and under on each dorsal strand. Continue this sequence until the body is completed. Remount the working thread to continue the tying process.

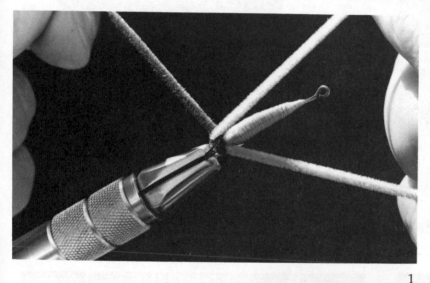
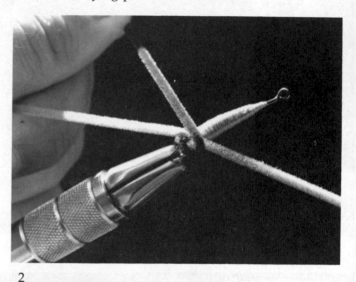

1   2

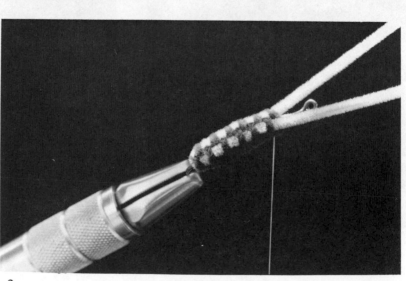

3

POTT'S WEAVE

The Mite series, tied by F. B. Pott of Missoula, Montana, made this running-loop wrap popular. In this wrap the body strand is encircled by a running loop each time it appears at a particular point. It is often used when a continuous dorsal or ventral band is required in a pattern. The body strand is white in the illustrations. Although not required, it may be more convenient to remove the tying thread before weaving.

1. Two contrasting strands are mounted in the rear. The white belly strand makes a complete body wrap.

2. When the body strand is vertical, the black dorsal strand comes up from the front.

3. The black strand tightly loops the white body strand and points forward.

4. After the back strand has looped forward, the white belly strand continues to encircle the shank.

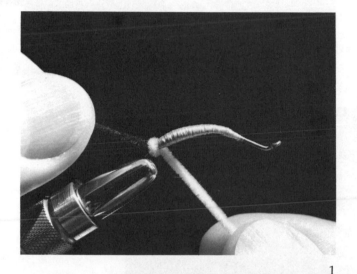

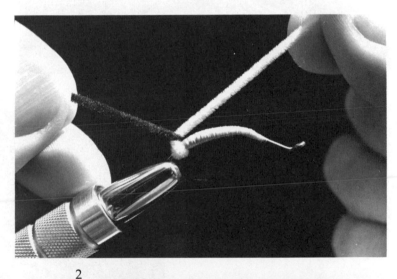

1

2

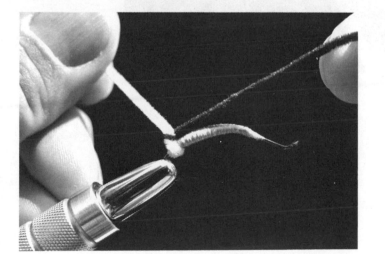

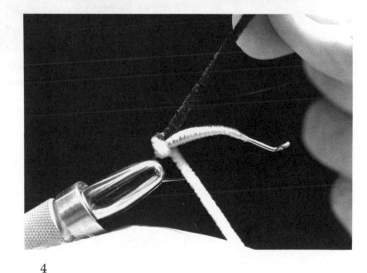

3

4

5. Again, the white belly strand encircles the shank only to be caught by the black back strand.

6. The black strand again loops completely around the white belly strand before it continues the encircling body wraps.

7. This sequence is continued until the body is built. Notice the continuous diamonds or squares created by the running loops of the black dorsal strand. The bobbin is remounted and the strand ends are tied before the tying process continues.

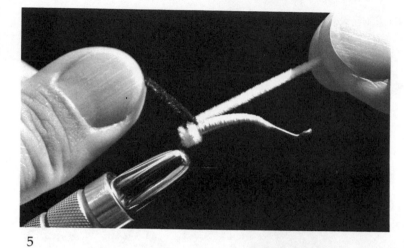

5

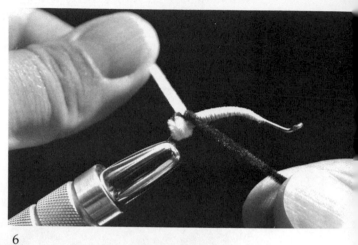

6

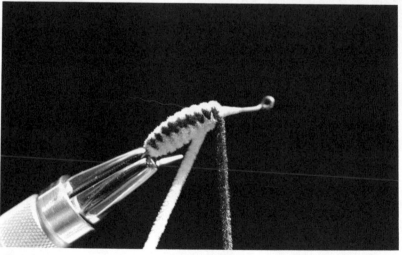

7

The Spun Marabou Method

With a dubbing whirl, even the fine, fragile marabou fibers may be spun, producing a thick, fluffy body.

1. In a spinning loop, mount a marabou section that has one side trimmed. For a fuller body, both sides may be used; merely fold one side upon the other. To create a variety of body colors, stack dyed marabou sections.

2. With whirl tension to secure the strands, trim the stem from the marabou. And, while maintaining the tension, spin the whirl.

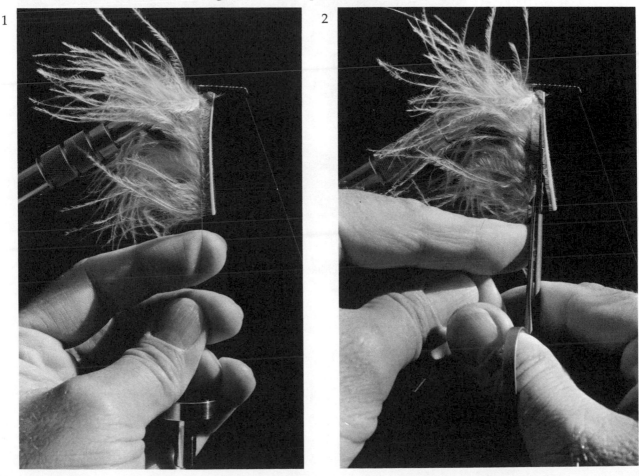

Finally, wrap the marabou carefully, folding back the fine fibers while wrapping.

The result is a plump marabou body appropriate for streamers and nymphs.

CHAPTER 23

The Spun Zonker Method

The spun zonker method, appropriate for steelhead, salmon, and nymph patterns, creates a thick body, a fur collar or, when sparsely spun, nymph legs. A thick zonker body can be trimmed to a variety of shapes, including sculpin and mice. Zonker strips—merely rabbit-hair strips on the hide—appear in a variety of natural and dyed colors. To fashion a thick body, allow the hair butts to extend beyond the spinning loop. This forms a dense "underfur" on the finished body.

1. Mount the appropriate length of zonker strip in the dubbing loop, as illustrated. Pull the whirl down to seize the strip, then slide the strip to the hook shank. Make certain that the zonker strip has a narrow hide section to prevent matting and bundling of the fibers.

2. The zonker strip may then be adjusted so that the correct fiber length extends beyond the loop. Next, carefully trim the hide base from the strip.

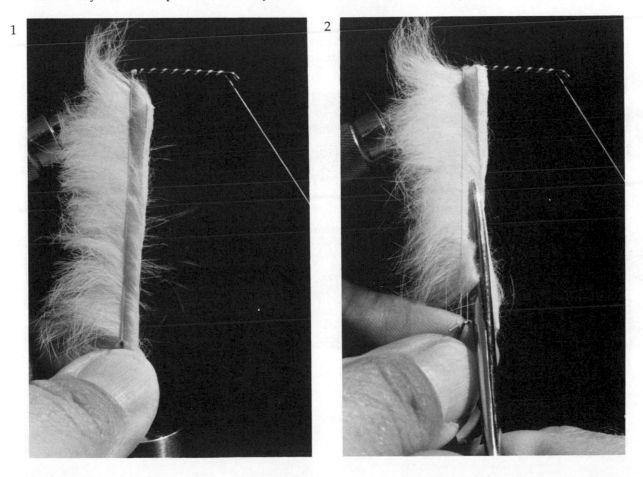

1

2

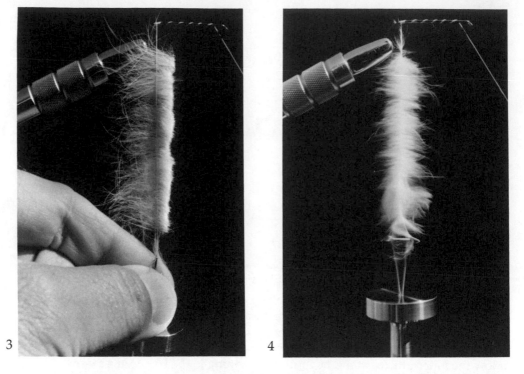

3

4

3. Only a short extension of fur should be left on the hide side. The length of extended fibers on both sides of the loop determine the density of the body.

4. While keeping the loop closed, spin the whirl.

5. When wrapping the body, make certain that the fibers are pulled back so as not to trap them in the ensuing wraps.

6. The result is a full spun-zonker body, appropriate for streamer, saltwater, and nymph patterns. Furthermore, the zonker strip may be mounted sparsely for nymph legs on large patterns, or mounted fully and trimmed to shape.

5

6

CHAPTER 24

The Spun Herl Method

A strong full body may be formed from several peacock herls spun with the dubbing whirl.

1. Remove the tender tips of several peacock herls. With the trimmed tips tied in at the shank, the peacock strands wedge in the loop and between the whirl hooks.

2. Slowly spin the strands to produce "chenilled" herls.

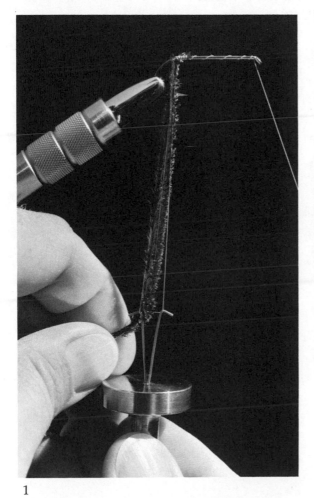

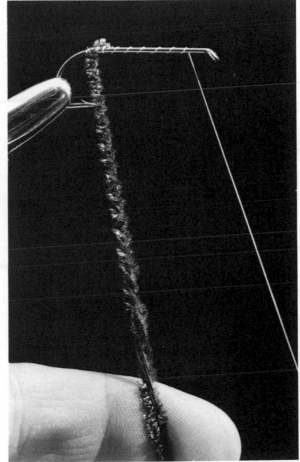

1

2

3. Wrap the corded strands firmly against any previous wraps to produce a plump herl body. To finish, merely secure the corded herls with several thread wraps and trim the excess.

The Stem-Loop Parachute Method

The stem-loop method, popularized by John Veniard and Donald Downs in *Fly-Tying Development and Progress* (1972), is also known as the Barlow gallows method. The concept is simple and unique: a light spring tension holds the looped stem to allow the hackle to wrap around itself to produce a knotted parachute hackle. A spring and hook suspended from a positioned gallows tool maintain the required stem-loop tension. It is important that the hook assembly is directly above the hackle-mounting position.

1. The base of the hackle is stripped of webbing and tied concave side down on a bare shank. This method, of course, may be used to mount a parachute hackle in place at the time. However, in the method illustrated, the hook is used only as a tying base for the parachute hackle; upon completion, the hackle disk is cut away and remounted in any position on a pattern. That is the reason why few thread wraps secure the hackle. If the hackle is tied on a fly and is to remain in position, then the initial wraps are firm. After the loop is made, the second wraps must still allow the stem to slide; however, after the parachute is completed, further wraps may secure the stem end.

2. The stem is looped as illustrated and secured by the spring hook; no more than four wraps are held in tension by the bobbin. This is important because the stem must be able to slide through these wraps during the knotting process.

3. The hackle is wrapped at the base of the loop several times while the loop is held in tension by the spring hook. After sufficient turns have been made, fine-tipped tweezers or hackle pliers draw the hackle tip through the stem loop. The tension hook is taken off the loop and, by gently pulling the hackle tip and stem end, the parachute is tied into a knot. The thread does not secure the parachute hackle in any way. If two hackles are wrapped and knotted in this manner, then the hackle tips may form the wings; otherwise, the stem end and hackle tip are cut off. Leave about one millimeter of excess ends for security. A razor blade can cut the bottom threads and the self-parachute may be taken off. Usually, it is best to place a drop of cement, such as Duro Quick Gel or Super Glue, in the hub of the parachute disk and press it for several hours between glass sheets. These parachute disks may then be sewn on with tying thread, like a button, in any desired position.

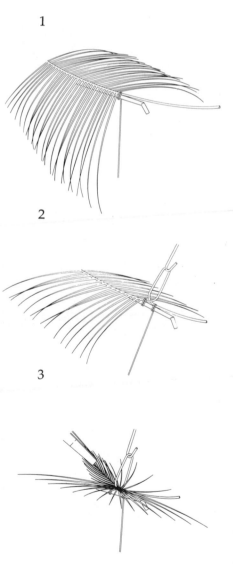

1

2

3

201

The Single-Thread Hair Spinning Method

Various animal body hairs—especially deer, caribou, antelope, and reindeer—may be spun with a single thread. The softer hairs, such as caribou and reindeer, produce the denser spun sections. Select a strong multistrand thread for spinning: it prevents cutting soft hairs or breaking thread during spinning.

1. Mount the hook securely in the vise and attach the thread with a small bead wrap so that all the spinning takes place on a bare shank. This allows each section to spin freely. If a tail is required, attach it with a small thread bead. Use a modest amount of hair—about one-half to three-fourths the diameter of a pencil. Clear all underfur from the hair, and place one relaxed thread wrap around the middle of the bundle and the hook shank.

2. Place another thread wrap around the bundle and shank. Slowly snug the thread.

3. Now, tighten the thread so the hair flares and encircles the hook shank. While tightening the thread, orbit the hand with the spinning hair.

4. After the rotation has stopped, tighten the thread and pass it between the flaired hairs and make a double shank wrap to lock the bundle.

5. Prepare and add another bundle as close as possible, and in the same manner.

6. As each section spins, continue to rotate the thread with the spinning bundle.

7. After two or three bundles have been spun in this manner, use a hair compactor to compress the spun section. Throughout the spinning process, periodically pack the spun bundles. Some tyers find that more force may be exerted during compaction if the hook is repositioned lower in the jaws so that the spun sections are forced against the jaw face. Be careful to avoid the hook point. Continue adding bundles and packing the sections until the pattern is completed, leaving adequate space for wings and hackle.

8. The spun hair, which is now actually denser than when on the animal, should be trimmed with serrated-blade scissors or razor blades. The fine serrations grip the fibers during cutting so that they are not merely pushed aside. Flexible razor blades, such as those taken from a twin-bladed razor, may be flexed to carve the curves required. Curved scissors will work as well.

1

2

3

4

5

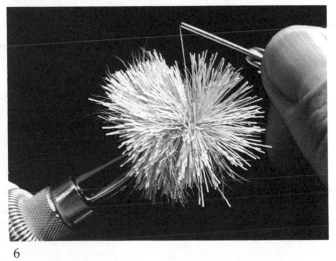

6

7

8

The Extended Body

Raphael Giraldo of Spain made a long cast over the expanding ring, a ring mottled by branch-broken sunlight. But I could not keep my mind on the cast or the quicksilver rise in the clear low water. I was still thinking about Raphael's fly box. I had never seen such small, delicate patterns. And one pattern, an *Emergente* or emerging mayfly, had a soft extended body without any support. I gently touched the extended body. To my delight, it moved; here was a soft and pliant body. What made this dubbed body cling to itself yet remain gentle to the touch? Raphael smiled and said that I would soon understand. But at present, he was more concerned about that trout's curiosity than mine. Later during the summer and true to his promise, Raphael Giraldo's friend, Raphael del Pozo, the creator of that unique pattern, would send me samples and instructions. It was a simple, effective method for creating soft, flexible bodies.

The American tyer can learn much from the Spanish tyers whose tradition goes back to that remarkable document of 1624, *El Manuscrito de Astorga* by Juan de Bergara, and beyond. This text lists forty-seven patterns, some of which were clearly hatch-matching and dry-dapping flies—all of which took place only 128 years after the *Treatise*, which had only 12 patterns. Spain has a long and rich history in fly fishing that is only now becoming known to us. And the modern patterns of Spain, such as the *Emergente*, continue Spanish tradition and artistry.

Frederic M. Halford, in *Floating Flies* (1886), constructed extended bodies out of boot bristles, Indian rubber (latex), horsehair, and maize (straw). Despite the delicateness of his text engravings of the extended-body mayflies, the patterns appear stiff and unnatural. There has always been an interest in producing the perfect extended body. And for years I had sought a simple solution to the problem. But the awkwardness of construction or the unnatural stiffness often made them less than acceptable. A few acceptable patterns, the extended-body grasshopper and the Green Drake, use twisted polypropylene yarn or deer body hair. And Dave Whitlock's damsel Wiggle-Nymph incorporates a dubbed body over a cut ring-eyed-hook shank.

The del Pozo technique creates the extended body from a tightly dubbed double strand, somewhat similar to the method that is used for the western extended-body grasshopper. However, the limitation of most extended bodies is in the difficulty of adding the tail fibers. I wondered whether or not it was possible to have fibers run through the center of the spiraled twist. If possible, this technique would be excellent for various adults, nymphs, and larvae. It could create the paddle tails of the damsel nymph, the long slender tails of the mayfly dun and spinner, the feathery tail of the midge larva. This technique could hatch a new generation of tailed and tailless imitations. When I touched Raphael's *Emergente,* I touched a perfect solution to the extended body design. All I had to do now was to solve the problem of mounting tail fibers within the twisted body itself. Such a fly design would have several distinct advantages:

1. The soft body may prevent trout rejection.
2. The pliable body and tail would fold during the take rather than be pushed away.
3. The method would allow a continuation of the abdominal dubbing into the thorax.
4. The method could be used for a wide variety of imitative patterns including midges, mayfly nymphs, damsels, duns, and spinners. The tail materials could be feather tips for damsels, Micro Fibetts for mayflies, and feather barbs for nymphs. Tailless patterns could create caddis and midge larva. And extended bodies could be created from various yarns and strands as well as dubbed loops.
5. The method uses common dubbing, which is available in a wide range of colors and, with blending, could produce any color required.

THE EXTENDED BODY

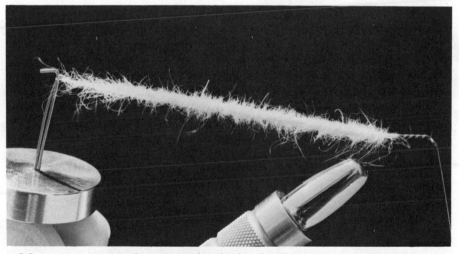

Mount a spinning loop on a hook shank. Place an appropriate amount of dubbing in the spinning loop. With a dubbing whirl or heavy hackle pliers, spin counterclockwise (as viewed from above). Note that the hook shank is merely a platform for spinning. The spun body will be cut off and mounted in a variety of positions.

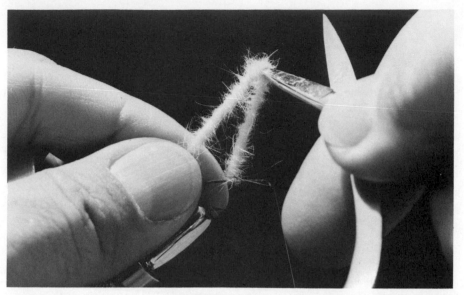

While keeping the "chenilled" dubbing tight, clip the excess dubbing for a smooth body. For a full, bushy body, do not trim the dubbing. With the tip of the scissors, fold the strand back on itself. When the tip of the scissors is withdrawn, the strand will furl upon itself. If the strand is tightly spun, then the body will cord tightly.

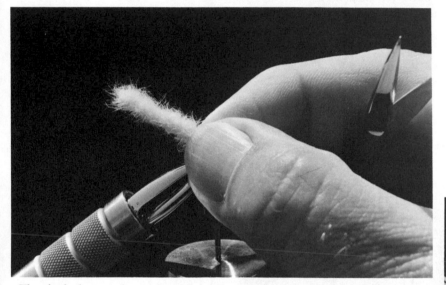

The furled strand may now be clipped from the shank and mounted in a variety of positions for various patterns.

The extended-body midge pupa incorporates the tailless, furled body.

THE TAILED EXTENDED BODY

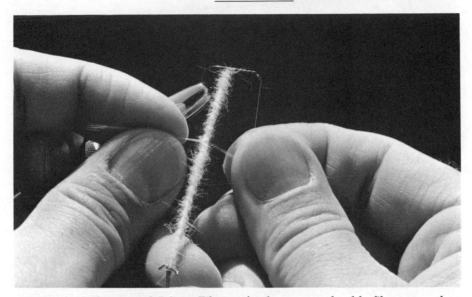

Take the tail material (Micro Fibetts, feather stems, hackle fibers, or other fibers) and press onto the middle of the dubbed strand.

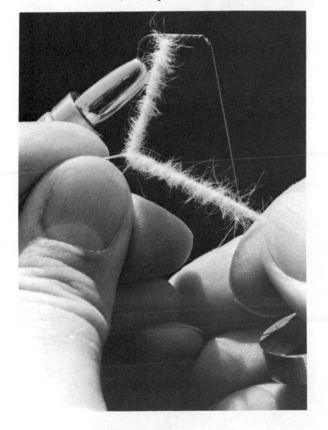

For a damselfly nymph, two, rather than three, hackle tips are used. The natural has three feathered gills, but the simplicity and balance of two work best.

It is best to pull the tail fibers against the strand so that the strands, which will naturally fold, furl over the tail fibers.

Next, twist the strand butt at the point where it touches the tail fibers. Allow the strand to encircle the tail fibers and enclose the fibers between the spiraling cords. Make certain that the tail fibers are between the doubled strands so that they are caught in the center of the spiraling. With a little practice this becomes fairly natural. If a mistake is made, merely straighten the dubbed strand by pulling it taut, and begin again.

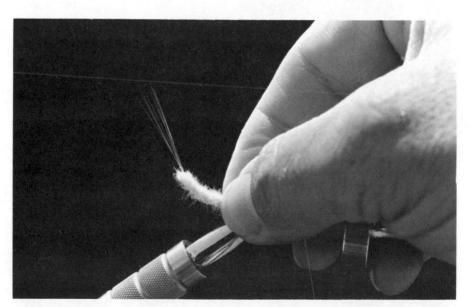

The soft-tailed extension makes a realistic mayfly body that may be mounted at various places along the shank.

Mount the body extension at the selected shank point and, for maximum strength, fold the tail fibers back and overwrap the ends to lock in.

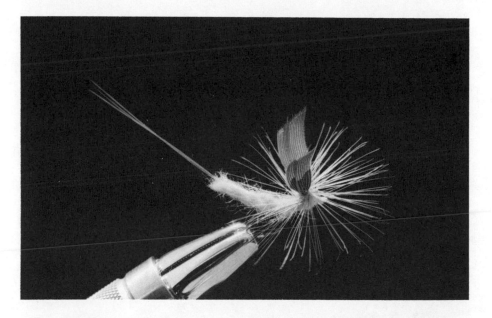

Because this is a fly *design* and not a fly pattern, all standard patterns may now have soft, delicate extended bodies—the Adams, the Cahill, the Hendrickson, the Green Drake. Any pattern type—mayfly, caddis, midge, or damsel—becomes more effective in that the hook curve, that barbed anathema of selective trout, is now more neatly concealed by the body. This is especially true when an extended-body dry is viewed from below.

Although I enjoy adventuring now and then, it is only through tying parsimony that we create a fly with simple methods and common materials. Another axiom of tying should be that a technique should not be made more complicated than absolutely necessary. Anything in tying that is simple and realistic is more likely to become standard. Raphael Giraldo did raise and net a beautiful trout that day from beneath the vaulted branches. But I remembered little of it. My mind was already casting another fly, one with tails and an extended body, beneath other sun-spattered branches half a world away.

PART FIVE

Imitations

CHAPTER 28

The Imitations

The following patterns, both traditional and novel, were selected because they gather into a single text a remarkable variety of methods and skills. By blending methods and substituting materials even a greater variety of patterns may be created. Most of the included patterns require only a modicum of skill. And the instructional detail is extensive enough so that even the complex patterns are clear. No tyer should become lost in a maze of methods and materials.

It is not enough to say that these patterns are effective—*any* pattern may provoke the odd rise. Effectiveness may be based as much upon the water, the trout, and the pattern size and color as upon the particular pattern. In any case, these patterns teach, in fine detail, methods for all fly tying. They require fine motor skills and spatial conception; they require a sense of color harmony and proportioning. Tying teaches an economy of materials and wraps. It teaches adapting and inventing to create strong and simple imitations.

Some patterns—such as the Humpy, the Adams, and the Pheasant Tail Nymph—are traditional; others—such as the Funneldun, the Woven Dragonfly Nymph, and the Lumini stonefly—are less standard. Also, the history of a few patterns, especially the Funneldun and the Hendrickson, is particularly interesting and for this reason is included. Most patterns explore the various methods—such as the techniques for dubbing, winging, and weaving—in the text. Other patterns and methods are included because they increase a tyer's total cache, a tyer's repertoire.

There will always be innovators in tying. No two tyers wrap the same pattern. There is always some difference, however slight—a difference based, in part, on angling conditions and tying traditions. In G. E. M. Skues's *The Way of a Trout with a Fly* (1921), there is a plate that depicts the various tying styles of the Blue Dun. The Hampshire Blue Dun is large and heavily hackled; the Derbyshire dun has less hackle and a vertical wing. The Usk dun has a swept wing, and the Devon dun is a wingless, hackled pattern. In Scotland, according to Skues's illustration, the sparse Tweed Blue Dun has a divided wing, while the Clyde dun is even sparser. The Tummel Blue Dun, a fly tied by fairy fingers, has only a whisper of fur and feather. Although tyers may not wrap the same pattern, every pattern should possess purpose and design. These patterns illustrate a tying range of purpose and design with adequate application for other possible patterns. These patterns should quicken your own waterborn theories and creations.

But while experimenting with the various tying styles and patterns, special attention should be given to avoid the twelve common tying errors:

1. Improper hook mounting
2. Improper proportioning of the tail, wing and hackle
3. Fraying the thread on the hook point
4. Cutting the natural fiber tips
5. Failure to employ slack or tension when required (this includes too-heavy or too-light-handed thread management for the particular method or material)
6. Excessive amount of thread wraps or material (Tying parsimony requires that each wrap and each fiber do its duty.)
7. Crowding the hackle and head toward the hook eye
8. Uneven stacking or matching of fibers and parts
9. Improper placement of body parts (beginners have a tendency to mount body parts slightly forward of their correct position)
10. Lack of appropriate materials or colors
11. Failure to keep the working thread advanced to the tie-off point
12. Failure to correct an error before continuing

Various hints, like the following, may help solve those small but persistent tying problems.

1. Use a cone-dish, a steeply concaved cup, for small hooks. The small hooks gather at the bottom for easier pick up.
2. Use petroleum jelly on the threads of a lacquer or head cement bottle. This seals the contents against air, yet allows ease of opening.
3. Apply adhesive Blu-Tack, a reusable and moldable Bostick plastic, on the vise as a material clip or weight.
4. Use a small rubber O-ring over the bobbin tube to secure the thread. This can be stored on the tube while tying.
5. Plump chenille and feathers with steam prior to tying.
6. Soften deer hair for spinning by steaming. Dave Whitlock produces densely spun bodies with this method. He also suggests lacquering the hooks to prevent rust that may arise from spinning the damp hair.
7. Sharpen the small flange end of a Matarelli whip finisher. If a small cutting V is filed into the flange, the notch can be used to cut the thread immediately after whipping the head.
8. Use Tupperware for cape storage. The rectangular boxes match the shape and are absolutely moth proof when sealed.

The charm of fly fishing has been described as "the pursuit of what is elusive but attainable, a perpetual series of occasions for hope." Perhaps this describes tying as well. Each session at the vise is an occasion for hope, an occasion for perfection.

THE ADAMS

According to Harold Smedley's *Fly Patterns and Their Origins* the first Adams was tied about 1922 by Leonard Halladay of Michigan and used by C. E. Adams on a local stream to imitate the flying ant. The ubiquitous Adams pattern, and its variations, has the neutral color of a caddis and the silhouette of a mayfly. It is one of North America's favorite patterns. It imitates caddis, stoneflies, mayflies, mosquitoes, and a wealth of nature's creatures. The true value of the pattern lies in its variegated, but neutral, colors. The wound hackle produces a mottled gray brown mix that effectively suggests a variety of insects, including the Spotted Winged *Callibaetis* (Baetidae), the Spotted Sedge (Hydropsychidae), and even midges (Ceratopogonidae) and Reed Smuts (Simuliidae). The banded grizzly-point wings may suggest the vibrant fluttering of an insect attempting to fly. It is an excellent pattern, not only for rainbows and browns, but also for grayling. The Adams has been praised on the English chalkstreams as an excellent pattern for shy, selective trout. Halladay's original dressing is enhanced by the availability of quality genetic capes from the Metz and Hoffman farms.

Hook: Mustad 94840, size 12–14; 94838, size 16–20; Partridge E1A, size 12–18; VMC 9288 and 9281, size 12–20
Thread: Black size 6/0 or 8/0
Body: Natural gray muskrat
Wings: Paired and divided grizzly points (hackle tips)
Tail: Mixed grizzly and brown, or ginger hackle barbs (fibers)
Hackle: Mixed grizzly and brown, or ginger hackles

The variations on the Adams are myriad. The female Adams, which is a traditional Adams with a small yellow-fur egg sack added to the end of the body, is an elegant pattern, especially useful in clear lakes and spring or chalkstream waters where minute imitative patterns are most effective. The "ovipositing" Adams egg sack, a bead of dubbing, should be slightly larger than the body diameter. Matty Vinceguerra's egg-sack Adams, described in Richard Talleur's *Mastering the Art of Fly-tying* (1979), incorporates a small loop of polypropylene yarn beneath the shank for the egg sack, which actually promotes flotation. The Adams is also tied as a spent pattern with the grizzly wings figure-eighted to produce downwings. The Reverend Dan Abrams uses elk hair for the tail and wing to make the Bastard Adams. Western variations of the Adams can have a parachute hackle around a white calf-tail wing, or a moose-mane tail. John F. McKim's Cheater Adams uses a cree hackle (a tricolored hackle that has the red-brown, gray, and white of both the brown and grizzly hackles) and no wings. The eastern variation is often a sparse and delicate dressing on fine-weight hooks, while the western Adams is slightly overdressed for the quick, nervous western waters.

The standard tie, however, should not be overdressed. It should have a slender body with a gentle taper and a hackle tied dry—that is, for the American, a hackle tied so that the dull side or concave side is toward the eye of the hook. This pushes the hackle tips forward for better balance. This modest fly with motley dress is one of the six most effective dry-fly patterns used in North America.

TYING THE ADAMS

1. First, lay down a thread foundation for the wings. Measure and match two grizzly hackle tips so that when mounted their length equals the shank length, excluding the head. Select hackle points that have dense bold barring and rounded tips. Slender hackle tips can become lost in the hackling. If the tips are matched and mounted "convex to convex," then the dry-fly wing arch appears. However, the bold barring is hidden between the wings. Straight hackle points, matched "concave to concave," place the darker barring on the outside, where it is preferred. Mount the hackle wings, tips pointing to the right, with authority; they should neither move nor rotate during mounting. Wings mounted in this manner resist wind pressure and maintain an erect stance. A thread bead in front of the wings correctly cocks them. Some tyers prefer to mount the hackle-tip wings pointing to the rear: this discourages wing twisting because the wings are channeled in the lateral pressure of the thumb and forefinger. A few tyers strip a length of the wing stem and overwrap it so that the correct wing length is achieved by drawing the stems to size the wings. The problem with this method, which works well at times, is that the stem is prone to twist while being pulled into place.

2. Next, wrap thread to the rear of the body, directly above the rear of the barb, for tail placement. Combine several stiff hackle barbs from the grizzly and the brown hackle. Cut off any soft webbing at barb base and align the tips with a hair stacker. Proportion the tails and securely wrap them in.

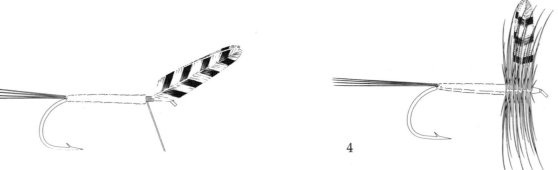

3. Add muskrat or medium gray rabbit fur for dubbing. Do not overdub the body. Mount the dubbing on a single thread and twist clockwise to attach the fibers to the thread. As you wrap on the body, continue to keep the dubbing taut. Complete body dubbing about one millimeter behind wing-mount point.

4. Mount and wrap in two hackles—one grizzly and one brown. The two hackle stems are usually tied along the foreside of the hook shank with the dull side of the hackle pointing toward the tyer. Both hackles are then bent sharply so the dull side is toward the hook eye. They are wrapped on at the same time. The Adams, with its double hackles, is usually wrapped thrice behind and twice in front of the wings. Larger patterns, often tailed with moose hair, are heavily hackled for western waters. On small patterns, especially those under size 18, it may be advantageous to offset the points for superior hooking.

THE BUCKTAIL CADDIS

The Bucktail Caddis, a pattern from the Pacific Northwest, marries simplicity with impressionism. Although there is some doubt as to the origin of the pattern, it has been ascribed to Don C. Harger of Salem, Oregon. It was tied to imitate the caddis, or sedge, on the Metolius and other western rivers. According to Smedley's *Fly Patterns and Their Origins*, the original pattern had an orange-wool body, a ginger palmered hackle and, despite the pattern name, deer body hair for the wing. The design, perhaps more a design than a pattern, first became popular about 1950, and since then has been adapted throughout the West to match local hatches. The design of the Bucktail Caddis makes it an excellent floater in the quick and heavy freestone rivers that rush down western slopes. Although originally developed to match the caddis, the neutral tones and downwing also imitate stoneflies, crickets, and grasshoppers. The body, hackle, wings, and hook size change to cover the imitative spectrum. The design can create the forty-four millimeter salmon fly, *Pteronarcys californica*, or the minuscule microcaddis.

The Bucktail Caddis has hatched a variety of second generation downwing patterns: the Montana Bucktail, the Traveling Sedge, and the Elk Hair Caddis. The Elk Hair Caddis, created by Al Troth of Montana, is a popular variation of this pattern. Troth's caddis, a match of the Hydropsychidae, usually has no overwrapped front hackle and the hairwing "head" is merely trimmed at an angle in alignment with the down-eye. A down-eyed hook is preferred for this pattern. It allows the tyer to clip the deer-hair base close to produce a small tapered head. The Elk Hair Caddis may or may not have the forward-hackle collar typical of the standard dry-fly pattern. When twitched, the clipped head of the Elk Hair Caddis creates a water disturbance somewhat similar to a struggling sedge.

Although not considered a consistent taker on spring creeks or selective waters, it is effective cast with a downstream slack line, tucked beneath the bank willows or skipped over the fast riffle water. Because the hook heel hides beneath the overwing, the Bucktail Caddis, if tied sparsely on small hooks, produces well in the braided riffles of spring creeks. The Bucktail Caddis is often used as a "damp" fly. It is cast up and across the stream. At the end of the drag-free drift, it is pulled under the current and fished throughout the rest of the swing as a wet fly. Thus it imitates the dry adult on the downward drift and the emerging pupa on the retrieve —one cast copies two stages of the natural. A hard backcast is all that is required to strip the pattern of water so that it will float well on another journey.

It is, furthermore, one of the simplest patterns to tie. The original Bucktail Caddis, as the name suggests, may have used the coarse hair from the base of a buck-deer tail. The name, however, is now a misnomer. The wing is seldom bucktail; the favored hair is the finely flecked coat of the coastal deer, the Columbia blacktail. This Pacific Coast deer hair has a gray base that shades into a rich gray-brown with a distinct yellow dun tip. Some of the European deer, such as fallow and roebuck, match this mottled coat well. Select the fibers that have soft, hollow bases. The soft hair base allows the fiber to flair and hold firmly. The stiff, slick base of some deer-hair fibers make mounting difficult, and the fibers often loosen.

The selection of thread for hairwing patterns is critical; it should be a strong, multistranded flat thread. A multistranded flat thread will not cut the soft overwing as easily as a tightly twisted single-strand thread. D. H. Thompson's multistrand Monobond in size 3/0 and 6/0 comes in a twelve spool kit on metal mini-spools and is available in a wide range of colors that include white, yellow, nickel, old gold, olive, mode, brown, beige, red, deer, burnt orange, and black. The characteristics and color range make Monobond excellent for hairwing patterns.

The important feature of the Bucktail Caddis is the palmered hackle, which, according to Smedley, gives the surface effect of the insect's hairwings. It is unlikely that the palmered barbs actually reproduce the surface effect. More likely, the barbs represent the trailing and clustered legs of the caddis. It is of interest to note that the palmer method is one of the oldest hackling methods and has been traced back to *The Treatise of Fishing with an Angle*. The palmered patterns, evidently imitating the palmer caterpillars, were popular in the sixteenth and seventeenth centuries. The hollow deer overwing has excellent float qualities and a stiff palmer makes this a worthy fast-water design. For heavy water, some western tyers combine two hackles, side by side, for palmering. Up to four hackles may be used for the forward collar. The floating merit allows the pattern to be bounced through thick runs or skipped across the surface to imitate the hatching struggle of the "traveling sedge."

The pattern is simple to tie and the variations make it interesting. Remember to tie the palmered hackle in by the tip and with the dull side, the concave side, toward the hook eye. This spreads the hackle forward for better support, leaves the gap free from long hackle, and places the long hackle in the thoracic area. Using the thumb to flatten the tip stem before tying in will usually result in properly angled barbs. Winding the hackle with the fingers for the first few turns before attaching the hackle pliers produces better barb angles. The palmer hackle may even be mounted in such a manner that the barbs cone forward toward the hook eye.

BUCKTAIL CADDIS (STANDARD)

Hook:	Mustad 94840 or Partridge D4A (bucktail hook)
Thread:	Thompson Monobond, nickel gray or matched to the body color
Body:	Orange yarn or dubbing
Overwing:	Blacktail, whitetail, or elk body hair
Palmer hackle:	Brown, ginger, or to match the hatch
Collar hackle:	Brown, ginger, or grizzly

TYING THE BUCKTAIL CADDIS

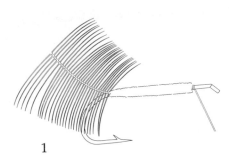

1. Wrap on the palmer hackle by the tip and add the body material (orange wool yarn, polypropylene yarn, or dubbing). Form a gently tapered body.

2. Palmer the body with running wraps and tie off the hackle. To achieve a heavy palmer, wrap the hackle twice as much as you would for standard ribbing.

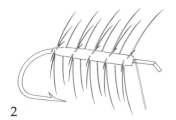

3. After making certain that the underfur is extracted, stack a deer-body bundle to align the natural tips. Depending upon the hook size, the hair bundle should be about one-third to one-half the diameter of a pencil. Mount the bundle firmly so that the fibers extend slightly "proud" of the hook bend. The key to a buoyant bucktail is the delta flair of the overwing: the hairs should arc 180 degrees over the body and down along the sides. The lateral hairs, like outriggers, support the pattern. After three wraps over the bundle, gently rock the wraps with the fingers to produce the delta flair. The overwing, especially a full overwing of a large pattern, may be mounted more securely by placing the wing butts into position and then passing the thread through the butt fibers several times before the thread passes over the entire butt to bind it down. In this method—a method often used for mounting dense hair clumps—the thick overwing is divided into tight, separate bundles. If the thread merely overwraps the butt, the center hairs may pull loose.

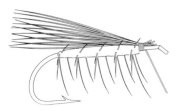

4. Add a full-hackle collar and whip-finish the head.

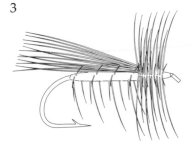

THE BURIED PALMER METHOD

The weakest part of the traditional Bucktail Caddis may well be the palmered hackle. Trout teeth often rip through the stem, allowing the hackle to unwind. To prevent this, the hackle and the body strand may be twisted together. The barbs will then grow randomly from the body, and the hackle stem will be buried. Woolly worms often incorporate this method. The softer the body material, such as chenille or dubbed strands, the deeper the stems. Hard, twisted yarn may expose the stem intermittently along the completed body.

1. Mount the body strip and hackle in the usual manner. Before combining and spinning the body and hackle, lay the hackle along the hook shank and wrap the body strand over the hackle mount point. This first, hackleless, body wrap produces a neat butt by avoiding splayed barbs.

2. The hackle and chenille are then combined and tightly spun as a single "strand."

3. Next, the combined "hackled" body is wrapped forward. To prevent trapping them beneath the ensuing wraps, stroke the barbs back (that is, to the left) while wrapping the hackled strand. Upon completion, the buried palmer body is whip-finished and trimmed.

THE DAMSELFLY NYMPH

Dave Whitlock's *Guide to Aquatic Trout Foods* (1982) taught this tyer the imitative value of Swiss straw. Wet Swiss straw has a spongy, almost gelatinous texture, similar to the natural nymph. The damsel's gills (the caudal lamellae or feathery paddles at the rear of the body) are well developed and appear as an extension of the body and should be part of any pattern. These nymphs swim by whipping body undulations with the gills functioning as sculling oars. No pattern can match the rippling writhes of the natural, but with a rhythmic retrieve the following pattern travels with a trouting tease. Damselfly nymphs vary in color, but they usually reflect their habitat: olives, browns, tans, and pale yellows. The high visibility of pale yellow, the color of this pattern, appears to attract lake trout from a distance.

The pattern is a "mild" variation of the Whitlock damsel nymph. The primary difference is the use of zonker sections for the tail and legs, instead of the ostrich-herl tail and hackle legs. Do not overdress this slender and sparse pattern. Remember, this nymph pattern should "swim" on the retrieve so that every rod twitch transfers into a wave of the "banner" tail. The shape and weight of the Partridge Limerick hook (sizes 6 and 8) is recommended.

Hook:	Partridge Limerick hook (code J1A), or Mustad Sproat 38941
Thread:	Pale yellow to match the body dubbing
Body:	Pale yellow Swiss straw and rabbit fur
Tail:	Pale yellow zonker strip tied in for a banner
Thorax and legs:	Zonker strip with guard hairs
Ribbing:	Medium to fine gold oval ribbing
Eyes:	Pale yellow knotted flock yarn (Vernille)

TYING THE DAMSEL NYMPH

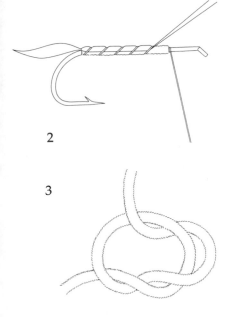

1

2

3

1. Mount some zonker hair for a "banner" tail, add oval gold ribbing, Swiss straw, and dubbing. Color match the Swiss straw, dubbing, flock yarn, and zonker strip.

2. Dub a slender body three-fourths shank length and fold the Swiss straw over the abdomen. Then spiral the oval ribbing forward. The width of the Swiss straw must be trimmed for small patterns. Fold the Swiss straw under to avoid jagged edges. Tie off the ribbing and Swiss straw at the three-fourths shank length. Next, prepare the flock yarn eyes.

3. Tie a double overhand knot in a length of flock yarn and tighten into a ball. Tie another double overhand knot and adjust by sliding the knot into position with a dubbing needle. Depending on the diameter of the hook wire, the eyes should be about two millimeters apart. On small patterns, the eyes may be made with a single overhand knot or may be a knotless lateral loop of flock yarn.

4 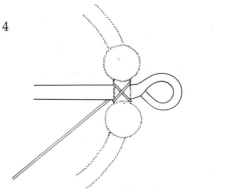 5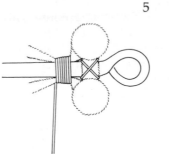

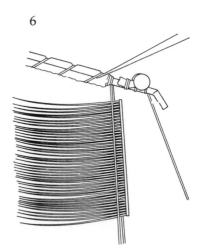

6

4. With a figure eight, mount the eyes directly behind the hook eye. Secure the eyes with several wraps. Pull the tag ends of the flock yarn against the shank and lock with wraps. Trim the excess yarn.

5. After mounting the eyes, add a spinning loop for a zonker section with guard hairs. With the spun-zonker method, spin and wrap the zonker for the thorax and legs. Trim the top of the thorax flat.

6. Fold the Swiss straw over the thorax and in front of the eyes. Lap it with thread and pass the thread behind the eyes. Cover the thread with sparse dubbing and, with the Swiss straw folded back for the wing pad, wrap directly behind the eyes. Now, advance the thread and whip finish. Trim the wing pad to one-half the body length.

THE FUNNELDUN

Neil Patterson, who lives on the Kennet, often views tying from "the other side of the stream." He is a remarkably creative and thoughtful tyer whose patterns are the culmination of original insight and creative simplicity. The funneldun grew out of his frustration in trying to produce the UpSide Down Paradun advocated by John Goddard and Brian Clark's *The Trout and Fly*. The valuable logic and insight expressed by this book finally found its way into Neil Patterson's Inverted Funneldun and Inverted Funneldun Spinner. In the beginning, Patterson found that there were three basic design faults that afflicted the traditional dry fly:

1. The traditional dry fly requires an expensive, hybrid hackle.
2. The traditional dry fly with the hackles mounted at right angles to the shank bears its full weight on the hackle tips, encouraging the tips to penetrate the water surface.
3. The traditional dry fly omits the distinct thorax of the natural.

The traditional dry fly, the Halford dry with the bend and point on the trout side, is a contradiction. On selective trout, the advantage is with the pattern that hides the hook. I can remember fishing a western spring creek one summer afternoon. The water was slow and clear—the trout were eager but selective. My conventional pattern swam through the rings like a feathered curse. Nothing took. As a minor experiment, I broke off the hook heel and point so that only the fly body was left. I cast this to the rings and one after another, trout hit. Surely the dangling hook heel and point was the cause of the original refusal. Although most are taken with dangling heel and spear, trout may, at times, discriminate. There appears then to be a need for an easily tied upside down fly pattern—a pattern that does not require the use of special tools or hooks.

The Funneldun, with its hackles coned over the eye, solves these problems with a simplicity, aptly described by Patterson as *Volkesfliegen*, "flies for the people." These are patterns dressed with a modicum of materials and manipulations. They are less contrived. The Funneldun makes sense in several ways, and it applies modern theories to pattern design. Patterson enumerates the advantages of the Funneldun design:

1. It offers the flattened edge of the hackle barb to the water surface, thereby supporting the pattern weight on a broader base.
2. It employs longer, and less expensive, webbed hackles.
3. It hides the hook beyond the body on the side away from the trout. It floats the fly with the hook curve up.
4. It creates a thorax in front of the wings, where it should be, and seen from all directions.
5. It creates a pattern with one-size-smaller hooks. The hackle barbs are coned forward, thus making it somewhat longer than if tied in the conventional manner. This is advantageous because it means that the hook is smaller and lighter in proportion to the fly size.

TYING THE FUNNELDUN

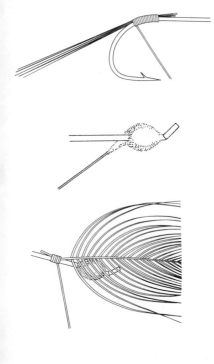

1. Tie in the tails a short distance down the hook bend, and wrap the tying thread forward to the eye. The tail should be tied in slightly down the hook bend, but not so much as to allow the pattern to float on its body. It should float on the tail tips. The distance down the hook heel will depend upon the hook style. The pattern may float parallel with the tail fibers, that is, the barbs lie directly along the water surface.

2. Dub on a fur thorax on the front quarter of the shank. Notice that this is dubbing from the right to the left so that the thread ends on the rear of the thorax.

3. Tie in the long-barbed hackle, dull side forward, about midpoint on the shank and clip excess hackle stem. The webbed base is wrapped over so that the stiff hackle tips reach about where a conventional hackle does. But, in this case, the hackle barbs are angled forward. This throws the fly support over a broader area for greater flotation. Pull the hackle barbs forward over the hook eye. Secure the hackles sloping forward with thread turns behind and over the hackle roots.

Cover the thread turns with a dubbed-fur collar to form the rear thorax. Wind the thread to the rear. Dubbing may be added to form the body.

4. Whip-finish at the tail-mount point. Now cut a small "V," with an approximately forty-five-degree arc, from the top center of the hackle. This will be the underside when the fly is cocked correctly upon the water. Patterson's favorite wing material is gray mallard-breast feather. After the tail is tied in, the thread passes forward to the eye. Hackle fibers with natural tips pointing to the right are laid beneath the shank and wrapped on, leaving space between the last wraps and the eye. The wings are sloped forward slightly and the thoracic ball dubbed in front. Then the thread is returned to the rear of the wings and the hackle is mounted behind the wings and "funneled" as described. More often, the Funneldun is wingless. Instead of wings, Patterson "winds hackles through one another and plays tunes with different color combinations." The "vibration" of interacting colors creates a sense of movement and life.

The pattern, designed according to pendular mechanics, rotates the lowest point, in this case the point where the shank meets the bend, below the points of support, the tail and hackle. The "V'd" section is a "stop" for pattern rotation. Other insect stages can be captured by this design. Patterson believes that "at no other stage is it more critical to have the hook in the air out of sight from the trout than when imitating the spinner, or imago, stage."

To convert a Funneldun into an Inverted Funnelspinner, simply over-hackle with long barbs and add two turns of red or blue hackle through the wings. Both hackles are then "funneled" forward, and the top barbs are barbered down to the shank. The hackles are then in a semicircle. Patterson describes the pattern mechanics: "You now have a spinner that stubbornly holds the hook high in the air and out of the water; the weight of the hook cunningly pressing the wings, thorax and body into the surface film where every good spinner . . . should be."

THE GOLD-RIBBED HARE'S EAR NYMPH

The ubiquitous Gold-Ribbed Hare's Ear nymph evolved from the nymphal pattern based upon the older dry and wet English flies. The origin is lost, but the dry pattern was popularized and preserved by Thomas Christopher Hofland's *British Anglers Manual* (1839), and Frederic M. Halford's *Floating Flies* (1886). Hofland referred to it as the Hare's Ear Dun, which was known in Scotland as the Hare's Lug. The term "lug" is Scottish and Northern England dialect for ear. It is, of course, a much earlier pattern. The nymph pattern was a rather logical outgrowth of the original dun pattern. The dun pattern described by Halford had no hackle; the legs were merely the pricked-out hare fibers. This is usually the same process by which the legs of the nymph are formed. It was more a low-floating dun design than a

pattern. Halford, later in life, discarded the design for more favorable ones.

This was surely one of the first no-hackle patterns—a design popularized later by the Swisher-Richards and Caucci-Nastasi teams. *Western Hatches* (1981) by Hafele and Hughes recommends the Gold-Ribbed Hare's Ear as a suggestive pattern for both the pupal and larval stages of the Hydropsychidae. The weighted larval pattern is tumbled along the bottom of the stream, while the unweighted pupal pattern is teased rhythmically to the surface in imitation of the ascending natural.

The Gold-Ribbed Hare's Ear is surely one of the most effective hatching-nymph patterns ever devised. If tied with a wide body weighted with lead, it imitates some of the *Rhithrogena* nymphs. In fact, the pattern claims a wide imitative palette from scuds and shrimp to the dark olive nymphs, the nascent or natant emergers such as the Heptageniidae, and the emerging caddis with the nymphal shroud still attached.

TYING THE GOLD-RIBBED HARE'S EAR NYMPH

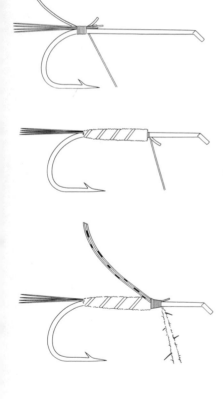

1. On a Mustad 3906 or Partridge Limerick, mount the thread and wrap in a tight bundle of hare guard hairs for the tail fibers. Because of the short length of the guard hairs, the tail may be shorter than the traditional one-half shank length.

2. Add medium-to-small oval gold or flat-tinsel ribbing.

3. With a spinning loop or single strand, dub on the pale hare's fur from the mask. Some tyers prefer the the shaggy results with a mixture of fur, underfur, and guard hair; others like a smoother taper without the guard hairs. Pale hare's fur is often used for the abdomen, and darker hare's fur is used for the thorax. End the body slightly, about one millimeter, beyond mid-shank, and spiral the ribbing forward. Secure the ribbing and trim the excess.

4. Add a section from a mottled oak turkey primary that has been Tuf-filmed. The width of the section should be about twice the body width at the front of the abdomen. The edges of the wing pad will just about extend, when folded halfway down the thorax on each side. Some traditional tyers omit the wing pad. After the wing pad is secure, wrap to the left of the initial wraps so that the thread passes over the body dubbing. This will make a smooth line between the abdomen and thorax when the wing pad is folded forward.

5. Dub the thorax fully but loosely with dark hare's ear mixed with guard hairs. The spikey guard hairs produce a translucent thorax section and form the legs. It may be necessary to tease the thorax with a dubbing needle for fullness. Fold the wing pad forward, whip-finish the head, and trim the excess.

THE HENDRICKSON

The Hendrickson, dated at 1918 by Austin Francis, is one of America's first classic patterns. The original Hendrickson—tied by Roy Steenrod of Liberty, New York, and named after his angling companion Albert Everett Hendrickson of Scarsdale, New York—had a golden-pheasant-tippet tail, wood-duck wings, fawn colored, red-fox belly-fur body, and, according to Roy Steenrod, an "almost transparent or water color" dun hackle. It is of interest that the "Father of American angling," Theodore Gordon, who converted many British wets into American dries, tied flies for A. E. Hendrickson. The Hendrickson, unlike other British "immigrants," would grow out of the search for an American pattern and an American technique. After Gordon's death in 1915, Roy Steenrod, a State Conservation Inspector, tied flies for Hendrickson. It was this angling-tying team that would give birth to the Hendrickson. The Hendrickson pattern imitates the female of the robust *Ephemerella subvaria*, a common spring mayfly of eastern and midwestern waters. Art Flick's Red Quill imitates the male companion of this species. Since that time when Steenrod and Hendrickson were fishing Ferdon's Pool on the lower Beaverkill, deep within the heavy hatches of *E. subvaria*, the pattern has undergone countless material and color changes. The original body, a cream pink fur from the urine-burned belly fur of a red fox vixen, is often replaced with pink-fawn or cream rabbit fur. But within the muted livery of today's Hendrickson is some of the history, if not the origin, of American angling.

THE HENDRICKSON (STANDARD)

Hook: Mustad 94840 or 94842, size 12–14; Partridge Code A, size 12–16
Thread: Waxed tan or pale yellow
Body: Cream fox fur (from the lower belly) or tan, olive, and yellow rabbit-fur mixture
Wings: Wood duck flank-feather fibers, rolled and divided. The mandarin drake flank feather, with its rich brown, is excellent if available.
Tail: Blue dun hackle fibers
Hackle: Blue dun

The hackle tail fibers should equal 2½ times the hook gap or the hook shank length. The wing should be twice the gap or equal to the hook shank. The hackle barb length is 1½ the hook gap or ¾ the hook shank. The head is traditionally equal to the eye length of the particular hook, and the sparse hackling is three turns behind the wings and two in front. Usually the head is not considered when determining shank length. Notice that the tail mount point is directly over the rear extension of the barb. The wing mount point is approximately at the front ⅕ point of the shank.

The Hendrickson, coming as it does from Catskill streams, may be tied according to the "Catskill style": a model perfect hook, a lean spare body, spun fur, divided wood duck wing, sparse wraps of a stiff, glassy blue dun hackle, wing set back from the eye (as much as twice the eye length of the particular hook), and a long, clean head. Harry Darbee describes the style in Francis's *Catskill Rivers*: ". . . the sustaining hackle is so close to the point of balance that the fly rides over broken, turbulent water like a Coast Guard lifeboat, so nearly balanced that often the tail of hackle whisk (originally, a little curlicue of several woodduck barbules) doesn't touch the water at all."

There are many variations on the Hendrickson theme. The female Hendrickson often has a pink fox-fur body. The Light Hendrickson has a cream fox and watery blue dun hackle. Some Hendricksons are dressed in borrowed robes, such as a red-gray or red-brown fur body.

The Hendrickson may be used to imitate several western mayflies, particularly some of the Western *Ephemerella* and *Heptagenia*. It is, in all its muted dress, a perfect pattern for the reluctant rise. Austin M. Francis, in *Catskill Rivers*, claims that Steenrod, the master of the Catskill style, had originated "what today may well be the most popular brown-trout fly in America, the Hendrickson."

TYING THE DRY HENDRICKSON

1. From the same stem level, select barbs from a wood duck flank feather. Each section, which will be rolled, constitutes an individual wing. Bundle and mount the wood duck barbs, with the natural ends aligned and pointing to the right. Wing length equals shank length.

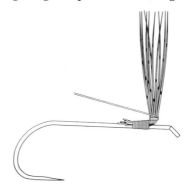

2. Figure eight and post by wrapping around each wing bundle to erect and divide. It may be necessary to "bead" the thread in front for wing erection.

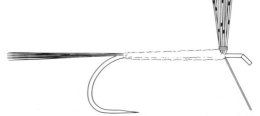

3. Spiral the thread down the shank, directly over the rear extension of the barb. Wrap in several wisps of blue dun barbs for the tail. Add appropriate dubbing and wrap a smooth, slender body. Traditionally, sparse

dubbing was spun in a spinning loop so that the thread color showed through the dubbing. Unfortunately, this interplay between the color of the thread and dubbing is seldom advocated today.

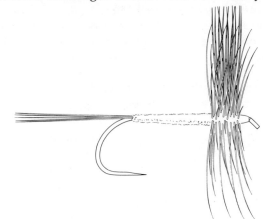

4. Mount the watery blue dun hackle behind the wings and wrap three times before passing the hackle in front of the wings. This will support the soft wing fibers. The Hendrickson dry is usually lightly hackled. Whip-finish to complete the pattern.

THE HUMPY

The Humpy is one of the most effective patterns in the fly wallet. In minuscule it imitates small terrestrials, mayflies, and caddis; larger sizes match caddis, stoneflies, and grasshoppers, as well as a hoard of other insects. The origin of the Humpy, sometimes called "Goofus," has been ascribed to several people and several protopatterns. However, in a discussion of origins, the argument usually leads to a tyer from San Francisco. The late Jack Horner, a member of the Golden Gate Angling and Casting Club, tied the Horner's Deer Fly, which had a folded-deer-hair body ribbed with thread while the natural tips of the hair formed the wings. As a master of deer hair, Horner also had created a popular deer-hair shrimp pattern about 1938. The term "Humpy," which comes from the pattern's distinctly humped body, may have originated near Jackson Hole, Wyoming, according to Jack Dennis. The term Goofus, popularized by Dan Bailey of Montana, often refers to a Humpy with mixed brown and grizzly hackles. However, Humpy and Goofus are usually used synonymously. Humpy variations are legion. It has appeared with various dyed hairs, hackle combinations, and underbelly colors. There is even a Royal Humpy that sports a red belly and white calf-tail wings.

In any case, the best qualities of the Humpy are its buoyancy and imitative capacity. Although typical Humpy water is quick and heavy, the pattern is realistic enough for slow streams and still waters. Perhaps, as Westerners say, the Humpy is effective because it imitates anything that the trout wants it to imitate. This popular pattern can constitute over thirty-percent of the total patterns sold during a season. A western angler who has not cast a Humpy is usually an angler without experience.

The Humpy is usually tied in hook sizes 10 to 18. Mustad hooks, especially 7957B and 94840, and Partridge's wide-gaped Captain Hamilton hooks are suitable for the standard and heavy-hackled Humpy. Many tyers prefer a "flat," multistrand thread, such as Thompson's Monobond, that will not cut the soft deer fibers. Monobond also has excellent elasticity for material binding. Dark mule deer, pale whitetail, and cream elk hair give a natural variety of body colors. Although various materials may be used for the tail, especially hackle barbs and deer hair, some tyers prefer straight, stiff moose body hair. The underbelly, which covers the underbody, can be floss, thread, or dubbing in various colors; perhaps the most common color is pale yellow.

The Humpy presents interesting tying problems in proportions and material manipulation. If the Humpy proportions are wrong, the pattern appears most awkward. Even a small error in proportion distorts its demeanor. A few tying methods make this durable pattern easier to tie.

Proportions. The deer-body-fiber length must account for the underbody, overbody, and wings. Having long, soft fibers for tying makes this pattern much easier to tie. The number of body fibers will determine, to some extent, the body length. And the more body fibers that are used, the wider the body bends will be; hence, more length will be required for those bends at the rear and the wing base. Fewer fibers, of course, bend more abruptly. The deer-hair length will constitute the underbody, the overbody, and the wings; therefore, correct length is critical.

Material Manipulation. The final problem is the separation of the body fibers from the tail fibers. This is especially critical if a dubbed or floss underbelly is added. Sometimes, especially in the smaller sizes, the underbelly is merely the thread itself. The length and manipulation of the overbody solves this problem.

TYING THE HUMPY

1. Using a hair stacker, align the natural tips of several moose body fibers. A size 10 hook will require about eight to ten moose fibers for the tail; a smaller hook would require fewer fibers. These fibers are small in diameter and remarkably stiff; they make excellent tails for hairwing patterns. Remove any underfur that adheres to the fiber base. Measure the tail fibers according to the shank length (which is the "known length") and firmly wrap the tail fibers on the shank immediately above the point. Some tyers advocate that the tail mount occupy half the shank length. This increases the diameter of the "humped" body. More delicate bodies are created by decreasing the number of fibers and the mounting space. The final wraps around the tail directly above the rear barb point should be "slack wrapped" to prevent any tail flare. The tail mount area will be about one-third to one-half the shank length. After mounting the tail, wrap the thread to midshank. The illustration shows the tail butts mounted directly above the rear of the barb.

1

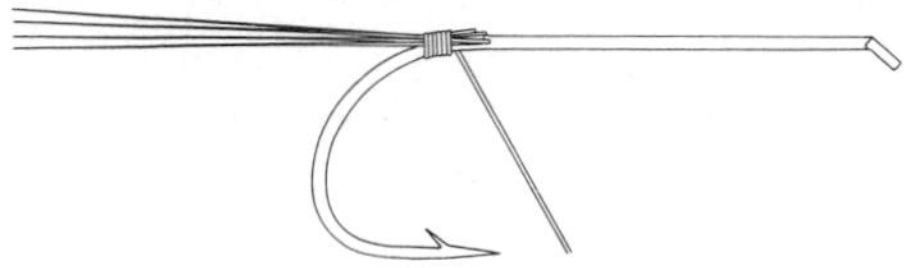

2. Next, take a bundle of deer body hair and remove the short fibers and underfur by hand and stack to even the natural tips. A size 10 hook will require about sixty deer-hair fibers with a bundle diameter approximately three millimeters without compression. Fewer fibers would be required for smaller hooks. Note also that the softer the fibers, the larger the fiber bundle. But like most tying, the tyer should strive for a delicate body— undertie rather than overtie. The length of the fibers should be long enough for easy handling. Body-hair length should be about two inches long. Anything under an inch and a half begins to make difficult handling. Measure the length of the deer-hair bundle from the head of the pattern to the tail tip; this is the correct length, assuming a standard hook and correct tail length, for the Humpy. This method of proportioning is presented by Kathy Buchner in Robert Boyle and Dave Whitlock's *The Fly-Tyer's Almanac* (1978). She emphasizes that "The key to the whole thing is the length of the tail. If the tail is the right length, everything else will come out right." She also mounts the tail butts at midshank so that they form a foundation for the underbody. A Kathy Buchner Humpy is harmony. The second illustration shows the correct length of the body bundle during mounting. The body butts mount firmly at midshank; do not allow the material to twist during wrapping. To avoid fiber twist, use firm wraps and finger pressure on the body bundle. Furthermore, it is important to keep the tail fibers from mixing with the body fibers. To accomplish this, hold the body bundle slightly above the tail fibers throughout the tying process. A little practice makes this natural.

2

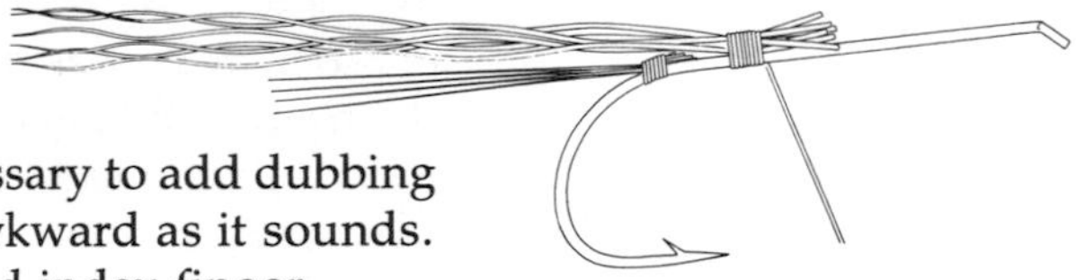

3. If a dubbed underbelly is required, it is then necessary to add dubbing with the right hand only. Such a method is not as awkward as it sounds. Twist the dubbing on firmly with the right thumb and index finger.

4. Dub the underbody forward, slightly beyond the mounted overbody, and tie off.

3

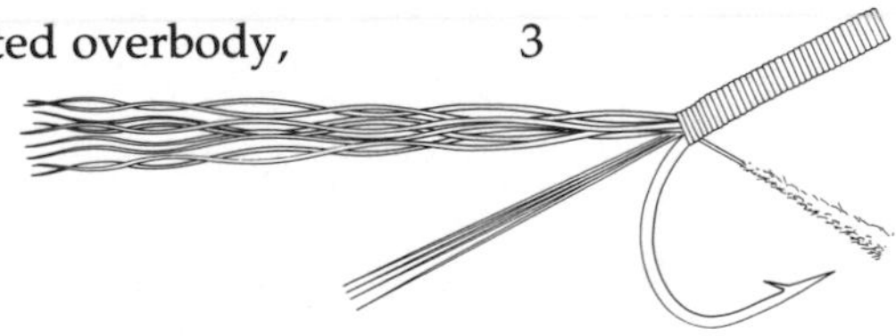

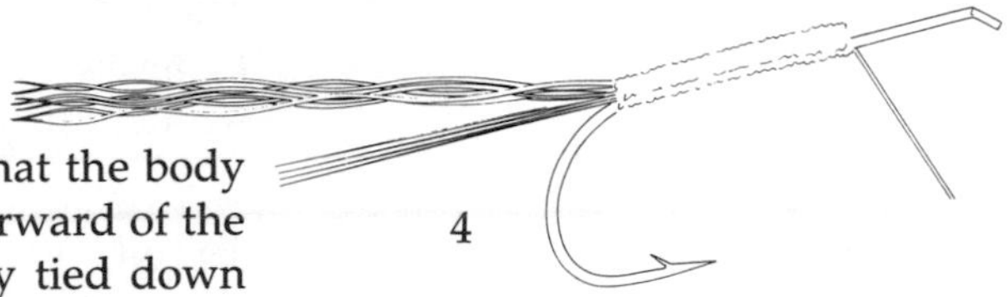

5. Next, firmly fold the overbody forward making certain that the body fibers are tight. Wrap the thread over the overbody slightly forward of the underbelly. The forward one-third of the body will be firmly tied down except for the wings. This firmly wrapped "platform," as Kathy Buchner calls it, forms the foundation for the hackle. Be certain to leave adequate space for hackle and head.

4

5

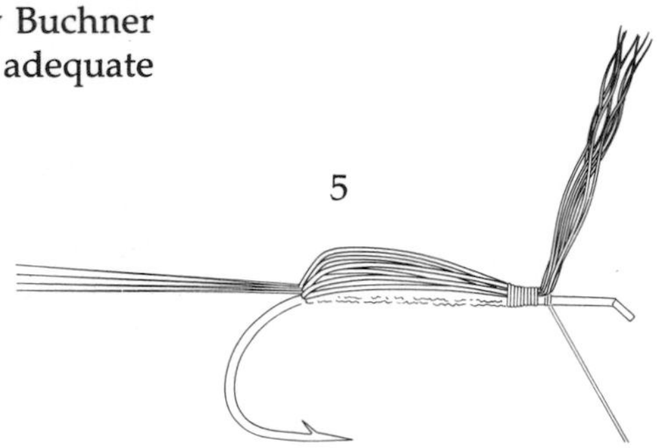

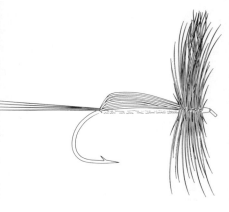

6. The wings are wrapped behind and beaded in front to make them erect. Divide the wings with a figure eight and post (several wraps around the wing base to gather or "bundle" the fibers) and, if necessary, cross anchor the thread to erect each wing. The hackles, a grizzly and a brown combination, are usually side mounted, but not against the wing, and wrapped with their dull sides toward the eye. Often two hackle pairs are wound on the Western Humpy for the heavy, rushing rivers. Two hackles may be wrapped at one time; however, it is most difficult to maintain tension on three hackles at the same time. When three are mounted, it is best to wrap two and then overwrap the third. The hackles fill up the entire thoracic area, which may be about one-third to one-half the shank length, and pass in front of the wings for the finishing wraps. The wings should appear to emerge from the center of the hackles. The illustration shows the completed Humpy with traditional dress and dubbed underbody. In a well-wrought Humpy the proportions are studied and exact.

The Humpy, with its full mottled hackle and neat overbody, is a westerner ready for the tumbling drive of swift currents. Or, in more delicate sizes, it is a ruffled caddis drifting like cottonwood "down" through trout rings. The Humpy is truly a fly for all seasons. My first encounter with the Humpy was many years ago on the Yellowstone River above Le Hardy Rapids. It was a million miles back in time and mind. My Humpy rode a swirling riffle into a cluster of trout rings until it disappeared in a slashing rise. The rod bent against the surging weight. Then it relaxed with a limp, dead line. The trout had broken off. A new Humpy and several casts later, another trout was on, surfacing and bucking against a reining line. Soon the trout came tame to the touch. It was a tawny cutthroat trout spattered with dots along the flank, and with the bright red-orange strip beneath the ruby gill plates. Like the Humpy in its jaw, it was a native of the American West.

LUMINI PATTERNS

Piero Lumini's stonefly and *Chironomid* patterns, presented in his *Dizionario delle Mosche Artificiali* (1984), contain tying simplicity and unique materials. The Italian "sliver" biots or *ali in quills* form the stonefly wings. And the *Chironomid* pattern employs the cul de canard feathers, the oil-gland "brush" feathers that require no floatant.

TYING THE LUMINI STONEFLY

1. On a standard-shank hook, such as Mustad 94831 or Partridge code E1A, dub a polypropylene body two-thirds the shank length.
2. Mount matched strips of "quill wings," the Italian *ali in quill*. Although matched turkey feather sections may be used, the thin, transparent *ali in quills* are flexible and realistic. Two pairs may be mounted for greater strength. To maintain flat wings, the wing mount point must be directly on top of the dubbed body. Slightly divide the wings over the shank and trim the ends as illustrated.

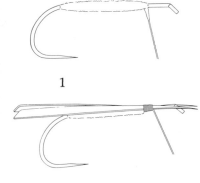

1

2

3. At least ten pheasant tail fibers and a dry hackle, especially brown or cree, are added for the thoracic segment. Piero Lumini leaves two naturally tapered pheasant-tail barbs for the antennae. This can only be done if the correct antennae length is established during mounting. Because the typical stonefly has insignificant antennae, they may be omitted. In small and medium patterns, the downwing and extended antennae copy the caddisfly as well.

4. The hackle is then wrapped forward with the concave or dull side toward the eye and secured. Clip excess hackle. Trim or flatten the dorsal hackle barbs.

5. Next, the thoracic case folds forward and the head wraps complete the pattern. If the antennae are desired, shear all except two matched pheasant-tail barbs.

TYING THE LUMINI *CHIRONOMID*

1. The Lumini *Chironomid* is a small emerger-midge pattern. Because it employs the unique cul de canard feathers, no floatant is required. The natural feathers, which have been permanently impregnated by the oil duct, float the pattern. On a Mustad 94840 or Partridge L4A, sizes 14 through 18, mount a stripped peacock herl, one with contrasting edge color, and lay down a tapered thread underbody. Fine-wire "sloped" hooks, such as the Partridge shrimp hook or the Tiemco nymph hook, are excellent for this floating pupa. Next, spiral the stripped herl forward to two-thirds the shank length. The thread underbody gives form to the pattern.

2. Dub a small thoracic segment with seal fur or polypropylene dubbing.

3. Add a bundle of cul de canard fibers and trim to approximately half the shank length. The unique water-resistant fibers will support a midge-range pattern without any floatant.

4. Whip the head and the pattern is complete.

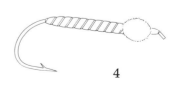

THE MICROCADDIS

The following pattern, designed for hook sizes 16 through 20, is simple and effective for the downwing microcaddis and midges. The tying sequence illustrates the parachute pattern; however, standard hackling, wound at a right angle to the shank axis, serves well, especially when sparsely wrapped. The overwing material—barbs from pheasant tail, wood duck, partridge, or various hackles—should equal 1½ the shank length so that the hook heel is hidden beneath the overwing. Synthetic overwings also may be used. The body can be dubbing or merely the tying thread. Tied on midge hooks, the pattern requires only meager materials and methods. Ernest Schwiebert's *Nymphs* (1973) includes a brief chapter on matching the pupae of the diminutive caddis: the Philopotamidae and the Hydroptilidae. Some of these microcaddis are smaller than a size 20 hook. Only scant attention has been granted the microcaddis, perhaps because of the assumption that all micropatterns are generic. Fishing the micropatterns has been considered either the inner sanctum of angling or trouting affectation. The folded overwing method appears in John Betts's *Flies with an "Edited Hackle"* (1982); however, the microcaddis uses the overwing base as a parachute hackle post. Betts's modest book has several unique methods for tying micropatterns.

TYING THE MICROCADDIS

1. First, measure and wrap in a bundle of barbs one eye-length behind the hook eye. On hooks smaller than 16, it may be easier to wrap the abdomen prior to mounting the overwing.

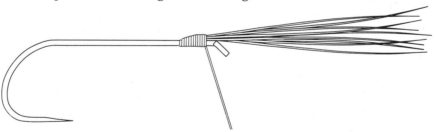

2. Then mount a hackle at the overwing base.

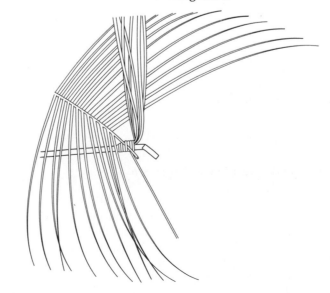

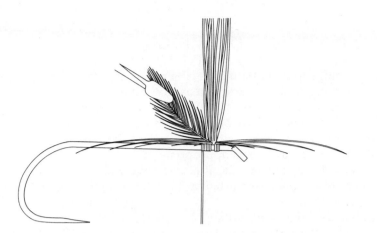

3. Firmly wrap the hackle around the base. With soft barbs, it may be necessary to tether the overwing with gallows while hackling. Only two or three hackle turns are necessary. Secure the hackle immediately behind the overwing base. Trim excess and dub or thread wrap a slender body.

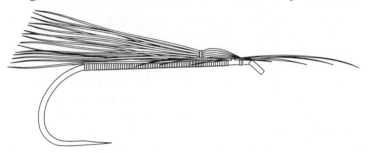

4. After completing the body, bring the thread forward to the thoracic position, approximately one-fourth the shank length from the eye. Pull the hackle barbs forward so they are not trapped under the overwing. Now, fold the overwing down and wrap two or three times over it. For greater pattern strength, whip-finish on the shank.

A microcaddis with dubbed body and dubbed thoracic thread.

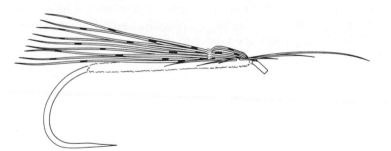

Top view showing pattern design.

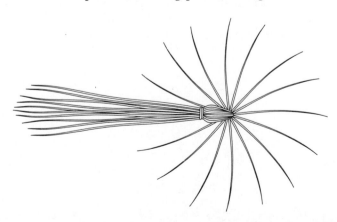

THE MIDGE

Fishing the midge in sizes 18 to 26 is either angling affectation or supreme sport. For stalking selective spring-creek trout, it is surely a supreme sport. It requires "far and fine" fishing and, sometimes, close and fine tying. Perhaps the pattern is effective because of the silhouette and hidden hook, or perhaps the minute midge, sometimes called the gnat, merely beguiles the trout. With fine thread and appropriate materials, the midge is a compliant pattern. Even into size 26, it is a relatively simple tie. The hackle, either gray or black, matches the body. It is interesting that Alfred Ronalds, in *The Fly-Fisher's Entomology*, writes of hackling the Black Gnat "with a light dun hackle tinged with brown" to make it "buzz." Theoretically, the sparse, light-shattering dun hackle gives the impression that the insect is buzzing on the surface. Various wing materials may be used, including Antron yarn. If Antron is used, it should be flattened into a fine veil over the back to imitate the glassy gossamer wings of the midge. Complete tying directions follow.

Another wing and body variation comes from Taff Price and the Jura region of Switzerland where anglers have used the moustique patterns for over one hundred years. The moustique flies use the cul de canard, the havana-colored preen feathers, for wings. Marjan Fratnik, an expatriated Slovian living in Milan, created a more durable moustique pattern. This pattern, popular in Germany, Austria, Switzerland, Italy, and Yugoslavia, is nearly unsinkable. Fratnik's pattern incorporates a thread or heron-barb body, and cul de canard overwings. Dyed pheasant-tail barbs should be used instead of the protected heron. Because the Fratnik Midge is simplicity personified, only a single drawing is included.

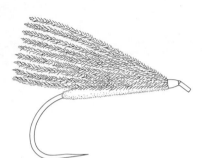

Fratnik Midge.

TYING THE MIDGE

1. On a Partridge sneck or wide gap, mount a white, Tuffilmed, duck-quill section.

2. Tie in the tip of a primary feather (gray or black, crow or goose) and, after wrapping a thread underbody, spiral the barb forward. The barb body should "fuzz" when wrapped. Secure the body and trim the excess.

3. Next, fold the quill wing over the top of the pattern so that the hook heel is completely covered. Fold the wing against a dubbing needle if a straight fold is desired.

4. Add a dry gray or black hackle, concave side forward, and hackle the pattern. After sparse hackling, secure the hackle and whip-finish the head.

Bottom view of the midge showing the concealed hook and tapered wings.

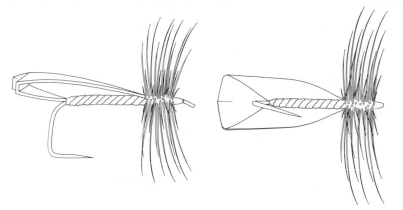

THE PHEASANT TAIL NYMPH

Originally developed for upstream dead-drift nymphing in the chalk-streams of southern England, Frank Sawyer's Pheasant Tail Nymph was designed to imitate the swimming olive mayfly nymph. It has become, within a quarter of a century, a small classic. The pattern, a weighted nymph, is tied with a fine reddish brown transformer wire. No tying thread is used. The spartan silhouette with the feathered tails and spindled body effectively imitates the *Baetis* and other small mayfly nymphs. The pattern is tied so that the strands of the pheasant-tail fibers constitute the tail, the body, and the oval thorax. The reddish brown body, when wet, closely matches the deep browns of some *Baetis* nymphs.

A Pheasant Tail Nymph tied with dyed olive-brown fibers would be a remarkable match for our stream and pond olives. Yet the pattern's original natural color remains productive. Sawyer felt that the color of the imitation was more effective than a dyed color: "The red of the pheasant tail body and wire tying that I use could not possibly be mistaken by us for an olive, or greenish yellow coloring. Yet fish take it readily when creatures with this latter coloring are hatching. It is not an exact copy of coloring, as we know it, but fish are deceived by it." The dressing presented here is from Frank Sawyer's *Nymphs and the Trout* (second American edition, 1973). Sawyer's unique tying method uses the fine reddish brown transformer wire with a .005-inch diameter instead of thread. Larger wire should not be used for patterns sized 16 and smaller. The original pattern, which imitated the smaller nymphs, is tied on hooks ranging from 14 to 16.

In Sawyer's nymphing technique, which he described as "the induced take method," the pattern is "pitched" upstream of a trout. After the nymph has sunk slightly below and in front of the trout, the rod is raised so that the ascending nymph passes before the nymphing trout. Such an action may "induce" a trout to take. This technique, and especially one in which the ascending nymph is twitched, simulates the *Baetis's* unique darting swim. The natural nymph's darting action results from the rapid flicking of the strong body and filamentous tails. Sometimes Sawyer would anoint the tippet and nymph with trout body slime to increase the sink and taste.

TYING THE PHEASANT TAIL NYMPH

1. After covering the hook with a few binding wraps of the fine wire, build the oval thorax on the front third of the shank. When the thorax is completed, wrap the wire to the rear. Do not overdress the nymph with excessive wraps of ballast. Unlike tying thread, the wire holds without constant finger tension.

2. Take four pheasant-tail fibers (barbs) and wrap in at the rear of the hook so that they extend about one-eighth inch beyond the hook bend. The natural barb tips will form the tails of the nymph. Next, spin the four fibers of the pheasant tail onto the wire so that they are reinforced.

3. Next, wrap the body firmly and evenly to the hook eye. Some tyers wrap the wire forward and then overwrap it with pheasant fibers. However, the spinning combines the colors and improves the body strength. Now, at the head, separate the fibers from the wire and wrap the wire back to the immediate rear of the thorax.

4. Bend the fibers back over the top and sides of the thorax and lap the wire, as illustrated, over the fibers.

5. Finally, wrap the wire to the eye position. Bend the fibers forward and wrap off the pattern with six turns of wire and cut the excess.

The result is a spindle-shaped pattern with a pronounced thoracic hump. The black pheasant-fiber base creates the dark wing pads typical of the nymph. Note that the correct length of fibers is critical so that the dark base becomes the wing pad. When wet, a reddish brown cast can be seen through the fibers. In still and slow waters, the pattern has good water entry and sinks to the required depth before line pull levels it off to address the trout. The hook point is not "muffled" by the dressing or hackles. Only light pressure is required to home the point during a take. The pattern is legless because the swimming nymphs relax their legs beneath them to achieve their torpedo taper.

THE REED SMUT LARVA

The smut, or black fly, larva (family Simuliidae) is about six millimeters long, approximately the shank length of a size 18 hook. Some are three millimeters and a rare few are over twelve millimeters long. The naturals attach themselves to rocks and vegetation by a posterior ring of hooks and prolegs, and travel by "rappelling" downstream on silk "ropes." An upstream presentation of a drifting, sunken smut on a delicate tippet imitates this act. Although patterns are not common, the insects are. Their slipper-shaped cocoons can carpet some river beds. The larval imitations, like the naturals, are cream, olive, gray, and black, with a cylindrical body and a swelled posterior. Any smut pattern should have enough weight for fast-water entry, yet be light enough for natural current drift. Wide-gaped hooks or curved hooks are required because the swelled body eliminates some gap. An excellent Spanish pattern has a thread body that is lacquered and a tuft of dubbing for the head. It drifts on a light tippet just beneath the surface. The following pattern incorporates fine plastic strips less than one millimeter in width. However, a variety of materials may be used for the body, including thread or fine flashabou strands.

TYING THE REED SMUT

1. On a size 18 to 22 Partridge E6A or VMC 9288 hook (both are short shanked and wide gaped), mount a plastic strip and build a tapered thread underbody. Wrap the stripping firmly forward and secure. Trim the excess.

2. Add two flue tips, or cul de canard tips, and dub a small thorax. Whip-finish to complete the pattern.

THE SOFT-HACKLED FLY

The soft-hackled fly, according to Sylvester Nemes, is the essence latent in all insects: it is a nymph, a larva, an emerger, a dun, and a dry. It is all, yet it is none. It is a pattern without a top or bottom, and a pattern without an insect. It is none because it is all. The beauty of the soft-hackled fly lies in its richness: the finely spattered barbs and the slender, Spartan proportions. In *The Soft-Hackled Fly*, Nemes describes how the soft barbs bring vitality to the pattern: "As the fly floats downstream, these barbs close in and out, squirm against the body of the fly, and react in a lifelike way to every little kind of pressure." The soft hackle, pushed away from the body by the swelled thorax, crawls and writhes with sinuous undulations. And, according to Nemes, its nobility goes back to the Donne fly recorded in the *Treatise* in 1496. First-time tyers find a complex simplicity in the soft-hackled fly. It requires the proper preparation of materials, a concern for proportions and the creation of slender bodies. Floss as well as dubbed body should barely cover the shank. And the thorax bud must lift and spread the hackle barbs. The particular pattern presented here is a thoracic variation of the Orange Partridge that appeared in T. E. Pritt's *Yorkshire Trout Flies* (1885). Although body and hackle colors change, the tying technique is similar for all ribbed and thoraxed soft-hackled patterns. Body hackles from various birds may be used—especially quail, grouse, pheasant, and the inexpensive hen back.

TYING THE SOFT-HACKLED PARTRIDGE AND ORANGE

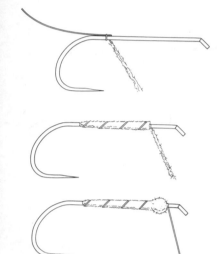

1. The Partridge and Orange may be fashioned from orange silk floss, black and brown hare's ear, and brown English partridge, as Nemes recommends. However, I prefer a Partridge J1A wet-fly Limerick hook, burnt orange rabbit dubbing for the body, hare's face for the thorax, and matching burnt orange thread. On hooks under size 14, tying thread, especially Pearsall's silk tying thread, makes an excellent body. Depending on the hook size, mount either gold wire or oval gold ribbing directly above the hook point. The naked heel and shank lend a delicate swirl to the finished pattern. Add the fine body dubbing.

2. Wrap a tight, tapered body forward two-thirds the distance to the eye. Then, spiral the ribbing forward and wrap off. Trim the excess ribbing and add the spikey hare's face dubbing.

3. Wrap a thorax, twice the diameter of the abdomen. The thoracic ball should extend to the hackle mount point, approximately twice the eye length along the shank. Nemes recommends that the fur thorax be no longer than one-eighth inch wide on a size 10 hook.

4. There are several methods used to prepare and mount the soft body hackle. To allow the body dubbing to show through between the barbs, only a few hackle wraps are used. The most difficult part of tying is wrapping the fragile hackle on; it requires good hackle pliers and a light hand. The "half-hackle" method allows each barb to arch over the body and work with the current. There should be no maverick barbs that fold back on themselves. Place the body-feather hackle on the tying table, tip toward you, with the convex side up, outside up. Carefully strip the barbs from the right side of the hackle. Anchor the hackle by the tip. Trim the tip back so that the first hackle barb equals the hook shank.

5. Orbit the hackle two to four times, so that the concave side of the barbs envelop the shank. Wrap off the stem and trim the excess hackle. Whip-finish to complete the pattern.

THE SWISHER-RICHARDS NO-HACKLE DUN

In recent decades, tyers have explored the problem of pattern profile; they sought a more realistic insect silhouette on the water. An interesting introduction to pattern profile theory may be found in Swisher and Richards's *Selective Trout*. Other works, such as Brian Clarke and John Goddard's *The Trout and the Fly*, continued the quest with patterns like the USD Paradun and Polyspinner. According to Swisher and Richards's theory, the hackle blurs the meaning of wing and body on smaller patterns. They "advocate no-hackle because the hackle fuzzes up the delicate sail-like outline and tilts the body at an unnatural angle." The acute flotation angle and the clean wing profile without the obscuring hackle produce a more imitative prey image for the trout. Such patterns, at times, can be remarkably effective; however, the simplicity and tying speed of the pattern are countered with other cares:

1. Precise proportions must be adhered to for correct cocking and flotation.
2. Wings must be mounted with care to prevent tippet twist during the cast.
3. Wings should be mounted so that the lower wing edges flare as outriggers.
4. The selection of materials is critical; light-wire hooks, matched wings, and fine dubbing blends, such as poly-beaver, should be used.
5. Dub firm and delicate bodies for buoyancy.

TYING THE NO-HACKLE DUN

1. At the tail mount point, wrap in a tightly dubbed ball.

2. Tie in the tail fibers (only one fiber per side for small patterns, two or three fibers for large patterns), and "crimp" them into the fur ball so that the tails splay approximately sixty degrees. The tails should occupy the same horizontal plane as the hook shank.

3. Dub the body forward, and swell it slightly at the wing mount point so that the wings have adequate separation and support.

4. For clarity, only the wings and hook appear in the drawing. Mount the wings, convex sides together, so that they straddle the shank and slant back approximately sixty degrees. Wing length should equal total shank length, including the eye. Bring the thread up between the wings and, with a soft loop, around the far wing and near wing as illustrated. The thumb and forefinger must maintain pressure, yet allow the thread passage. The thread wraps, unlike the illustration, will be close together and vertical.

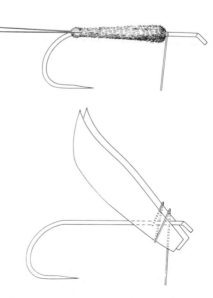

5. Select matched and opposite (each from the opposite second primary feather) dark gray duck-quill slips from wings. For durability, cement the wing base with polyurethane or spray with Tuffilm. Now, with lateral thumb and forefinger pressure on the wings, tighten the thread so that the wing base flares against the dubbing. Slowly tighten the thread and add more wraps to secure the wing base. Finally, trim the wing butts and add thoracic dubbing. Whip the head to complete.

6. The divided wings on the completed pattern may be left natural, as illustrated, or trimmed to a more realistic shape.

7. René Harrop of St. Anthony, Idaho, developed the Swisher-Richards Double-Wing No-Hackle. The durable double wings grant more support and durability to the pattern. For the Double-Wing No-Hackle Dun, Dave Whitlock sprays the wings with Tuffilm and mounts each side pair, a short and a long wing, at the same time.

THE THOMPSON RIVER CADDIS

Some patterns proclaim their heritage. Harry Lemire's Thompson River Caddis is one that does. Its autumnal colors—the bronze and burnt orange, the bands of gray—herald the Northwest fall. With traditional greased line technique, this "damp" pattern swims slowly across the currents. The splayed moose hairs create a surface commotion that contributes to its effectiveness. This "steelhead caddis" imitates the large fall caddis; however, in trout sizes and with dyed grizzly breast feathers, it may also suggest the stonefly and grasshopper. The pattern incorporates the broad-banded grizzly breast feather that is seldom used in tying. Lemire saturates the pattern in Scotchgard after tying and dresses it with silicone before fishing.

TYING THE THOMPSON RIVER CADDIS

1. Mount thin bronze mylar ribbing and burnt orange dry-fly dubbing on a Partridge single Wilson dry-fly hook, or Partridge S. E. B. Steelhead and Salmon, down-eye, wet-fly hook, size 8. Trout sizes may also be used.

2. Dub a full body about three-fourths the shank length, and then wind the ribbing in the opposite direction of the dubbing.

3. Directly on top, mount the underwing, the short hair from the base of a fox squirrel tail, the length of the body.

4. "Tent" the grizzly breast feather overwings against the body and underwing. Wrap the feather butts firmly and clip the excess short to leave a bare shank.

5. On the bare shank, spin fine moose-body fibers, slightly longer than the overwings, for a hair hackle. As no other fibers are added, make certain that an adequate bundle has been spun for the head. Trim the head to taper forward. Clip the top and bottom to "sparse" the fibers and to expose the wings and body.

THE VERMICULAR

This pattern simulates the slender, segmented, wormlike (or vermicular) larva of various aquatic insects: the scavenger beetle larva (Hydrophilidae); the riffle beetle larva (Elmidae); the campodeiform caddis larva (Rhyaco-philidae); the crane fly larva (Tipulidae); the midge larva (Chironomidae) and to a lesser extent, the whirligig beetle larva (Gyrinidae); the predaceous diving beetle larva (Dystiscidae); the alderfly larva (Sialidae); the fishfly larva (Chauliodinae); and the dobson fly larva (Corydalidae). The pronounced overbody suggests the sclerotized body plates; the thread suggests the underbody and sutures. With dyed deer hair and varied thread colors, a host of larval imitations arise. Color and texture of the overbody and thread combine and contrast into a swarm of forms. Certain color combinations suggest themselves—dark green overbody and pale green thread, cream overbody and red thread, and brown overbody and cream thread.

The number of overbody fibers will vary according to their diameter and the hook size; however, a typical size 10 Partridge grub-shrimp hook requires about twenty fibers. The body should be sparse and carried down into the hook heel. Nature abhors a straight line; therefore, the recommended hooks for the larva imitation include the Partridge Yorkshire sedge hook, the Partridge grub-shrimp hook, and the Orvis nymph hook. A thick multistrand thread like Kevlar or Monobond works best. It constructs the body quickly and does not cut the soft deer hair. Pattern durability increases with a coat or two of flexible cement on the overbody. The Vermicular, with dressing, hangs from the surface similar to some naturals. Otherwise, it is cast deep and slowly retrieved.

TYING THE VERMICULAR

1. After mounting the thread, wrap a smoothly tapered thread underbody. The thread color determines the underbody and suture color.

2. Add deer-hair body fibers tip first. It may be necessary to clip the fine solid ends before mounting. The number of fibers depends upon the hook size. Then wrap the thread forward on the underbody to the first suture point.

3. Fold the body firmly over the back and wrap the thread over the body case. Notice that the overbody wraps do not travel forward. Now wrap the thread around the underbody to the next suture point.

4. Continue the overbody wraps and underbody traveling wraps until the body is formed.

5. Add a dry hackle, convex side toward the eye, and finish with a tapered head. Apply a flexible cement to the overbody.

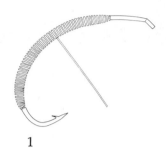

1

2

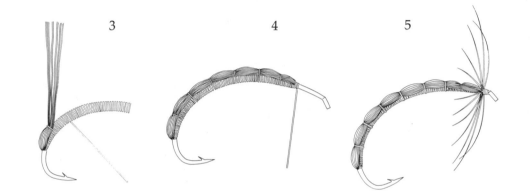

3

4

5

THE WOVEN DRAGONFLY

My first rendezvous with trout and the woven dragonfly nymph still rings and ripples my imagination. I had parked the car and trudged the quarter of a mile to a basin lake hidden in sand and sage. Footprints faded in the soft sand and the dust evaporated in the wind. Evening was coming, but there would be time to cast a few theories upon still waters. A slender dragonfly danced past me with wings that spoke like crackling cellophane. The lake was enameled against the tawny hills and radiating rings spotted the plant beds. Small swallows dipped near the lake on emphatic wings. There was still time before the lake would breathe softly in the darkness. I assembled my rod and tied on a clinger pattern—it was a shallow lake with abundant plant life.

I cast carefully along a moss blanket and worked the nymph with short, staccato strips. Just beyond my cast rings red-winged blackbirds balanced upon slender swishing cattails and interrupted the evening with their crisp ''o-ka-lings.'' But my mind was deep within the lake. In that strange, sunken world, every predator becomes prey for another predator. Using the hand-twist method, I palmed figure eights of line into my left hand and tried to work the nymph through the open troughs between the plant beds. I cast a couple of times. Each time the nymph twitched through a dozen feet of clear water. I watched the cast rings slowly dissolve from my third cast farther along the ledge. Then the tip flicked and the rod bent into muscle. The line cut deeply away. The figure-eights melted in my palm. The reel sang line into the lake. I pressed my palm against the whirring rim. A tender tippet held. I had not set the hook; there was neither time nor need. Taut line fled the reel and the rod lived. A run through a plant ledge picked up a moss pennant: surely the trout would break loose now. After circling in open water, the trout again fled toward the dark moss caves, but the tippet tugged the trout back into the trough. The bent rod and dragging pennant slowly tired the trout. I tried to remember to bring the trout to net—not the net to trout. Yet, I missed with an awkward attempt. Finally, despite my fumbling, there was an enmeshed rainbow, about three pounds, speaking silently before its release to open water. I removed the dragonfly nymph from the pink mouth and watched the scarlet flank melt into a porcelain pool. It may be that only fables catch large trout, but for me, fly and method wove another tale for tomorrow. Darkness pushed the warmth from the land, and nighthawks floated heavily against a falling sun that burnished the water. Now and then a whirring tumble, the mating stoop of a nighthawk, was heard. And the evening, like distant dragons, faded into the dark.

TYING THE WOVEN DRAGONFLY NYMPH

1. This woven nymph mimics the mottled camouflage of the plant-clinging Aeschnidae. And the transluscent fibers of the flock yarn create volume without excessive casting weight. To tie the pattern, the shank of a size 6 hook (Mustad 79580, 3X long) is arched to increase the gap, and the front third is bent down. The pattern may also be woven, as illustrated, on the appropriately sized slope-shanked hook. Seldom does nature work in straight lines. The legs are formed from several strands of pheasant-tail fibers misted with Tuffilm and tied in a simple overhand knot. Overspraying will make the legs too brittle. The extended length of the legs is just to the hook point. Although all insects have six legs, only four are tied in to avoid bulk. This is enough for realism and, if correctly mounted beneath the shank, creates a near weedless hook. The legs should be soft enough to fold beneath the pattern on the retrieve. Mount the legs about one-fourth the shank length from the eye. Wraps may have to be made in front of the legs to place them correctly. Tie in a pair on each side. In the illustration, the off-legs have been omitted for clarity.

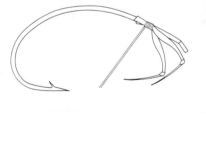

2. The Woven Dragonfly Nymph pattern features the parallel or "shuttle" weave and the corpulent, ovoid body of the natural. After the shank is well threaded, two diamond sections of leather—three-ounce leather approximately six millimeters by twelve millimeters—are wrapped along the rear sides of the shank to create the body shape. The flock yarn, which is remarkably durable, imitates the color and texture of the chitinous plates and junctures along the nymph's back and belly. Some of the better color combinations are olive and insect green, or olive and brown. With a parallel weave, advance the body to the rear of the legs. It is possible to actually weave through the legs so that they appear to grow out of the body. Remember to weave each band slightly over the edge of the previous band for a dense body.

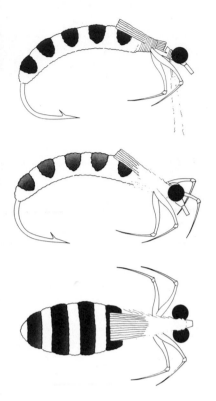

3. Mount a short wing pad—merely a folded gray quill section that has been Tuffilmed—and wrap on two large eyes. Taxidermy bead eyes are excellent; however, flock yarn eyes, made from the dark flock yarn, are simple and soft. Consult the Damselfly nymph directions for making the eyes. After the eyes are mounted, add rabbit dubbing that matches the color of the dark flock yarn.

4. Dub between the eyes and the thoracic area to complete the pattern. Further leg adjustment may be made by dubbing between and around them. To complete the pattern, whip-finish the head.

5. Notice, in this dorsal view, the lozenge shape created by the under-body and weave.

PART SIX

THE
COMPLETE
TYER

CHAPTER 29

The Streamside Tyer

The Itchen at East Lodge is a classic meadow river. Purple comfrey bells hang mutely. Ochre meadowsweet flares along the bank, and sedge heads nod in the warm late-afternoon wind. The river runs flat with sweeping curves troubled only by the purrucking of fretful moorhens and the vacant cooing of wood pigeons. Afternoon shadows press the waters, and trout rise along the dark banks. On one midsummer evening, Blue-Winged Olives, Lunn's Particulars, and Tup's Indispensables hatched at the end of my tippet. And no trout took. Almost imperceptibly, gauze galaxies of black gnats danced with the breeze. But the congregation in my fly box was the wrong denomination: I was gnatless.

The solution was simple. The field kit opened. The vise mounted. A crow strip built a body. A feather folded for a wing, and a dun hackle became legs. Soon, a barbed black gnat rode the currents—currents already robed with naturals—until it disappeared in a dimple. A trout had taken. When trout are "thoughtful" and patterns are critical, then the open-air approach to imitative fly tying may be the simple solution.

There are anglers who reject the concept of field tying. After all, a wanton wind can capture a finely engraved wood duck feather, or sly scissors can hide in a grass grotto. Some tyers believe that accurate imitative tying is best done on a calm evening table. And still others claim that a good tyer, one who has done his fur-and-feather homework, has no need to tie along the waters. Yet even the complete and confident angler seldom carries an imitative arsenal that accounts for every stage of every insect on every water. Nature offers the fly tyer endless variety and variation. Nature is the master tyer. If fly fishing is the craft of deception, then the open-air tyer, the *plein air* tyer, has a place on the bank.

One of the most significant, yet subtle, advantages for the open-air tyer is the birth of the pattern under the same ambient light conditions as the natural insect. The plein air painters of the late nineteenth century knew the advantages of working in natural light. A single color seen under different light conditions may become, in fact, two distinct colors. The texture of an object and its transparency or opaqueness make a dramatic difference in how the eye registers the color. The diffused light of nature allows the complete color to appear. For example, under artificial light, on a highly reflective surface such as the chitinous plates of an insect, we see the color and a reflected highlight. Smooth surfaces reflect light at an acute angle much like the reflected image in a mirror. When the light is totally reflected back at its source, there appears the color white. A single artificial light smudges the true color. Only in natural light is there natural color. And the problem is further complicated with faded specimens. It is established that selective trout can make critical color distinctions. So when the spectral colors of an insect are important to a trout, then field tying during a hush in the hatch may be advantageous.

Another reason for open-air tying is pattern experimentation. Of course, such experimentation is most applicable to slow waters with abundant insect life, complex currents, and selective trout. These conditions require creative pattern changes to challenge difficult trout. At times, the tyer must penetrate the false, masking hatch that the trout are *not* taking in order to determine what they *are* taking. The vagaries of multiple hatches can be the most challenging of trouting conditions. Also, a tyer can determine the dimensions of imitation—what will or will not seduce selective trout. There are times when a rapidly wrapped chimera ends in a heavy net. And field tying offers creative freedom at that moment when it is most productive —on the water with rhythmically rising trout. In addition, the field tyer is most productive during the two problem periods of fly fishing, the emergence and the spinner fall. A deftly dubbed body, a few wisps for bursting wing bulbs, can turn swirls into takes.

The field tyer can also modify existing patterns. The act of creation, even tying itself, has always been either by augmentation or elimination of materials. The tyer can add different dubbing, wings or hackle to create a different stage or insect. Or the tyer can subtract material to find the productive imitation. Within the feathered form of a fully dressed pattern may be an effective nymph. It is merely a matter of sculpting, of subtracting material until you arrive at the form that emphasizes the element that causes trout to take. Streamside sculpturing can create virtually any insect if hook size and color are appropriate. This may be done in several ways:

1. Cutting the wing back at an angle and pricking out dorsal dubbing can turn a dry into an emerger.
2. Cutting the wing back and clipping the dorsal and ventral hackles while leaving a few lateral wisps can create an emerger.
3. Cutting the wings off and clipping the dorsal and ventral hackles parallel turns a dry into a spinner.
4. Cutting the dorsal and ventral hackles and figure-eighting the wings to a down position turns a dry fly into a spent spinner.
5. Clipping the tail fibers off and shortening the wings can turn a dry into a midge pupa.
6. Clipping the ventral hackles often produces a more realistic float angle for duns.
7. Cutting the tail to half its length and clipping all the hackle while leaving a small wing bud turns a dry into a nymph.
8. Trimming a larger pattern can more closely match the precise size of emergers and duns. Even a millimeter or so may make a difference. Sculpting to change wing or body shape may be significant.
9. Carrying a midge bobbin can also be of value. It can be used for tying the wings in a spinner position, or tying the wings back for a stillborn

pattern. It can also, after the wings have been clipped off, anchor the hackles back to enclose the body, thereby creating an ascending nymph or pupa pattern.

10. Clipping some hackles off a fully battle-dressed pattern can create a more delicate and realistic surface impression for wary trout.

11. Pricking out dorsal and ventral dubbing can imitate the nymphal shuck of emergers.

Often a rumpled, well-worn pattern, even for selective trout, works better than a virgin tie. This is one of the mysteries of angling. Most of our private theories are washed downstream as soon as a trout rises when he should not and does not rise when he should. Sometimes within a virgin dry there lives a tantalizing nymph. Table tying is often complex and realistic—the field tyer is taken back to the basics of imitation. He must simplify and substitute. He must modify. Fly tying is a manipulative art, and the field tyer is in the perfect position to take advantage of the creative freshness of open-air tying.

The field tyer is a greater participant in nature. He solves the problems as they hatch. A modern traveling angler can fish three watersheds or more in one day. And any water can quickly change the *carte du jour*. Tying is the central act in a three-act drama—observing, imitating, and trouting. And, although not all trouting strategies require field tying, the advantages are evident. The open-air tyer cannot solve every angling problem—the reticent rise, the difficult drift, and the sporadic hatch—but he is an actor on the stage.

There is a historic precedent for field tying. G. E. M. Skues, the English angler who had a way with nymph patterns, used a small tying vise that was held in his mouth by a horn plate. All tying took place about six inches from his face. As awkward as this sounds, it is an ingenious solution for a field mount. Most modern field vises are either hand-held or mounted into wood. And there are adapters that convert some standard vises, such as the Thompson vise, for field work. There has even been a field vise that mounts to a leg strap so that the angler, when seated, can convert his lap into a tying table. There is also the "Irish vise," merely the thumb and forefinger. Lee Wulff has demonstrated that it is entirely possible to tie patterns even as small as size 28 merely by holding the hook in the hand. However, this does require some skill and is generally not practical for patterns smaller than 14.

The Croyden hand vise, marketed by John Veniard, Limited, of England, has been the standard field vise for years. It is light and compact, essentials for a field vise. Like many such vises, it holds the hook by a screw sleeve. Although the screw sleeve is not designed for commercial tying because it is a relatively slow method, its simplicity makes it appropriate for the field. Diamond tweezers, available from the jewelry trade, have slip sleeves that jam against the jaws. They do make effective vises for micropatterns, size 16 and smaller. Yet, with care, it is possible to tie size 12 patterns with them. And the jaw heads may be unscrewed from the handle to achieve an overall length of three inches. Again, however, the diamond tweezers must be hand held during the tying process.

The majority of field patterns for selective trout will be sizes 14 to 22. And, although most field vises will accommodate extra-long nymph hooks and larger hooks, such as the low-water salmon series, the field need for such hooks is usually limited. My field vise, which has given years of service, is made from tempered stainless steel. It fits, complete with wood-screw mount, in a seven-inch holster. Field mounting such a vise usually requires care. The wood screw must be used only on dead wood—stumps, fallen posts, or logs, and should never be twisted into vital growth. Once the wood screw is mounted, the hook is then clamped in the jaws. Afterward, the vise is connected to the already mounted wood screw. Excessive leverage would occur if the complete unit is screwed into the wood. Remember that only mild pressure is required to produce a stable tying position.

My field-tying kit is made from domestic kid leather, which is scuff resistant and durable. The leather is so constructed as to wrap around a Wheatley fly case, which is devoid of dividers, and fastened with a solid brass harness button. The leather-wrapped case contains twenty or more material packs, which connect by Velcro and may be changed or supplemented. For example, I have several packs that include tying materials for freestone river and lake patterns. The kit is approximately five by five by three inches. For a field kit to be useful, it must be small enough to be carried in the fly vest at all times, perhaps protected by a waterproof bag. A case in hand, rather than in the car or motel, is worth its weight in gold. And with judicious selection, the tools and materials contained in the case can create a remarkable variety of patterns. The Wheatley case contains the tools of the craft:

1. Dorin nippers, light and compact scissors
2. Matarelli midge bobbin
3. Two charged spools, one each of charcoal and cream (for light and dark patterns)
4. Small teardrop hackle pliers
5. Matarelli whip-finisher or a shortened Veniard whip-finisher (both excellent for small patterns)
6. Bobbin threader and cleaner

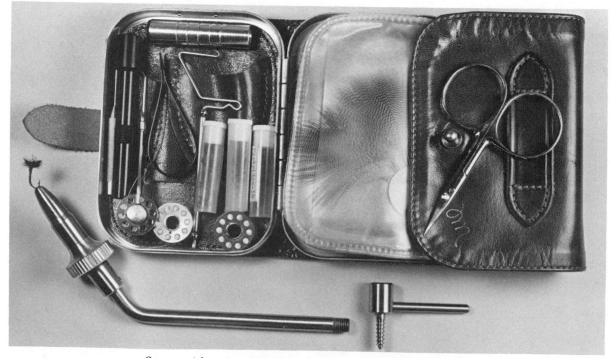

Streamside tying kit with portable vise and field mount.

7. Needle for dubbing and tying the extended-body patterns
8. Half-hitch tool for compressing spun deer hair
9. Hook tubes containing about twenty-five hooks each, sizes 12 to 22; especially recommended are Mustad 3913B and Partridge code B for small-pattern hooks. And add a few specialty hooks for streamers, caddis, and larger patterns. The hook tubes should contain a slip of paper identifying the size, style, and hook maker.

The material contents of a field kit will vary according to the season, the water, the trout, and the angler. An angler's experience and technique may often dictate certain materials and tools. Spring creeks usually demand a different gathering of goods than the round-rock rushing rivers. But remember that the primary difference between a compact field kit and a large table-top tying case is not in the selection of materials, it is in the amount of materials. Only a small amount, perhaps enough for ten patterns, is really necessary. Some materials may be so basic to your tying methods and patterns that more may be required.

A full range of dubbing materials is essential. Dubbing can take the place of chenille, floss, and yarn. It can create bodies for a variety of patterns, and, by blending, it can create any color. A field kit is the tyer's palette from which he blends and combines to create. And the tying tools that accompany the kit should be familiar friends. An open-air tyer does not want to complicate field tying with inferior or unfamiliar tools. Even periodic practice at home with the field kit will make open-air tying easier. A remarkable variety of patterns can be tied from the following materials if imagination is included:

1. Wood duck breast feathers
2. Hackles: grizzly, black, cream, ginger, and brown
3. Yarns: six-inch lengths of natural and synthetic yarns in the basic colors
4. Dubbing materials: natural and synthetics, especially wool, rabbit, hare, mohair, sparkle yarn; Herculon and poly in a range of colors including cream, beige, tobacco, brown, white, yellow, olive, burnt orange, red, wine, pink, green, dark olive, claret, black, and gray
5. Peacock eyes: dyed and wax-dipped in natural, yellow, green, brown, and black. The dyed eyes are merely dipped in hot wax to make them waterproof and resilient. The flue is then easily stripped with the fingernail.
6. Turkey flue (marabou): natural black and white, brown, green, and pale pink
7. Body-hair sections: deer, moose, and caribou
8. Peacock herls: the plump strands near the eye
9. Calf-tail section: white
10. Goose biots: black and brown
11. Floss: six-inch lengths of the basic colors
12. Wing sections: turkey and matched duck primary oversprayed with Grumbacher Tuffilm
13. Grouse and pheasant feathers: assorted
14. Tinsel: fine and medium
15. Chenille: fine and medium strands of black, olive, brown, and green
16. Pheasant-tail section

Not all tyers will agree on the correct collection of materials. And some of the previous materials, such as yarn, floss, and chenille, could be easily omitted. Experience and trout will help determine what should or should not be included. Adhesive disks are excellent for material storage. Merely fold the disks, available from most stationery shops, down the middle and press the adhesive sides around hackle stems and material ends. A complete field kit might also contain various pattern parts ready for mounting. In any case, the following pattern parts have been useful to me for field tying:

1. Leather body sections: trigonal leather sections are cut from heavy leather in various sizes and are wrapped on each side of the shank to build the bodies of dragonfly and damselfly nymphs
2. Burnt or cut wings in various sizes, shapes, and colors for mayfly, midge, and caddis patterns
3. Eyes: burnt and lacquered monofilament eyes for dragonfly, stonefly, and shrimp patterns. Lengths of Vernille may be knotted for eyes.
4. Knotted legs: pheasant-tail wisps tied and Tuffilmed

Field tying does slow down the act of fishing. But it is usually done during slow and difficult conditions so that the total tying time does not interfere with taking trout. In fact, the open-air approach should increase the angler's effectiveness on the water. And certainly, it will make a more observant angler. After all, "there is more to fishing than fishing." Finally, the following suggestions should make the open-air approach easier:

1. Tie with the wind at your back.
2. Take out from the case only the tool or material that you need at the moment, and return any tool or material when not needed.
3. Remember that creative substitution is essential in field tying—simplify the patterns and use materials creatively. This, in itself, can refresh your entire approach to fly tying.

A comprehensive field kit can be a close companion. And, at times, tying along a stream can create significant insight into a trout rise. But not all waters and conditions require the open-air approach. Our attitudes are often expressed by the trouting conditions we seek. When hatches are legion, and perhaps even legend, and when trout rise reluctantly, then the field tyer opens his skill among the mosaic of summer insects. He is with the flirting wagtails, matte gray and chrome yellow against the dark flow. And he is captured by the evening choreography of caddis.

CHAPTER 30

Sans-Vise Tying

Fly tying without a vise has a long tradition. It was especially common where poverty precluded even the modest cost of a vise and where large patterns, especially salmon patterns, were used. In the past, large salmon irons were often wrapped with heavy thread, thickened with adhesive wax. The thread held without tension. Simple patterns could be tied, even on the day's water, with minimal bother. Such tying was often functional, a refreshing contrast to the full battle dress of the Jock Scott, which included round silver tinsel, yellow floss, golden pheasant crest, Indian crow, dyed ostrich, toucan, silver lace, black cock, gallina, bustard, golden pheasant tail, peacock sword, red macaw, dyed swan, mallard, jungle cock, and kingfisher—a complex tie even for a Victorian with a vise. The hand tradition is still maintained, to a modest extent, in Ireland. To this day, neither vise nor hackle pliers are found on the tying tables of Rogan of Donegal. There is only a foot of silk, scissors, and materials. Michael Rogan, dubbed "Lord of the Flies," is a fourth generation tyer who believes that fingers are more sensitive than any steel tool. His salmon flies, once aptly described as "pieces of jewelry," are matched within five minutes by his size 16 Iron Blue Dun.

Although the vise is not required in some patterns, it may be absolutely indispensable in more difficult tying procedures. But tying sans vise does have its own strengths. A finger vise is infinitely adjustable. The pattern may be turned in almost any angle for mounting materials or examination. Lee Wulff points out that two hands can move together while the body moves, but it is very difficult for them to move in conjunction with an object not held in the hands. This offers a freedom not usually granted in tying. The skills acquired in viseless tying can be used to modify existing patterns; the wings of a dun may be tied down to imitate a natal or stillborn stage. A hackle may be figure eighted to create a spinner.

I am not advocating tying without a vise, but I do advocate viseless tying as a means to discovery. Practice gained from viseless tying may be applicable to vise work. It gives the tyer a new sense of materials and methods in a different dimension. And it does require some rethinking of methods. Tying sans vise is not as difficult as one might expect. After watching some accomplished hand tyers ply their tactics, and after modest practice, tying with the fingers is achievable. It offers problems, yet it also offers original solutions. And originality may be described as giving freshness to what is. Some patterns and sizes are readymade for hand tying; others, because of the small hook size or complex methods, demand a fixed vise and special tools.

There are different ways by which viseless tying may be accomplished. The two methods presented here may be seen as somewhat typical. Halford, in *Floating Flies and How to Dress Them*, remarks that "No one, amateur or professional, after once experiencing the advantages of having the hook rigidly held by a process which leaves the hands free, would ever revert to the old and uncomfortable plan of holding the bend of the hook between the thumb and forefinger of the left hand throughout the operation of tying." Yet it is a rather simple matter to finger-tie patterns with a hook size of 14 and larger.

There are hand vises that allow further freedom. With a hand vise and hanging bobbin most difficulties are erased. The advantage of a hand-held vise is that it allows the tyer to keep his hand well back from the hook bend and to use some of the vise fingers for holding materials. The complete length of a hand vise is about six inches. Tying history has seen thumb vises, mouth vises, and leg vises. *The Hardy's Anglers' Guide* of 1909 illustrates a small vise with thumb clip and table screw. But in true sans-vise tying, the fingers are the vise.

Lee Wulff of America and Donald Downs of England have quietly encouraged the art of hand tying. Although the methods are different, both may be considered as standard.

THE WULFF METHOD: THE HAIRWING PATTERN

Lee Wulff, while flying over Newfoundland in a small Air Force plane during the Second World War, perfected his hand tying of salmon patterns for General Hap Arnold, who would cast them into the cold drifts for salmon. The following modified Wulff method can create a variety of patterns, depending upon the type, color, and size of materials.

1. While holding the hook eye between the nail of the left thumb and the forefinger, mount a sufficient length of thread. Anchor the tag end of the thread in the fold at the base of the small finger and clamp it by folding over the fingers that are not holding the hook. This will maintain the thread tension when mounting the thread to the shank. For most patterns with a tail, body, hackle, and wings, gripping the hook eye frees the entire shank length for material mounting. According to Wulff, holding a hook by the heel, the low half of the hook bend, makes the finishing wraps more difficult and less neat. For wrapping strength, the tie-off point should be close to the left thumb and forefinger. A few patterns, such as Bivisibles and spiders, are held by the heel and tied off at the hook bend.

2. After wrapping a number of turns on the shank for a base, the tail is wrapped on. Mount the tail along the shank and cement to prevent twist. I find that if the wings are added now, the wing base will be covered by the body, producing a neater tie; Wulff, however, often adds the body before the wings.

3. The wing fibers or feathers are laid into position and held there with a pinch of the thumb and forefinger while they are wrapped. Wet-fly wings are done one at a time, and dry-fly wings are mounted as a unit.

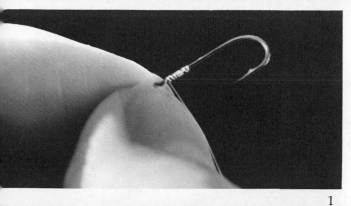

1

2

3

4

5

6

4. The wings are then made vertical by a thread buttress in front. Split and figure eight the wings in position. Cement the wing base.

5. Next, the body, tapered from the tail to the wing, is added. The body usually consists of yarn or dubbing. Half hitches are added if the pattern needs to be laid down. Partly finished patterns may be held in the lips to prevent unraveling without half-hitching. Such a practice, however, is not recommended by Lee Wulff because of possible disease transmission. Remember that during the actual tying process, thread tension is maintained by the fingers not holding the hook.

6. Place two hackles in front with their stripped butts between the erected wings, and secure. Until now there has been freedom in holding the fly. But once the hackles are added, Wulff limits the grip to the hook eye. Now, the first hackle is passed between the wings and wound behind them. The hackle tip is then brought back through the wings and tied down.

7   8

7. The second hackle is then wound over the tip of the first hackle directly in front of the wings. The grip is reversed in the photograph to show the hackling. The second hackle tip is then tied down beside the first one. Reverse the fly to expose the eye for three half hitches.

8. Cement the head to finish the Wulff.

A viseless Wulff tied by Lee Wulff.

THE DOWNS METHOD: THE QUILL WING PATTERN

Donald Downs, who ties either viseless or with a small pin vise mounted in an antler tine, practices the winging method advocated by Halford. Downs, a "country squire" and raconteur of field sports, stuffs his snuff boxes with modern methods and traditional touches. This method is particularly appropriate for hand tying. A bobbin may or may not be used in this procedure; however, the bobbin weight makes half hitches unnecessary.

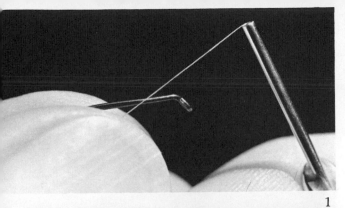 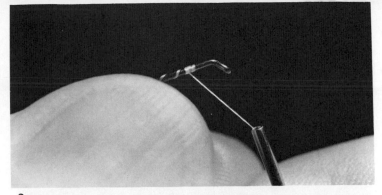

1 2

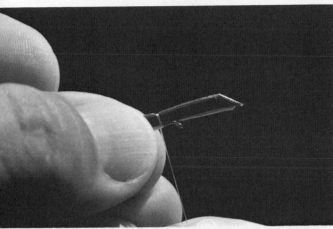 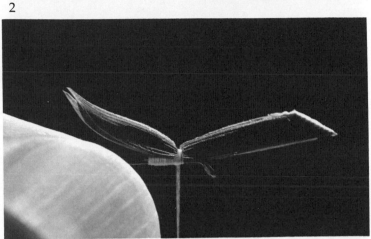

3 4

6

1. The hook is held by the heel between the left thumb and forefinger. The thread, anchored with hook heel, passes over the shank.

2. A thread base is laid down on the forward third of the shank.

3. Matched wings are mounted with the base pointing forward and the front edge pointing up. If each wing is Tuffilmed and each wing slip still has the stem base attached, the slips will not splay. Photograph five shows the attached stem section. Two thread wraps are passed over them to compress the fibers directly on top of the shank.

4. The wing length should equal the shank.

5. The butt ends are folded back on their respective sides and the wings are pulled up.

6. The thread is then wrapped directly behind the wings to erect them. The wings are now, as Downs phrases it, "caught in a basket." The "basket" base should be kept as small as possible.

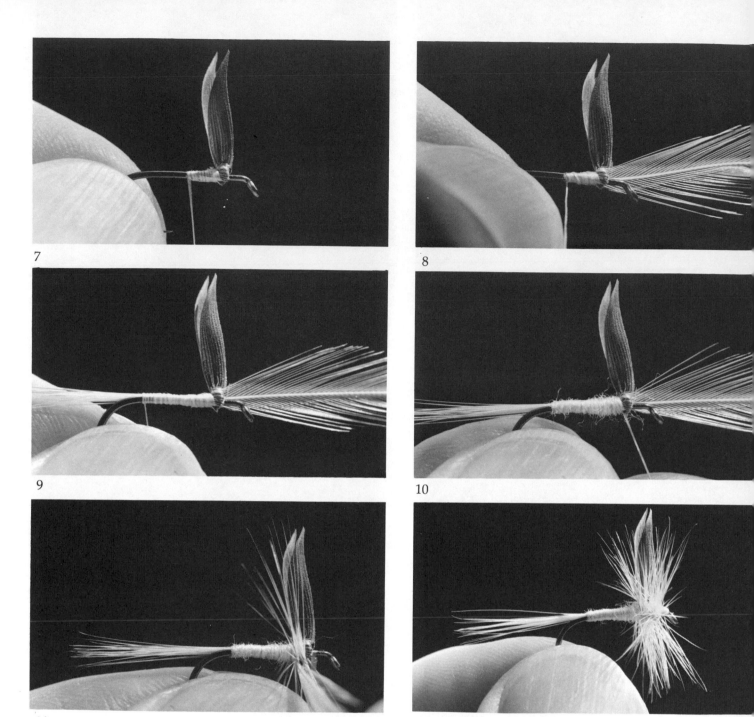

7

8

9

10

11

The completed Quill Wing.

7. The wing butts are trimmed and the foundation is wrapped.

8. At this time, wrap on the hackle on the offside with the dull or concave side pointing toward the tyer. Mounted in this manner, the bulky hackle butt is buried beneath the body.

9. Spiral the thread to the rear and add the tail fibers.

10. Dubbing is added to the thread and the body is wrapped forward to a point immediately behind the wings. Free the thread of any dubbing and wrap firmly two times behind the wings.

11. Then cross the thread over to the eye position and wrap the hackle, concave side forward, behind and in front of the wings. When hackling is complete, wrap the thread over the hackle tip, trim excess and complete with a hand whip or half hitch.

CHAPTER 31

The Spinning Knot

This unique method of connecting the fly to the tippet is a new twist on an old knot. The spinning knot can be tied in ten seconds and, once the tippet passes through the hook eye, in total darkness. Furthermore (unlike traditional knots), the smaller the pattern, the easier it is to tie with the spinning knot. The knot, which is similar to a uni-knot tied inside out, is spun or "woven" in the loom of the hand. For even greater strength, the tippet may be looped twice through the eye or once around the hook shank. With brief practice, the result is a swift and solid knot. The spinning knot should be tied with a smooth and continuous movement.

TYING THE SPINNING KNOT

1. After passing the tippet end through the eye of the fly, hold the tippet tag between the thumb and the forefinger of the left hand. Slide the fly down the tippet and over the palm of the hand.

1

2. Pass a loop, with the fly riding on it, around the little finger, over the back of the hand, and between the index and middle fingers. Hold the fly in the palm with the tippet looping back between the index and middle fingers.

3. Next, hold the looped fly with the right hand and tighten the tippet section across the palm of the hand.

4. All that is necessary now is for the looped fly to be wound five times or more, in either direction, around the taut tippet held in the palm. Arc the fingers to create spinning space and to keep the tippet tight. Then with the fly in the right hand and while still holding the tag end of the tippet with the thumb and the index finger, relax the other finger of the left hand and slip them out of the loop.

5. Continue to hold the tag end of the tippet as the hand rotates to grasp the wraps made around the tippet. With the right hand, slowly pull the fly away from the knot. Do not pull the tippet tag. Pulling both the tippet tag and the fly will increase tippet waste.

6. Once the knot has been loosely drawn up as illustrated, continue to pull the fly to slide the knot against the hook eye. Snug the knot firmly against the eye. If the knot is tightened before it is snugged against the eye, then a crinkle may result as the knot slides over the extended tippet.

7. After clinching the knot against the eye, trim the excess. Do not forget to place the tippet clippings in a pocket and not along the stream.

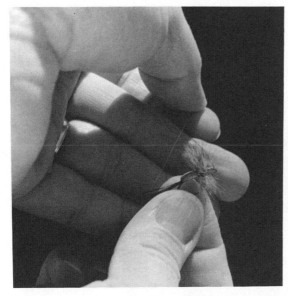

2

3

4   5

6

7

Glossary: A Fly Fisher's Lexicon

The modern fly fisher is constantly confronted with technical and historical terms. And writers often assume a literate audience familiar with these angling terms. Modern fly fishing is a curious combination of art and science. An angling term may be obscure music, objective fact, or both. It may tell a tale or illuminate the social background from which it sprang. It is important to recognize that some words have various meanings and that the fly fisher may endow a scientific term with a nontechnical meaning or even an erroneous meaning. But anything used long enough, even in error, may become the accepted standard. The study of angling terms is freighted with pleasure and problems. A lexicon gathers the nuances and subtleties of specialized terms: it gathers their etymologies, multiple cognates and, sometimes, their social origins. In this manner, angling enters semantics, the science of meanings. It may be important, sometimes, to know the genesis of the term even though time itself has corrupted the origins. Furthermore, it may be important to know the original spelling as well as the history. It is through words that we know our world. Some words are clear, but other words, the obscure and problematic words, whisper too quietly. Some terms, through growth or decay, have been so transformed as to mean their opposite. Furthermore, a few terms have become more specific (specialization), while others have become more general (generalization). Some are natives; others, naturalized foreigners. And a few are aliens. But an angler should collect words as he collects fly patterns. Fly fishing is rich with words. Words mirror the act of angling. They reflect the historical development of fly fishing in different lands, in different times. They show where the rod has been. They add a richness to the act of angling and a broth to time.

A glossary is a reference work that should be clear and certain. But words relating to fly fishing are myriad, coming, as they do, from several fields of study, different time periods, and different cultures. The following glossary, which includes angling and fly tying as well as some biological words, attempts to clarify those technical and historical terms often found in present and past angling writing. Angling is a branch of science. And word precision is essential to the learning process. Bioscientific words are precise and universal. A hellgrammite can be half a dozen creatures, but the *Corydalus cognata* larva is only one. Like science, fly fishing requires a vocabulary, an imagery of words that express the facts and the concepts. Meaningful dialogue results from precise and meaningful words.

Where there is a significant quote or reference, the source is indicated. The semicolon in the entry usually separates the various meanings, or shades of a meaning, of a term. Such a limited glossary will always be judged by what is included and what is left out. No matter, one man's midge is another man's smut.

Aerobic: A habitat with free and available oxygen.

Aftershaft: The small, soft undershaft or underfeather directly beneath and attached to another feather; the *hyporachis*, the insulating accessory plume connected to the underside base of a feather; the term *aftershaft* and the synonym *hyporachis* should be restricted to the auxiliary shaft only; aftershaft has also been called an accessory plume, a *hypoptile* (*hypoptilum*); the term *afterfeather* is a direct translation of the German term, *afterfeder*, introduced by Studer (1878); the afterfeather or aftershaft consists of an aftershaft (hyporachis) with its own aftervanes (*hypovexillum, -a*); the aftershaft is a soft feather that varies in type—in grouse, quail, and pheasant, the aftershaft is long and narrow with barbs relatively short; in the turkey, the aftershaft is often oval or elliptical with long, fine barbs that are one-third to two-thirds the length of the main vane; in ducks, the afterfeather is very short with no central stem or hyporachis.

Anadromous: Ascending from the sea for reproduction; said of fish, such as salmon and steelhead, that migrate annually into fresh water for reproduction.

Anaerobic: Living without free oxygen; a habitat with no oxygen such as occurs in the profundal areas of deep lakes.

Anastomosed: The condensed wing vein network; the "coming together" or channeled vein connections, said of insect wings.

Apolysis: The separation, but not the casting, of the larval integument from the pupal integument. The actual shedding of the larval integument is called *ecdysis*.

Badger: A white, cream, or silver feather with a black center; a cape of badger feathers; a badger feather may have a black list or edge; the term probably comes from the Old English *broc(k)*, a reference to the light and dark fur of a badger; E. Muller suggests that the term badger (from *badge* plus *-ard*) is derived from the reference to the white badge mark on the animal's forehead; earlier names for the animal were *brock* (appears in Middle English, c. 1230) and *bauson*.

Barbicel: The hook or clawlike projection of the barbule.

Barb: The lateral feather fiber branching from the rachis or shaft.

Barbule: The lateral projection of the barb; the interlaced webbing.

Benthic: An adjective describing the flora or fauna inhabiting or associated with the bottom or substratum of a body of water; bottom dwelling.

Biot: The leading lateral barb of a goose quill; the stiff and rapidly tapering barb, usually on the leading edge of a primary feather.

Bite: The distance between the hook point and the rearmost part of the hook bend; the distance between the rearmost part of the heel and the hook point.

Bivisible: Term credited to Edward Ringwood Hewitt in "Telling on the Trout," (1926). The Bivisible consists of a double palmer, usually with a forward white palmer; "The white wisp enables the angler to see the fly readily, hence the name I gave it—Bivisible because I can see it and the trout can see it." (Hewitt, 1948, quoted by Smedley.)

Bloa: "Pertaining to the color of the clouds, leaden, bluish purple, or pale blue, was used to mean dun colored" (Smedley, 1950); the *blae* of the Scottish patterns and the *bloa* of the Yorkshire patterns; "the color of the lowery clouds of a threatening sky" (Smedley); compare Old Norse *blar*, bluish black, and *blautr*, soaked or wet; term used in such patterns as the Bloa and Red, the Blae and Silver.

Bobbin: In fly tying, usually a tension thread holder with a thread tube. The weight of the tool eliminates the need for half hitches during tying. The thread tube is usually beveled at the ends for smoothness, and the thread tension adjustable.

Bulla: The bubble node usually found midway along the subcostal vein of an insect wing.

Caddis: The Trichoptera; the term *cadew* is of unknown origin, chiefly dialect and dated 1651 in reference to the cased Trichoptera; from the Old French *cadas*, meaning silk floss with reference to the caddis case; the Middle English *cadas* (from the Old French) and *cadace* refer to the coarse, variegated worsted yarn; "Both the caddis or artificial fly and the caddis fly (and caddis worm) derive from caddis, caddice, floss silk, cotton wool, worsted yarn, especially ribbon. . . ." (Eric Partridge, *Origins*); also probable origin is the relation to the Greek *cadus*, meaning case or vessel, perhaps in reference to the cylindrical case of the caddis larva.

Camlet: originally a costly Eastern fabric, popularly associated with camel hair and silk; a dubbing, yarn, or fabric made of various combinations of wool, silk, hair, cotton, or linen; stuff from the angora goat (Oliver Goldsmith); "Theakston has a dressing for the female Stone-fly (usually preferred): 'Body of yellow camlet, with eight or nine rounds of brown floss silk, or camlet thread wrapt over it; head and shoulders yellow camlet, darkened on the upper parts, *etcetera*, with the brown bear's hair; wings selected from the feathers of a wild drake, partridge, or hen pheasant; legged with hairs or stiff hen hackle.' He means mohair by 'camlet'. . . ." (Arthur Ransome)

Cape: The dorsal cervical feathers; a neck "patch" with hackles attached.

Carapace: The shieldlike dorsal body plate or plates of insects.

Cerci: The tail or caudal filaments; the paired terminal appendages; the tail of an insect; technically, the two lateral "tails" are cerci, but the medial "tail" is a median caudal filament or *telofilum*; (*cercus*, singular).

Cervix: The neck, pertaining to the neck area or especially the back of the neck of insects.

Chenille: The soft, tufted yarn having fibers that spiral from a central, twisted core; from the French *chenille*, meaning hairy caterpillar.

Chitin: The outer skin of an insect; the material of the cuticle.

Claspers: The paired appendages of the male insect used to hold the female during copulation.

Coachman: A dark mahogany-colored feather often with a back center; a cape of such coloration; term derived from the pattern of a mothlike imitation created by Harding, a stagecoach driver (1867); some attribute the color red in the pattern to the red livery of a coachman; Francis Francis noted that the coachman pattern was "one of the best evening and night flies." (1880)

Coch-y-bondhu: A furnace feather or cape with a black center and black listing or edge; from the Welsh, meaning red (*coch*) and black (*du* or *dhu*); *coch a bon ddu*, meaning "red with black (*du*) trunk or stem (*pon*)"; an "angler's artificial fly," dated 1852; the Welsh term for the terrestrial june bug (*Phylopertha horticola*), known also as the Brachen Clock; an insect that is red or reddish brown with a black belly; a term descriptive of such coloration; a pattern with red hackle or red wings and black body; variant spellings including cock y bondhu; "A coch-y-bondhu hackle is one having a black center or list with red (reddish brown) or brown outer fibers tipped with black. This hackle is the same as the 'furnace' with the exception of the black outer edge." (Smedley)

Complete metamorphosis: The physical changes in the development of an insect that include ova, larva, pupa, and adult.

Compound eye: The insect eye, which is composed of numerous simple eyes functioning collectively; the oculi; see *simple eye*.

Costa: The major, frontal forewing vein; the costal vein that forms the leading or anterior margin of an insect wing; the costal vein is one of the three nearly parallel longitudinal veins that include the *subcosta* and *radius*.

Coxa: The basal or body segment of an insect leg (*coxae*, plural).

Cree: A tricolored feather with cream or pale ginger, red game and black or gray; a hackle with black-and-red bars on a white ground; a mottled ginger; a cape of such coloration.

Creel: A feather or hackle with red bars on a white ground; sometimes called a ginger grizzly (i.e., a white feather with red bars rather than black bars), a ginger chinchilla, or barred red game; term is from a now-rare Old English Game bird. The shortened name cree is also given to this bird; however, the cree feather should have black and red bars on a white ground.

Cutaneous respiration: The respiration directly through the outer skin or cuticle of an insect; such respiration is through the body wall itself.

Dapping: To fish with a silk blow line where the line is often attached directly to the end of the rod, traditionally twelve to eighteen feet long, which allows the line to drift and dance in the wind as the fly gently touches the water; dapping, also dape or dib (1653); dapping flies are usually fully dressed with stiff and heavy hackles on an extended hook; traditional loch dapping in Scotland and Ireland, where the boat drifts with a drogue, favors the large, palmered artificials and naturals, mayflies,

and daddy longlegs; an angling method in which the natural or artificial is raised and dropped periodically on the water surface rather than cast. "To fish by letting the bait dip and bob lightly on the water" (*Oxford English Dictionary*).

Detrivore: A consumer of disintegrated or decayed plant mass.

Diapause: The period of suspended development of an insect.

Dinging: To mount the thread to the bare hook; ". . . my first step is to pick up the hook and start the dinging with a piece of thread long enough to tie the fly" ("The Wulff Fly Patterns," Lee Wulff in *Roundtable*, January/ February, 1979); perhaps from the implication of "to knock," "to hit upon," "to strike" (*Oxford English Dictionary*); ding, with a variant dent, "to strike or hurl" (Eric Partridge, *Origins*).

Distal: The outermost apex of a structure; opposed to basal or proximal, said of insect parts.

Diurnal: Occurring in daytime, adapted for daytime or daylight; opposed to nocturnal.

Dorsal: The top or back side of an organism.

Drake: Any member of a number of specific, large mayflies, i.e., Brown Drake (*Ephemera simulans*) and Green Drake (*Ephemera guttulata, Ephemerella grandis, et al.*); probably derived from Old English *draca*, meaning dragon, compare dragonfly and drake; the male duck (Old English *duce*, to dive); the term appears to describe any large flier, and appeared as an angling term in 1658. Drake was first applied to mayflies because their wings could be imitated with feathers from the mallard drake (Smedley); Smedley also quotes the line, "A dun is a half done drake," with the implication that a drake is a sexually mature mayfly.

Draper hook: A hook bend characterized by a double shank brazed at the bend to produce a "flat-bodied" nymph hook. The concept, originated by Keith Draper of New Zealand, was refined and produced by Partridge & Sons in 1980. The "shoulders" of the hook body have fine serrations to prevent material movement.

Dressing: The material, such as furs or feathers, or the process of mounting the material on the hook; the recipe, which may include methods as well as materials, used in tying a particular pattern.

Drogue: A drift anchor usually made of canvas about three or four feet square that slows the natural drift of a boat; the drogue, a term of unknown origin, was used to check the speed of a whale (1725), and was a hooped canvas bag towed at the stern of a boat to prevent broaching (until 1875).

Dry fly: An imitation that floats on the surface of the water. The traditional historical requirements for a dry fly are: 1) an imitation of the winged stage of an adult insect (subimago or imago); 2) an upstream presentation, usually to an individual trout or trout rise; 3) a natural float of the imitation; and 4) the drying of the imitation during the backcast. John Waller Hills dates the 1851 edition of Pulman's *Vade Mecum of Fly Fishing for Trout* as the first published observations on the dry fly. He also adds that dry fly fishing was probably practiced on the River Itchen in England during the 1840s. By 1865 the practice of the dry fly was prevalent on the Southern Hampshire streams in England. The modern dry fly may include patterns that "swim" in the surface; the so-called "flymphs" or "damp" patterns, such as emerging nymphs; parachute patterns; as well as other imitations that penetrate the water surface with the body or hook, such as the Swisher-Richards No-Hackle patterns. Hence, any patterns with parts that extend above the water surface may be considered dry. Generally considered, the dry fly is a pattern that is visible above the water surface. The distinction between the dry fly and the wet fly is not as clear as it was in the last century. With the advent of fishing the various stages of the particular insect, fly patterns and fly hooks have become more specific. And some patterns, in fact, are fished as dry, emerging, and wet in a single cast. Furthermore, a few "flutter" patterns are neither wet nor dry; they are "damp" patterns scraped along the water surface. At the end of a dry float, a Humpy might be tugged beneath the surface to imitate an emerging caddis on the retrieve. Thus, the manner of presentation and line technique may also define or determine the fly type. Usually, a nymph and larva are specialized wet-fly patterns, and floating emerges, such as the Swisher and Richards No-Hackle Dun, are wet flies. Generically, any pattern without a completely sunk hook may be considered a dry fly. The characteristics of the dry fly include:

1. Any pattern with a rigid or supporting tail and hackle that elevates the hook above the water surface.
2. Any pattern that incorporates nonabsorbant materials, or any pattern that has a floatant added prior to presentation.
3. Any pattern proportioned so that the hook does not touch or penetrate the water surface.
4. Any pattern tied in such a manner that the natural tips touch but do not penetrate the water surface, i.e., any pattern based upon the principle of hydrofuge.
5. Any pattern tied in such a manner that the dull side or concave side of a stiff hackle points toward the hook eye.
6. Any pattern with vertical or forward wings.
7. Any pattern that occupies three dimensions, i.e., any pattern hackled so that the barbs radiate at right angles from the shank axis.
8. Any pattern tied on a light sneck, perfect, or sproat hook, often forged and up-eyed.

Dubbing: The soft body fibers; the application or technique for applying such fibers; the twisting of soft fibers on a thread or thread loop to form a chenille-like strand; the dressing of an artificial fly, hook, or line with an artificial fly (dated 1450); to dress or adorn a fly (dated 1540).

Dun: The sexually immature adult mayfly, the subimago; the gray color of the subimago wing; the color iron gray or grayish brown derived from the Old English term *dunn*, first used in angling in 1681 to describe the dusky colored natural fly; compare the term dusk.

Dystrophic: The aquatic environment that contains organic matter and scant nutritives for flora and fauna; an environment characterized by poor tissue production; a term to describe lakes that lack the productive nutrients like nitrates and phosphates; the term means "ill nourishing."

Ecdysis: The act of casting or shedding the integument or outer skin; molting, to shed the exoskeleton, said of insects.

Eclosion: The act of hatching from the egg or from the pupal stage; the hatching into the adult stage, said of insects.

Elytron: The platelike forewing of beetles that covers the membranous underwing; the anterior, chitinous wings of a beetle (*elytra*, plural).

Epilimnion: The oxygenated and warm surface zone of a lake; extends as deeply as the mixing effect of the wind and the penetration of the light, said of lakes.

Eutrophic: A rich aquatic environment producing abundant organic tissue, the term means "well nourishing," said of lakes.

Exuvia: The insect "shuck"; the cast cuticle or outer skin during ecdysis: the skin of an insect is composed of four main layers—the epicuticle (the outer layer), the exocuticle, the endocuticle, and the epidermis (the inner layer composed of cells).

Femur: The third leg segment of an insect, numbering from the body axis outward, which is usually broad.

Filiform: Threadlike or hairlike.

Filoplume: A hairlike feather; the mature filoplume has a threadlike shaft with a tuft of short basal barbs or barbules. Unlike a bristle, the filoplume has a tuft of barbs (the apical barbs) at the tip; a degenerate feather bearing apical barbs. There are usually two or three filoplumes with each body contour feather or semiplume, and they are more numerous near the remiges and rectrices.

Fleck: Any feather or cape having specks or dotting that contrast with the hackle shade; probable origin of term may be Old Norse *flekkr* and others, meaning flake or speck (1750).

Flue: The soft downlike fibers at the base of a feather; the down mass or feather itself; the soft, immature feather; the term comes from the Flemish *vluwe*, of the same meaning; compare the term *fluff*.

Fur: Fur consists of several kinds of hairs: the guard hairs are straight and taper to a fine point; the bristle or awn hairs also taper to a fine point, but they are thinner than guard hairs and have a characteristic swelling just below the tip. Both the guard hairs and the awn hairs are known as overhairs. The underfur—the down or wool hairs—are the thinnest of the hair types. The underfur has an even diameter throughout its length and is crimped or curvy. The tightly crimped underfur acts as an insulatory sheet, while the stiff overhairs create a protective shield to the soft underfur.

Furnace: A reddish brown feather with a black center or list; not to be confused with a coch-y-bondhu, which has a black list, a red outside, and black-tipped barbs. A furnace lacks the black-tipped barbs; also a brown feather with a black center; a cape of furnace feathers.

Fusiform: A streamlined shape, often pointed at both ends, torpedo or spindle shaped, said of nymphs.

Gap: The distance across the hook bend between the hook point and the shank; also called gape.

Genitalia: The sexual organs and appendages.

Gravid: Possessing fertile eggs, pregnant.

Greenwell: A ginger hackle with a black center; a ginger badger hackle; a Greenwell can have a pale red edge; however, if the edge is dark red, the hackle is often considered to be a furnace hackle, not a Greenwell hackle; named after the hackle used in the Greenwell's Glory pattern first tied by the professional tyer James Wright of Sprouston in England and christened and popularized by Canon Greenwell of Durham in England; there is doubt as to the true originator and John Goddard finds Mark Aitken's dressing earlier and similar to Greenwell's Glory; "a glorified Blue Dun" (Smedley); an English term seldom encountered in American tying.

Grizzly: The barred Plymouth Rock feather or cape; a bicolored feather with white bars on a dark gray or black field; the term comes from Middle English *grisel* and French *gris*, meaning gray; from the fourteenth to sixteenth centuries, a gray fur; according to the British Poultry Standards, the points of excellence are straight bars, high contrast of bars, bar and ground color of equal widths, barring carried down into underfluff, and black tip bar; the barred Plymouth Rock was first exhibited in 1869; the barred rock was developed, as an exhibition ideal, to secure the long, narrow, finely-barred feather rather than body size or conformation. Note that the ground color is white, often with a bluish tinge, and the barring, which should be moderately narrow and straight, is a beetle-green black. Every feather should finish with a black tip; also called the cuckoo, a term derived from the breast markings of the European cuckoo; Frank Elder, *The Book of the Hackle* (1979), maintains that the term grizzly should be used for the barred marking on the hackle rather than the hackle color—dun grizzly, ginger grizzly, or others. The Belgium campine has barred body feather but not barred neck hackles. The dark cuckoo marans, from France, is black barred. The golden cuckoo marans has bluish gray hackles with gold-and-black bars.

Guard hairs: The long, stiff, and lustrous body hair of a fur bearer; the "shield" shaped overhair of mammals; see *fur*.

Hackle: The narrow, glossy feather, the dorsal cervical tract feather, on the neck back of a bird; from Old English *hacele* or *haecile*, meaning cloak or mantle; a "hackle-fly," dated 1676; to dress a fly with a hackle feather, dated 1867; other body feathers from a bird are the spey hackles (the long lateral sickle feathers at the tail base), the spade hackles (the wide shoulder hackles), and the saddle hackles (the dorsopelvic tract feathers), the long flank hackles between the spade hackles and tail feathers; a feather mounted to imitate the wings or legs of insects.

Hackle Gauge: In fly tying, a template or scale that measures the length of hackle barbs and indicates the proportionate hook size.

Hackle guards: In fly tying, a small cone-shaped disk that is placed over the eye of the hook to keep the hackle away from the whip-finishing process.

Hackle pliers: In fly tying, a spring clip or clamp used to manipulate the hackle feather during mounting. Several shapes and sizes are available, many with a finger ring for ease of rotating the hackle around the hook shank. The traditional shape is that associated with Herb Howard pliers or Veniard's of England. Hackle pliers should hold firmly without cutting the hackle, should be large enough for handling and weight. Such pliers may also be used to hold the tying thread during the tying process.

Hair: hair grows out of the skin of mammals; some hairs have specialized names such as fur (see *fur*), fleece (the dense, soft hair of sheep), bristles (the short, stiff hairs of hogs), and quills (the sharp, spiny hairs of porcupines and hedgehogs), and whiskers (the tactile hairs on various mammals); a flat hair shaft, which grows at uneven rate, is curly; straight hair has a round shaft. Hair may be used in all parts of a fly pattern—the tail fibers, the dubbed body, the wings, and the legs or hackle.

Hair compactor: A cylindrical or disklike tying tool

usually with a slit or hole for the hook shank, thereby compressing the spun animal body hair radiating from the hook shank.

Hair compressor: A cylindrical tying tool for compressing bullet heads before wrapping the collar thread.

Hair stacker: A cylindrical tying tool that aligns the natural tapered hair tips by gently tapping the tool on the table.

Half hitch tool: In fly tying, a tapered tube that allows thread loops to slide off and form a locking head knot. If a series of single loops are used, usually head cement is added to make certain they will not unravel. A variation of the half hitch is a double or triple hitch. Instead of a single wrap around the half hitch tube, two or three are made and passed over the fly head and tightened. This, in effect, produces a mini-whip that holds better than a single-loop hitch.

Halteres: The knobbed appendages in place of the hind wings on Diptera; believed to be either vestigial wings or balancing knobs.

Herl: The long fuzzy barb of a peacock tail feather or ostrich plume; from the Low German *harl*, meaning a filament or fiber of hemp or flax; hence "a herl of silk"; a feather barb or fiber (dated 1450); a type of feather, such as peacock or ostrich herl, with a specialized structure called a *flue*. Also spelled "hurl" or "harl."

Hyaline: Transparent or clear, said of insect wings.

Hypolimnion: The profundal or deep zone of a lake, characterized by cold temperatures, slow decomposition of tissue, and a relative absence of oxygen.

Incomplete metamorphosis: The physical changes in the development of an insect that include ova, nymph, and adult.

Instar: The immature insect during a stadia (*which see*) between molts; such nymphs are further classified as junior (immature) or senior (mature) instars.

Integument: The skin of an insect; see *exuvia*.

Intercalary: See *veinlet*.

Interstitial: Occurring in interstices, a small or narrow space between objects; located in a crevice or fissure; usually said of insect habits and insect body parts.

Keel hook: A hook bend, developed by Dick Probst, characterized by an offset shank so as to produce a "weedless" design. The dressed keel hook floats with the hook point on top, opposite to the traditional tie.

Kirby: A hook bend characterized by a semiangular shape and an offset where the point is turned away from the bend plane. The Kirby offset points to the left if the bend is up and the point faces you. The opposite bend, where the offset points to the right, is a reversed bend. Although the Kirby hooks, originated by Charles Kirby of London, are not common, they are excellent for small wet patterns.

Labrum: The upper or front lip of an insect.

Lemnetic: The open water zone of a lake that is penetrated by light; the lake zone beyond the littoral zone.

Lentic: Static or slowly moving water; said in relation to very slow streams or static lakes; from the Latin *lent*, meaning "slow" or "thick."

Limerick: A hook bend characterized by an acutely angled bend where the sharpest curve is at the rear of the spear. The bend merges imperceptibly with the shank. Because of the mechanically weak acute bend and streamer use, the hook is usually made from heavy wire. The Limerick salmon hook is bronzed rather than black enamel. The term is attributed to the town of Limerick, in Ireland.

Listing: The term is correctly applied to the center or lateral strips running on each side of the feather stem that are darker than the rest of the feather; also used for any feather or hackle, regardless of color, that has a black edge or list without a black center; list is sometimes used only for the black edge of the barbs; a furnace has a black list with red margins, and a badger has a black list with silver or white margins. The demarcation of color is the margin between the barbs and the barbules of the feather. Term origin is from Old English, *liste*, meaning border, edging, or strip. The general meaning was established by 1696. As it has come to mean both a band as well as an edge, the term has appeared in angling history as a feather with either a dark center strip or a dark edge strip; Eric Partridge's *Origins* defines list as "an edge or border," which derives from Old High German *lista*, meaning a strip or border; Walshe's *A Concise German Etymological Dictionary* (1956) suggests the origin in the Latin *litus*, seashore or border of the ocean.

Littoral: The shore zone of lentic waters where the plants are rooted; used to describe inhabitants of this zone.

Lotic: Moving, as in lotic water, for instance, a stream or river.

Mandibles: The outer or paired jaws of an insect.

Mayfly: The aquatic insect classified as Ephemeridae, meaning "lasting but a day," hence also called "dayfly"; the English term mayfly was so given because of the major appearance of the insect during the month of May; also called drake (see *drake*); the mayfly develops from ova to nymph to dun (subimago) to spinner (imago) and finally to spent spinner. The mayfly is the only insect to hatch again (from dun to spinner) after emergence.

Marabou: The fluffy immature turkey feather; the "blood feather" is the long, underdeveloped feather with barbs parallel to the feather stem; such feathers are often three or four inches long; the term comes from the similar long fluffy feather from the marabou stork.

Marrying: In fly tying, the joining of different wing sections by engaging the hook projections.

Microbiota: Microscopic organisms not visible to the unaided eye.

Midge: A generic term used to describe any minute insect; the term usually and more correctly refers to a *Chironomid*; the larger *Chironomids* are often called "buzzers," the English term, or gnats. Some English anglers reserve the term midge just for the terrestrial diptera, *Biblio johannis*. However, in general angling usage, the midge has come to mean any of a variety of minute insects including *Chironomids*, reed smuts, black gnats, buffalo gnats, black flies, and dixa midges as well as microcaddis and other microinvertebrates, including tiny terrestrials; the term is related to the Latin *musca*, meaning "fly." Ed Koch, in *Fishing the Midge* (1972), defines midge as "an artificial imitation of any small aquatic or terrestrial insect that a trout would find acceptable as food."

Naiad: The aquatic nymph; also *naid*, from the Greek mythological river spirits; compare Old French *noiant*, from Latin, *natare*, "to swim."

Natant: The floating or swimming insect stage, especially floating on the surface of the water; the emergent nymphal stage, the term is related to the Latin *nare*, meaning "to swim"; see *naiad*.

Notum: The dorsal plates of a thorax, said of insects.

Nymph: The immature stage of an insect having an incomplete metamorphosis; an artificial that imitates the nymphal stage of the insect; nymph imitations usually require: a) heavy down-eyed extended-shank hooks; b) absorbent materials; and c) correct nymphal proportion and coloration.

Occiput: The dorsal posterior of the head, the rear or hind area of the insect head.

Ocelli: The two or three simple eyes of an insect, (*ocellus*, singular).

Oligotrophic: An aquatic environment low in nutrients for flora and fauna, typically deep and cold and often well oxygenated in all zones; such lakes can possess an appropriate environment for salmonids; the term means "few nutritives."

Operculate: A cover often in the form of fused nymphal gills; the lid gill or gill shield; a cover (*opercula*, plural).

Ova: Insect eggs.

Ovipositing: The act of laying or depositing insect eggs.

Palmer: The tying technique of a spiraling hackle wrapped laterally along the shank or body of a fly; an artificial fly resembling a Palmer-worm (a hairy, wandering moth larva especially of the tineid moth); the hackled, artificial fly resembling the Palmer-worm, dated 1651; an artificial resembling a Palmer-worm, a hairy, wandering tineid moth larva; the term *palmer* comes from the wandering pilgrim-beggar or palmer; ". . . the palmer got its name from the pilgrims who walked . . . to the Holyland in fulfillment of a vow. When they came back home they wore pieces of palm leaves in their hats to signify they had made that long journey and were called palmers. . . . Because a caterpillar, with all its legs, does a lot of walking, it likewise became a palmer" (Smedley); the medieval palmer wore crossed palm leaves to indicate his travels.

Palps: The small, jointed sensory organs projecting from the maxilla or labium of an insect; an appendage.

Parachute: The tying technique of horizontal hackling on a vertical stem, such as the wing base.

Pattern: A specific artificial fly; a list of the materials and methods for dressing a particular fly.

Perfect bend: A hook bend characterized by a rounded heel that distributes the stress for optimum mechanical strength. Also called the round bend. The long bite on a perfect hook allows deep penetration; however, the deep bite and long spear can result in poor strike penetration. Some hook designers, such as Mustad, have adopted a modified perfect bend to reduce the claimed disadvantages. The term origin is probably based on this design as a solution to the earlier faults found in angular hooks, especially the sneck bend.

Periphyton: The organic slime on submerged objects, the benthic plant system. Dr. C. E. Cushing, a Northwest stream ecologist, notes that the term "periphyton" technically refers to *phyton* (plants) and *peri* (around). The German term *Aufwuchs* may be more accurate because it includes the detritus, bacteria, algae, and invertebrates that constitute the complete community. "The German term 'Aufwuchs' has a much broader connotation than the closest English equivalent 'periphyton.' *Aufwuchs* comprises all attached organisms . . . which are usually considered as benthos by American authors. . . ." (G. E. Hutchinson, *A Treatise on Limnology*, Volume 1, 1957)

Periwinkle: The cased Trichoptera; term probably related to the European intertidal snail with a thick, spiraled, cone-shaped shell; term from Old English *pinewincle* and Latin *pina*, a mussel.

Pharate: The recently emerged adult still clinging to the pupal husk; the recently hatched adult, said of insects.

Photoperiod: The length of daylight; the seasonal length of daylight said to be a factor in insect emergence.

Phototropism: The response to light; flora and fauna that avoid light are said to be negatively phototropic.

Plastron: The air sack or film covering during submergence, the air cloak held on by hairs or scales, usually said of water beetles.

Plumose: Plume or featherlike, often said of antenna or gills.

Postero-lateral spines: The spines located on the hind, lateral edge of body segments, said of insects.

Profundal: The deep-water lentic zone of a lake beyond the penetration of light.

Puparium: The pupal case, (*puparia*, plural), of insects.

Quill: The rachis or stem of a feather or hackle; the barb sections mounted as wings, for instance, the quill wing; the stripped herl from the eyed tail of the peacock. Notice the three basic meanings of quill in fly tying.

Rachis: The central shaft of a feather, the vane stem.

Raptorial: Adapted for predation; predatory, relating to birds of prey.

Rectrices: The tail feathers that direct the flight (1768); large, stiff, asymmetrical pennaceous feathers along the posterior edges of the tail. See *remiges*.

Remiges: The primary and secondary wing feathers which, with the rectrices, comprise most of the airfoil for flying; the large flight feathers along the posterior edge of the wing. Primary remiges differ from secondary remiges in being more pointed, more stiff and, usually, more asymmetrical. Both the rectrices and the remiges include the largest feathers of a flying bird.

Rheophilic: Associated with currents or flowing water; see *rheotropism*.

Rheotropism: The response to current flow; a trout that must keep its head upstream is said to possess positive rheotropism. A more accurate term might be rheotaxis—*rheo* (current) and *taxis* (arrangement or orientation); the term *tropism* is usually restricted to botanical phenomena. Cecil E. Heacox's *The Compleat Brown Trout* (1974) popularized the various tropisms of trout.

Riparian: Associated with the bank or margin of a stream or river; the inhabitants of the bank side.

Saddle feather: The elongated and tapered saddle hackles (the dorsopelvic tract feathers) are upper tail coverts. And, as they are designed to droop, the stems are thin and soft. They are used for large dry-fly hackles, palmer hackles, salmon and streamer wings. The barbs, although usually not as stiff and straight as the spade hackle, often serve as dry-fly tails. Technically, the term saddle applies only to the dorsopelvic feathers of the male; the dorsopelvic feathers of the female form a soft back slope and are collectively called the "cushion."

Schlappen hackle: A long webby hackle about twenty-four centimeters long with a fine diameter stem (about .012 inch) used for the Defeo-style beards, Spey hackles, and streamer wings. Chinese schlappen are usually strung and often dyed; the term schlappen comes from the German word meaning "to dangle or to hang loosely"; the all-web or nearly-all-web hackle found between the saddle and the tail feathers.

Sclerite: The chitinous body plates of the insect exoskeleton connected by the flexible sutures.

Sclerotized: The hardening of insect body plates or sclerites.

Scutum: The middle section or segment of the insect thoracic notum.

Sessile: Rooted, stalked, or fixed in place.

Seston: The suspended matter, including both flora and fauna, in water.

Seta: Bristlelike; a bristle, often said of body hair (*setae*, plural).

Sickle feather: The cock tail feathers (the rectrices) and the upper major tail coverts form, respectively, the greater and lesser sickle feathers. The sickles serve as streamer wings and, sometimes, Spey hackles. The term *sickle* is derived from the crescent or "sickle-blade" droop of the feather.

Simple eyes: The ocelli of an insect, see *compound eyes*.

Smut: The term refers to a variety of small insects, especially the reed smut or black fly (*Simulium spp.*); the early English origin of the term is related to smudge and soot, a small black particle, perhaps related to Gaelic *smuid*, smoke, and Early Irish *smut*, a cloud; the term has been used in trouting since 1889, the trout rise to a small insect, and 1899, a minute black insect; the smutting rise, a slowly expanding ring with minimal water disturbance, see *midge*.

Sneck: A hook bend characterized by an angular or square bend that allows the longest possible straight shank length, *i.e.*, the shank length being equal to the hook length. The weakest point, the angled bend between the shank and the heel, would sometimes break and the hook shape fell into disfavor. The origin of the term is obscure, perhaps relating to the Scottish and Northern dialect term *sneck*, the L-shaped latch or catch of a door or gate, the angular shape of a door catch; Middle English *snecchen* with derivative *snekkle*, meaning "the latch of a door," perhaps, as Eric Partridge indicates in *Origins* (1983), "from the 'snap' or click it makes."

Spade hackle: These rounded back feathers take their name from the digging spade. The spade hackle comes from the scapulars, which are between the back and the wing. Sometimes the medium coverts are also called spades. The spades furnish nymph legs, nymph cases, and sometimes beards and soft hackles.

Spent spinner: The spinner after ovipositing and with wings extended, adrift on the water; the spent imago.

Spider: A fly design characterized by a long palmer hackle at the head only; also called the Michigan style (Smedley); W. C. Stewart, in *The Practical Angler* (1857), described the "spider" and recommended that the hackle barbs, which were soft and sparsely tied, be total hook length.

Spinner: The sexually mature adult mayfly, the imago; so called because of the "spinning" nuptial flights of the adult mayfly; "a spinner is a done dun" (Smedley).

Spiracles: Breathing pores of insects.

Sp.: Abbreviation for *species*; used when referring to several species or unknown species in a given genus; plural form is *spp.*

Sproat: A hook bend characterized by a semiangular shape, one of the most common hook shapes used in fly tying. Hans Hurum, in *A History of the Fish Hook*, quoting Dick Orton of The Angling Foundation, identifies the term with a Mr. Sproat of Ambleside, near Kendal, England. A more fabulous tale comes from the managing director of Partridge, Alan Bramley. According to Bramley, Gerard de Sproat was a Dutchman who fled Switzerland during World War I and later became an Admiral in the Swiss Navy. After casting to roach on the Dutch dikes, Sproat adapted his downstream wet-fly techniques to the trout in the Bernese glacial streams. He developed the angled, unforged Sproat bend to "enhance" the fly movement as it tumbled through heavy torrents. Alan Bramley goes on to describe Sproat's "tumble technique": "Casting down across the stream at an angle of about forty-five degrees [Mr. Sproat] then raced along the bank so that he came below the fly thus slowing down its speed through the torrent." It must be added that Mr. Bramley's tale was concocted on April Fool's Day in 1980. It makes an interesting story and now the Patridge company refers to these hooks as "De Sproat" hooks in honor of the mythical Swiss Admiral. The disadvantage of the Sproat bend is the significant amount of hook heel that extends beyond the fly body; however, for wet flies, bucktails, and streamers, the extension poses no problems. The Sproat bend has more bite than a perfect bend, and the gradual curve between the heel and shank makes the Sproat a relatively strong hook design.

Stadia: The nymphal period between molts, said of insects.

Sternite: The ventral sclerite of insects.

Stigmatic area: The apex of the front margin of the wing, usually of a mayfly.

Suture: The flexible seam that connects the body plates of an insect.

Swedish hook: A hook bend characterized by an angular shank loop for mounting a parachute hackle with the eye wire returning to the shank line. The dressed hook is designed to float with the point on top and without water penetration, producing a more realistic float angle. The design was created by Nils E. Eriksson and Gunnar Johnson of Sweden. The hook was made by Partridge & Sons in 1979.

Tarsal claw: The claw at the apex of the tarsus on insects.

Tarsus: The final leg segment of an insect, the tarsal claw joins distally; the tarsus contains one to five segments, often a consideration in taxonomy (*tarsi*, plural)

Taxonomy: The science of classification; usually a binomial system of classification, often descriptive and referring to size, color, habits, or morphology, which includes a capitalized genus name and a lower case species or subspecies name, for instance, *Epeorus longimanus*; note that genus names and higher are capitalized; the suffix *idae* indicates a family, as in Baetidae; the suffix *inae* indicates a subfamily, as in Hydrophilinae; other endings are *oidea* for superfamily, and *ini* for tribe; species and subspecies derived from geological names are formed by adding the genitive or adjectival endings such as *-ae*, *-icus*, *-ica*, *-icum*, *-ensis* or *-ense*; the taxonomic order is phylum, class, order, family, genus, and species, with various subdivisions; the terms are usually derived from Latin and Greek, but may also come from other languages as well as people and place names; the genus and species are always underlined or italicized.

Teneral adult: In the Odonata, the recently emerged pale adult before full coloration; from the Latin *tener*, meaning tender.

Tergite: A back body plate of an insect; a dorsal sclerite.

Thermocline: The narrow lake zone connecting the epilimnion and the hypolimnion; during calm weather when the epilimnion is not oxygenated by the wind, there is a tendency for trout to seek the cooler, oxygenated thermocline belt.

Thermotropism: The response to temperature.

Thigmotropism: The response to touch; the trout that avoids direct contact with objects in the water is said to be negatively thigmotropic.

Tibia: The fourth segment of an insect leg connected between the femur and tarsus (*tibiae*, plural).

Tippet: The terminal leader section to which the fly is tied, probably derived from Late Middle English *tippe*, meaning tip, end, tail, or slender extremity; a long, narrow strip of cloth usually worn hanging from the hood or sleeve (thirteenth century); the level tippet section tied to the smaller terminus of a leader; in England the term *cast* is often used for the word tippet; the term is dated 1825 in relation to the artificial fly; also the hackle fibers of a golden pheasant, hence "golden pheasant tippet fibers."

Tracheal gills: The plumose gills of the nymph; the respiratory gills or tubes of an insect.

Trochanter: The second section of an insect leg connected between the coxa and the femur.

Tubercles: The rounded nodules, a knoblike body elevation of an insect.

Turbinate: The shape like an inverted cone frustum, often stalked, said of the stalked, turbanlike eyes of some insects.

Underfur: The fine, dense hair near the hair base of fur bearers; the soft, basal hair, see *fur*.

Univoltine: Having but one brood or hatch a year, said of insects.

Variant: Any feather or cape with more than one color; a fly pattern with extended proportions.

Veinlet: The short, detached, and narrow veins occurring along the trailing margin of some insect wings.

Ventral: The bottom side, beneath.

Vernal: Occurring only in spring, pertaining to springtime.

Vise: A jawed tool that holds a hook firmly while materials are mounted. Vises differ according to jaw mechanism (draw cam, push cam, spring lever, and screw knob), mounting systems (C-clamp, table base, hand held), and materials (brass, steel, aluminum).

Webbing: The dense barbules devoid of barbicels occurring at the feather base and tapering toward the tip.

Wet fly: Categorically, any pattern fished beneath the water surface; originally, the wet fly was designed to imitate; a) drowned surface flies such as duns and spinners; b) emerging nymph and pupa; c) ovipositing adult insects; and d) small crustaceans and beetles. Nymphs and streamers, while dressed for subsurface angling, are best considered separately. Traditionally, the wet fly should be dressed sparsely with absorbent materials on a heavy, down-eyed hook. Soft-hackled patterns and variants (spiders) may be considered wet flies. The wet fly, the most antique pattern type, usually has reverse wings that are tied on last. Major books on nymph fishing include *Nymph Fishing for Chalk Stream Trout* (1939) by G. E. M. Skues, *Nymphs and the Trout* (1958) by Frank Sawyer, and *Nymphs* (1973) by Ernest Schwiebert. The characteristics of the wet fly include:

1. Any pattern characterized by a "heavy" or "bushy" tie of absorbent materials that may include added weight.
2. Any pattern in which the wings and hackle fold back or point rearward; any pattern in which the dull or concave side of a soft hen hackle points to the rear.
3. Any pattern with a short, soft tail.
4. Any pattern tied on a heavy, and often down-eyed, hook.
5. Any "flat" pattern or pattern whose material occupies a single plane congruent with the shank and point.
6. Any pattern tied on a heavy Sproat or Limerick hook, often without a forged bend.
7. Any pattern with special parts such as beard (wet fly and salmon fly) or thorax (nymph and larva).

Whip-finisher: In fly tying, a tool that wraps one thread several times over another so that the under thread may eventually be tightened to produce the whip-finish head knot. Some whip-finishers work by a spring-lever side hook, such as the Thompson and the Veniard, or by a rigid side hook, such as the Matarelli. A fundamental advantage to the mechanical whip-finisher, once mastered, is the rapidity, control, and thread pressure of the whip process.

Wing burners: A metal template that holds either feather or fabric so that the flame burns the surplus, thereby leaving a shaped wing for fly tying. Butane lighters are usually used with the tools that come in a variety of sizes and shapes.

Wing cutter: A bladed tying tool that cuts feathers or fabric into wing shapes. Cutting is normally done upon a soft pad to prevent dulling the blade. Usually, wing cutters are available in different sizes and have replaceable blades.

Wing pad: The wing pods or buds; the underdeveloped wing nodule of an immature insect.

Wulff: A fly type usually characterized by a fully dressed pattern with bucktail wings and tail and a yarn body with various hackle colors; pattern that incorporates a yarn body and a calf-tail wing; the viseless Wulff patterns were created by Lee Wulff in 1929, who had studied engineering at Stanford University and art in Paris (Smedley).

Yorkshire Flybody hooks: A hook bend characterized by the rear extension of the eye-wire so as to form a "detached" body. The hook was developed by Peter Mackenzie-Philps of Yorkshire in 1973. The hook is available only in sizes 12, "the large dayfly size"; 14, "the dayfly size"; and 16, "the midge size."

Bibliography

ARBONA, FRED. *Mayflies, the Angler, and the Trout*. Tulsa, Oklahoma: Winchester Press, 1980.

AUDOUYS, BERNARD, and JEAN-LOUIS PELLETIER. *Je Monte Mes Mouches en 15 Lecons*. Paris: S.E.D.E.T.E.C. S.A., 1972.

AYERS, DONALD M. *Bioscientific Terminology*. Tucson, Arizona: The University of Arizona Press, 1979.

BEHRENDT, ALEX. *The Management of Angling Waters*. London: Andre Deutsch, 1977.

BETTS, JOHN. *Flies with an "Edited Hackle."* Red Bank, New Jersey: J. V. Graphics, 1982.

BORGER, GARY A. *Naturals*. Harrisburg, Pennsylvania: Stackpole Books, 1980.

BORROR, DONALD J., and DWIGHT M. DELONG. *An Introduction to the Study of Insects*. New York: Holt, Rinehart, and Winston, 1954.

BOYLE, ROBERT H., and DAVE WHITLOCK. *The Second Fly-Tyer's Almanac*. New York: J. B. Lippincott Company, 1978.

BREDOW, KLAUS V. *Das Grosse Buch vom Fliegenbinden*. Ruschlikon-Zurich: Albert Muller Verlag, 1981.

CAUCCI, AL, and BOB NASTASI. *Hatches*. New York: Comparahatch Ltd., 1975.

CLARKE, BRIAN, and JOHN GODDARD. *The Trout and the Fly*. London: Ernest Benn, Ltd., 1980; New York: Nick Lyons Books, 1981.

CUMMINS, K. W., and R. W. MERRITT, eds. *An Introduction to the Aquatic Insects of North America*. Dubuque, Iowa: Kendall/Hunt Publishing Company, 1978.

DAWES, MIKE. *The Fly Tier's Manual*. Illustrations by Taff Price. London: William Collins Sons & Co. Ltd., 1985.

DIEZ, JESUS PARIENTE. *La Pesca de la Trucha en Los Rios Leoneses*. Spain-Argentina: Editorial Nebrija, S. A. 1979.

DERKATSCH, INESSA. *Transparent Watercolor*. Englewood Cliffs, New Jersey: Prentice-Hall, 1980.

ELDER, FRANK. *The Book of the Hackle*. Edinburgh: R & R Clark, 1979.

FASSETT, NORMAN C. *A Manual of Aquatic Plants*. Wisconsin: The University of Wisconsin Press, 1957.

FLICK, ART, et al. *Master Fly-Tying Guide*. New York: Crown Publishers, Inc., 1972; New York: Nick Lyons Books, 1983.

FRANCIS, AUSTIN M. *Catskill Rivers*. New York: Nick Lyons Books/Winchester Press, 1983.

GARRISON, EVERETT, with Hoagy B. Carmichael. *A Master's Guide to Building A Bamboo Fly Rod*. New York: Martha's Glen Publishing Company, 1977; New York: Nick Lyons Books, 1986.

GODDARD, JOHN, et al. *Stillwater Flies: How & When to Fish Them*. London: Ernest Benn, 1982.

GODDARD, JOHN. *Trout Flies of Still Water*. London: Adam and Charles Black, Ltd., 1977.

———. *Trout Fly Recognition*. London: Adam and Charles Black, Ltd., 1976.

HAFELE, RICK, and DAVE HUGHES. *The Complete Book of Western Hatches*. Portland, Oregon: Frank Amato Publications, 1981.

HALFORD, F. M. *Floating Flies*. London: Sampson Low, et al., 1886.

HARRIS, J. R. *An Angler's Entomology*. New York: A. S. Barnes & Company, 1973.

HAWKSWORTH, DAVID. *British Poultry Standards*. London: Butterworth Scientific, 1982.

HEACOX, CECIL E. *The Compleat Brown Trout*. New York: Winchester Press, 1974.

HOTCHKISS, NEIL. *Underwater and Floating-leaved Plants of the United States and Canada*. Washington, D. C.: Bureau of Sport Fisheries and Wildlife, 1976.

HURUM, HANS JORGEN. *A History of the Fish Hook*. London: Adam & Charles Black Ltd., 1977.

HYNES, H. B. N. *The Ecology of Running Waters*. Toronto: The University of Toronto Press, 1970.

IVENS, T. C. *Stillwater Fly-Fishing*. London: Andre Deutsch, 1975.

JORGENSEN, POUL. *Salmon Flies*. Harrisburg, Pennsylvania: Stackpole Books, 1978.

KOCH, ED. *Fishing the Midge*. New York: Freshet Press, Inc., 1972.

LaFontaine, Gary. *Challenge of the Trout*. Missoula, Montana: Mountain Press Publishing Company, 1976.

Leiser, Eric. *Fly-Tying Materials*. New York: Crown Publishers, Inc., 1973; New York: Nick Lyons Books, 1985.

Lucas, Alfred M. and Peter R. Stettenheim. *Avian Anatomy*. Washington, D. C.: United States Government Printing Office. 1972.

Lumini, P., M. Gigi, and A. Del Bono. *Manuale del Costruttore di Mosche Artificiale*. Florence, Italy: Editoriale Olimpia—Viale Milton, 7—50129, 1981.

Marinaro, Vincent C. *In the Ring of the Rise*. New York: Crown Publishers, Inc., 1976.

McCafferty, W. Patrick. *Aquatic Entomology*. Illustrated by Arwin V. Provonska. Boston: Science Books International, 1981.

McClelland, H. G. *How to Tie Flies for Trout*. London: Fishing Gazette, 1939.

Merwin, John, ed. *Stillwater Trout*. New York: Nick Lyons Books/Doubleday & Company, Inc., 1980.

Mosely, Martin E. *The Dry-Fly Fisherman's Entomology*. London: George Routledge and Sons, Ltd., 1932.

Mottram, J. C. *Fly-Fishing: Some New Arts and Mysteries*. London: The Field & Queen (Horace Cox), Ltd., 1915.

Muenscher, Walter Conrad. *Aquatic Plants of the United States*. Ithaca, New York: Comstock Publishing Associates, Cornell University Press, 1976.

Nemes, Sylvester. *The Soft-Hackled Fly*. Old Greenwich, Connecticut: The Chatham Press, 1975.

Partridge, Eric. *Origins: A Short Etymological Dictionary of Modern English*. New York: Greenwich House, 1983.

Pethe, H. *Traite Pratique de Montage des Mouches Artificielles*. Paris: H. Pethe, 1971.

Prescott, G. W. *How to Know the Aquatic Plants*. Dubuque, Iowa: William C. Brown Company Publishers, 1969.

Price, S. D. (Taff). *Rough Stream Trout Flies*. London: Adam and Charles Black, Ltd., 1976.

———. *Stillwater Flies*. London: Ernest Benn, Ltd., 1979.

———. *Fly Patterns: An International Guide*. Illustrations by George Thompson. London: Ward Lock Limited, 1986.

Proper, Datus C. *What the Trout Said*. New York: Alfred A. Knopf, Inc., 1982; New York: Nick Lyons Books, 1987.

Richards, Carl, Doug Swisher, and Fred Arbona. *Stoneflies*. New York: Nick Lyons/Winchester Press, 1980.

Ronalds, Alfred. *The Fly-Fisher's Entomology*. London: Longman, et al., 1844.

Roskelley, Fenton, ed. *Flies of the Northwest*. Spokane, Washington: Inland Empire Fishing Club Publication, 1979.

Sawyer, Frank. *Nymphs and the Trout*. New York: Crown Publishers, Inc., 1973.

Schwiebert, Ernest. *Matching the Hatch*. New York: The Macmillan Company, 1969.

———. *Nymphs*. New York: Winchester Press, 1973.

———. *Trout*. New York: E. P. Dutton, 1978.

Skues, G. E. M. *Minor Tactics of the Chalk Stream*. London: Adam and Charles Black, 1910.

———. *Nymph Fishing for Chalk Stream Trout & Minor Tactics of the Chalk Stream*. London: Adam and Charles Black, 1974.

Smedley, Harold Hinsdill. *Fly Patterns and Their Origins*. Muskegon, Michigan: Westshore Publications, 1950.

Solomon, Larry, and Eric Leiser. *The Caddis and the Angler*. Harrisburg, Pennsylvania: Stackpole Books, 1979.

Stewart, Dick. *The Hook Book*. Intervale, New Hampshire: Northland Press, Inc., 1986.

Swisher, Doug, and Carl Richards. *Selective Trout*. New York: Crown Publishers, Inc., 1971; New York: Nick Lyons Books, 1983.

———. *Fly Fishing Strategy*. New York: Crown Publishers, Inc., 1975; New York: Nick Lyons Books, 1983.

Taverner, Eric. *Fly-tying for Salmon*. London: Seeley Service & Company, Ltd., 1942.

Usinger, Robert L., ed. *Aquatic Insects of California*. Berkeley: University of California Press, 1974.

Veniard, John. *Fly Dressers' Guide*. Illustrated by Donald Downs. London: Adam & Charles Black, 1972.

———. *Fly-dressing Materials*. Illustrated by Donald Downs. London: Adam and Charles Black, 1977.

Veniard, John, and Donald Downs. *Fly-Tying, Development and Progress*. London: Adam and Charles Black, 1972.

Wakeford, Jacqueline. *Flytying Techniques*. New York: Nick Lyons Books/Doubleday & Company, Inc., 1981.

Whitlock, Dave. *Dave Whitlock's Guide to Aquatic Trout Foods*. New York: Nick Lyons Books/Winchester Press, 1982.

Wigglesworth, V. B. *Insect Physiology*. London: Chapman and Hall, Ltd., 1974.

Willers, W. B. *Trout Biology*. Wisconsin: The University of Wisconsin Press, 1981.

Williams, A. Courtney. *A Dictionary of Trout Flies*. London: Adam & Charles Black, 1982.

Wood, Phyllis. *Scientific Illustration*. New York: Van Nostrand Reinhold Company, 1979.

Wright, D. Macer. *The Fly-Fisher's Plants*. Newton Abbot, England: David and Charles (Holdings) Ltd., 1973.

Wright, Leonard M., Jr., *The Ways of Trout*. New York: Nick Lyons Books/Winchester Press, 1985.

Index